"This book shows Vygotsky in a new light - not ⏷ the creator of the revolutionary theory of the ⏷ sciousness but also as a magnificent practitioner, ⏷ glad that this brilliantly written book continues the ⏷ theory and practice for the 21st century. The book shows that Vygotsky's ideas are not outdated and even now can serve as a fundamental basis for transforming existing educational practices for the sustainable development of humans and society."

- **Nikolai Veresov, Associate Professor of Early Childhood Education, Monash University. Author of** *Undiscovered Vygotsky*

"With elegance and meticulous attention to detail, Myra Barrs takes us on a careful path through the writings of Vygotsky that have come to light at various points over the last 80 years. She gives us a rich and nuanced understanding of the complex interplay of emotion, cognition and art in Vygotsky's work, revealing, as she does so, how limited and one-dimensional are many earlier accounts."

- **Henrietta Dombey, Professor Emerita of Primary Literacy at the University of Brighton. Author of** *Teaching Writing: What the Evidence Says*

"Vygotsky is usually considered one of the most original psychologists of the last century, but often his theoretical perspective is highlighted rather than the concrete application of his ideas. Instead Myra Barrs, through a systematic analysis of the original Vygotskyan texts and the most up-to-date literature on the Russian psychologist, definitively shows the close circular relationship between theory and practice in his thought: Vygotsky is a "teacher" not only for his personal experience in schools and universities, but also for his promotion of the psychological and social growth of new generations, a perspective of increasing relevance for contemporary psychology."

- **Luciano Mecacci, Former Professor of General Psychology, University of Florence, Italy. Author of** *Lev Vygotskij: sviluppo, educazione e patologia della mente*

"Myra Barrs's book sails right into areas that have been at the centre of controversy in recent times, and she puts everything in the context of the *whole* of Vygotsky's work. It would seem that she has produced a definitive textbook on Vygotsky's ideas for his principal readership, teachers."

- **Andy Blunden, author of** *Hegel for Social Movements*

Vygotsky the Teacher

This highly accessible guide to the varied aspects of Vygotsky's psychology emphasises his abiding interest in education. Vygotsky was a teacher, a researcher and educational psychologist who worked in special needs education, and his interest in pedagogy was fundamental to all his work. *Vygotsky the Teacher* analyses and discusses the full range of his ideas and their far-reaching educational implications.

Drawing on new work, research and fresh translations, this unique text foregrounds key Vygotskian perspectives on play, imagination and creativity, poetry, literature and drama, the emotions, and the role of language in the development of thought. It explains the textual issues surrounding Vygotsky's publications that have, until recently, obscured some of the theoretical links between his ideas. It underlines Vygotsky's determination to create a psychology that is capable of explaining all aspects of the development of mind.

Vygotsky the Teacher is essential reading for students on education and psychology courses at all levels, and for all practitioners wanting to know more about Vygotsky's theories and their roots in research and practice. It offers a unique road map of his work, connecting its different aspects, and placing them in the context of his life and the times in which he lived.

Myra Barrs is a freelance writer and consultant. She is Honorary Senior Research Associate at the UCL Institute of Education, UK, and former director of the Centre for Literacy in Primary Education.

Vygotsky the Teacher

A Companion to His Psychology for Teachers and Other Practitioners

Myra Barrs

Myra Barrs

29.3.22

Routledge
Taylor & Francis Group

LONDON AND NEW YORK

First published
by Routledge
2 Park Square, Milton Park, Abingdon, Oxon OX14 4RN

and by Routledge
52 Vanderbilt Avenue, New York, NY 10017

Routledge is an imprint of the Taylor & Francis Group, an informa business

© 2022 Myra Barrs

British Library Cataloguing in Publication Data
A catalogue record for this book is available from the British Library

Library of Congress Cataloging-in-Publication Data
Names: Barrs, Myra, author.
Title: Vygotsky the teacher : a companion to his psychology for teachers and other practitioners / Myra Barrs.
Description: First edition. | Abingdon, Oxon ; New York, NY : Routledge, 2022.
Identifiers: LCCN 2021008144 (print) | LCCN 2021008145 (ebook) | ISBN 9780367195403 (hardback) | ISBN 9780367195410 (paperback) | ISBN 9780429203046 (ebook)
Subjects: LCSH: Vygotskii, L. S. (Lev Semenovich), 1896-1934. | Educational psychologists–Soviet Union–Biography. | Educational psychology–Soviet Union.
Classification: LCC LB775.V942 B37 2022 (print) | LCC LB775.V942 (ebook) | DDC 370.15–dc23
LC record available at https://lccn.loc.gov/2021008144
LC ebook record available at https://lccn.loc.gov/2021008145

ISBN: 978-0-367-19540-3 (hbk)
ISBN: 978-0-367-19541-0 (pbk)
ISBN: 978-0-429-20304-6 (ebk)

DOI: 10.4324/9780429203046

Typeset in Bembo
by Taylor & Francis Books

In memory of Gordon Pradl
my friend and teacher
(1943–2020)
who urged me to write this book

and
of James Berry
my beloved partner
(1924–2017)
who has been with me all the way

Contents

Figures

Acknowledgements

Acknowledgements are due to the following holders of copyright material:

Andy Byford, for a quotation from his '*Lechebnaia pedagogika*: the concept and practice of therapy in Russian defectology, c.1880–1936', *Medical History*, 62(1).

MIT Press, for quotations from Vygotsky's *The psychology of art*, and for the reproduction of 'Leontiev's parallelogram' and the use of part of the diagram's caption, from *Acting with technology: activity theory and interaction design*, by V. Kaptelinin and B.A. Nardi.

Springer, for quotations from the six English volumes of Vygotsky's *Collected works* and from *Vygotsky's notebooks: a selection*, edited by E. Zavershneva and R. Van der Veer.

The Marxists Internet Archive, for the cover photograph and for quotations from A. Meshcheryakov's *Awakening to life: forming behaviour and the mind in deaf-blind children*.

Luciano Mecacci, for the use of the comprehensive bibliography of Vygotsky's works in his *Lev Vygotskii: Sviluppo, educazione e patologia della mente*.

PsyAnima, *Dubna Psychological Journal*, 3, for quotations from L. Mecacci's 'Russian psychology and Italian psychology and psychiatry in the second half of the 20th century'.

International Research in Early Childhood Education, 7(2), for extracts from Vygotsky's 'Play and its role in the mental development of the child', translated by N. Veresov and M. Barrs.

History of Education Quarterly, 41(4), for quotations from E.T. Ewing's 'Restoring teachers to their rights: Soviet education and the 1936 denunciation of pedology'.

Journal of Cognitive Education and Psychology, 10(2), for extracts from Vygotsky's 'The dynamics of the schoolchild's mental development in relation to teaching and learning', translated by A. Kozulin.

Psychological Thought, 5(2), for quotations from E. Minkova's 'Pedology as a complex science devoted to the study of children in Russia: the history of its origin and elimination'.

Revue internationale du CRIRES: innover dans la tradition de Vygotsky, 4(1), for quotations from V. Sobkin's 'Lev Vygotsky: from theater to psychology'.

School Psychology International, 16(2), for quotations from G.L. Vygodskaya's 'His life'.

European Journal of Psychology of Education, 9(4), for quotations from B. Schneuwly's 'Contradiction and development: Vygotsky and paedology'.

Taylor and Francis, for quotations from articles by various authors in *Journal of Russian and Eastern European Psychology; Changing English; Mind, Culture and Activity*; and *Estudos de Psicologia*.

Cultural-Historical Psychology, 12(3), for quotations from M. Dafermos's 'Critical reflection on the reception of Vygotsky's theory in the international academic community'.

Max-Planck-Institut für Wissenschaftsgeschichte, for quotations from L. Hyman's 'Vygotsky on scientific observation'.

The author would be glad to hear from the copyright owner of the English translation of Vygotsky's *Educational psychology*, whom she has been unable to trace.

Introduction

Vygotsky the teacher

At the heart of Vygotsky's work was education. He began his career as a provincial teacher, by all accounts an outstanding and unforgettable teacher and teacher educator. Later, as a psychologist in Moscow, he held conferences that were attended by students, teachers, doctors and other psychologists from all over the city. His teaching was often based on case studies; his work in child psychology and educational psychology was grounded in his experience of teaching and his observations of children, particularly children with special needs. Behind the careful design of his experiments with children was a highly developed interest in pedagogy, and this practical experience with children and with teachers lay behind all of his subsequent work in psychology and in 'child science' or 'pedology'. His whole project was an evolving approach to studying the development of mind. His work was not completed when he died of tuberculosis at the age of 37, but he left a clear picture of his intentions, his priorities and his methods.

This book sets out to be an accessible guide to Vygotsky's work. It pays serious attention to the full range of Vygotsky's ideas and their educational implications. Vygotsky wanted to ensure that psychology in general, and the psychology of education in particular, was broad enough to include the importance of play, the role of creativity, imagination and emotion, and the fundamental part played by language in the development of concepts and of consciousness. To this end he set out to change psychology.

Vygotsky's Russian texts

Vygotsky is widely considered to be the most important educational psychologist of the twentieth century, yet until recently it has been difficult to read his work in authentic versions. The story of his publications, both in Russia and in the West, is a complicated one; several of his texts were not published during his own lifetime and his published work was suppressed or censored after his death in 1934. Although after Stalin's death in 1953 his books started being published again, the texts that were published in the late 1950s and early 1960s were not based on original sources, but were heavily edited and censored. The particular reason why Vygotsky's work continued to be regarded as problematic, even after it was no longer officially banned, was his interest in 'child science' or 'pedology' (see Chapter 7). Even in the 1980s and 1990s reliable texts were limited. The *Collected works* in Russian, published in the 1980s, avoided the question of pedology and omitted several essential texts from the collection. Most Vygotskyan commentators now regard this edition as incomplete and inaccurate.

Sometimes the original publication dates of Vygotsky's works are disputed. When I discuss these cases later in the book, I mention the grounds for dispute. I have relied throughout on the outstanding bibliography provided by Luciano Mecacci in his recent book about Vygotsky (Mecacci, 2017).

The English translations

The six volumes of the Russian *Collected works* were then translated into English, without any alteration, and published from 1987 to 1999. Prior to that, the main English texts available were *Thought and language*, which was published in a heavily cut version in 1962, and then in a very good – but still incomplete – translation in 1986, before appearing, as *Thinking and speech* (Vygotsky, 1987a), in volume 1 of the English *Collected works* in 1987. (In this book I shall refer to *Thinking and speech*, unless a text I am quoting uses the title *Thought and language*.)

Although there are now more possibilities of access to Vygotsky's work, many readers of Vygotsky in English have not read much further than *Thought and language/Thinking and speech* and *Mind in society* (a very flawed set of heavily edited excerpts from Vygotsky published in the USA in 1978, which is still in print).

Luciano Mecacci (1992), who has studied the way in which Vygotsky's original texts were edited and changed in the 1960s, has commented on the fact that later editions in Russian perpetuated the interventive editing of the Soviet-era editors, and then became the basis of all subsequent translations. In recent years there has been a much more sustained effort to return to authentic texts and to present them in faithful translations. The translation of Vygotsky's complete pedological works, for instance, which he himself regarded as just as important as his work in psychology, is being carried out now by David Kellogg and Nikolai Veresov (Vygotsky, 2019). Although some pedological texts were included in volume 5 of the *Collected works* (Vygotsky, 1998), they were heavily cut and edited.

It is only quite recently that we have been able to read most of Vygotsky's work – and in the past twenty years Vygotsky studies have been transformed.

Commentaries on Vygotsky

Initially, Vygotsky studies in the West were dominated by a small number of North American commentators, whose version of Vygotsky was limited by their own theoretical perspectives. These earlier commentators were also influenced in their view of Vygotsky by some of the leading Soviet psychologists that they encountered in the USSR in the 1970s and 1980s, who, earlier in their careers, had criticised and disparaged Vygotsky's work for political reasons.

But in more recent years the field of Vygotsky studies has greatly expanded, and there are now important Vygotskyan commentators in many parts of the world. This book draws on many such commentators, from Australia, Brazil, Canada, Finland, France, Greece, Israel, Italy, the Netherlands, Russia, South Africa, South Korea, Switzerland, the UK and the USA. As a consequence of these wider perspectives, the Vygotskyan debate has broadened, so that this is a particularly appropriate time to review the development of Vygotsky's life's work and the continuing relevance and importance of his contribution to educational theory and practice.

The outstanding new publication in this field is *Vygotsky's notebooks* (Zavershneva and Van der Veer, 2018), which gives remarkable insights into Vygotsky's thinking processes and the drafting stage of his ideas.

Another aspect of Vygotsky's thinking that has not until now been adequately recognised, its roots in philosophy and particularly the philosophy of Hegel and Spinoza, has been foregrounded by Jan Derry's book *Vygotsky: Philosophy and education* (Derry, 2013).

Extensive exploration of the seminal concept of *'perezhivanie'* in Vygotsky's work (see below) has been carried out in publications by Fernando González Rey, Nikolai Veresov, Marilyn Freer and others.

This wider view of Vygotsky's work has led to the inclusion in the Vygotskyan canon of some books once regarded as irrelevant to his psychology, such as *The psychology of art* (Vygotsky, 1971) and several of his pedological works. It has also foregrounded certain key Vygotskyan themes which were given too little emphasis by earlier psychologist commentators, themes such as consciousness, and the role of language in the development of mind.

The result of all this activity has been that what we might call the 'foundational concepts' of Vygotsky's work are now much more clearly in view.

Foundational concepts

Vygotsky's strong focus on the arts and on play, creativity and imagination, the emotions, and their role in thinking, is a central component of his psychological theory that still needs more emphasis in Vygotskyan studies, and in practice.

His detailed analysis of the teaching and learning of scientific concepts, as a major element in the development of mature thinking, has huge implications for the school curriculum (especially at secondary level), and for pedagogy.

His theory of the zone of proximal/proximate development, although it has sometimes been confusingly interpreted (see Chapter 9), is nonetheless full of brilliant insights into the relationship between teaching and potential development.

Vygotsky's view of language as the main route by which human beings become conscious of their own behaviour, and therefore able to regulate *and reconstruct* their behaviour and their mental operations, was essential to his theory of mental development and education:

> speech, being initially the means of communication, the means of association, the means of organisation of group behaviour, later becomes the basic means of thinking and of all higher mental functions, the basic means of personality formation.
>
> (Vygotsky, 1998a, p. 169)

This fundamental insight also has the potential to unify and restructure educational practice. Yet the centrality of speech and language in Vygotsky's theory was downplayed and airbrushed out by many commentators in both Russia and the West in the late twentieth century. (For a detailed account of how Vygotsky's legacy was misunderstood, misinterpreted and actually distorted in the 'secondary literature' of that time, see Ronald Miller's 2011 book *Vygotsky in perspective*.)

And finally, from his earliest psychological writings, Vygotsky was explicit about the need for psychology to recognise the role of consciousness in the creation and organisation of mind:

> Vygotsky's life goal was to create a psychology that would be theoretically and methodologically adequate for the investigation of consciousness.
>
> (Lee, 1985, p. 66)

Like Marx, his view of the relationship between consciousness and activity was interactionist. Mind is formed through interaction with others, through experience in the world and in relation to human culture. The role of language is fundamental to this interaction. Through language, higher mental functions are internalised and developed. Consciousness is thus the product of these social and cultural processes. Higher mental functions, interacting in increasingly complex psychological systems, are then integrated in the continuing development of mind, in a process of constant dialectical change:

> Vygotsky viewed development as the gradual reorganization of consciousness.
>
> (Lee, 1985, p. 71)

In this book I have given full weight to these foundational concepts.

Terminology

Translation from the Russian has led to some mistranslations of particular terms, and consequent misunderstandings. Among these has been the translation of the word '*obuchenie*', which in Russian means both teaching and learning. This has led to different interpretations. The full implications of this crux in translation are spelt out in Chapter 9 of this book, which deals with the zone of proximal (or proximate) development, frequently called the ZPD.

The 'zone of proximal development', mentioned frequently in the book, is probably the most famous phrase associated with Vygotsky. The Russian original of the phrase is *zona bližajšego razvitija,* meaning 'the zone of nearest (or next) development'. The Italian phrase, *zona di sviluppo prossimo,* is a direct translation from the Russian. But 'proximal' in the English phrase is a rather obscure term from anatomy, first used by the translators of an article in *Mind in society* (Vygotsky, 1978). The recent translation of this article by Stanley Mitchell (Vygotsky, 2017), discussed at length in Chapter 9, uses the translation 'proximate'. In this book I have used the expression 'zone of proximal development' whenever it is used by other authors. But otherwise I have used 'zone of proximal/proximate development', both to make the meaning clearer, and to indicate that there is an issue of translation here.

Another Russian word which does not translate easily into English is *per-ezhivanie*, a noun from the verb *perezhivat,* which means to 'live through a (difficult) experience'. *Perezhivanie* is sometimes translated as 'lived experience', but there are disagreements about its exact meaning and how it can best be conveyed in translation. As this word is very relevant to child psychology and the understanding of children's interpretation of their experience, it has become a disputed term. It is discussed in full in Chapter 7.

An unfamiliar term that will arise early in the course of this book is 'defectology', which was a familiar term for many years in Russia and is still in use today. It describes the study of children's developmental pathologies, disabilities and special needs. Although Vygotsky acknowledged that the word carried within it unacceptable implications, he used it in his work because it was the current term. Vygotsky was known as a defectologist and taught in defectological institutions. His writings in defectology are discussed in Chapter 3.

Allied to defectology was the multi-disciplinary science of 'pedology', the subject of Chapter 7. This is sometimes known as 'child science', including all the specialisms concerned with childhood, such as paediatrics, child psychology and teaching. Vygotsky became a leading pedologist.

The structure of this book

This book is organised chronologically and each chapter focuses on one area of Vygotsky's psychology, often through an analysis of a single book or a small group of publications. Apart from the account of Vygotsky's early life given in Chapter 1, the book is not a biography, but it does offer some glimpses of Vygotsky's life, his personality, and his ways of working and thinking. I have also tried, at occasional points in the book, to give a sense of the times in which

Vygotsky was working, and of the changes in the political climate in Soviet Russia that were the background to his work.

I am hoping, in this way, to 'put Vygotsky together'. For want of a map of his work such as I mean to provide, I believe that many readers of Vygotsky, including those who have read several of his books, are not always aware of the relationships between the different aspects of his work, and do not have enough information about the textual issues surrounding some of his publications. Indeed, through the process of writing this book I have gained hugely from being able to see the connections between different aspects of Vygotsky's psychology, particularly the connections between his later work and his earlier writings in aesthetics and in defectology.

Manolis Dafermos regards Vygotsky as an extraordinary example of creativity in science. He quotes Alexander Zaporozhets, originally one of Vygotsky's research students, who saw Vygotsky's main quality as creativity and the ability to make connections:

> If you were to ask what was Vygotsky's dominant quality as a scientist, i.e. the quality that made the greatest impression on those around him, the answer might be his extremely creative capacity for productive synthesis, the ability to put things together in a creative way. One can say that this creativity was no extraordinary episode in Vygotsky's life: it was in his blood, it was the permanent mode of his everyday scientific life and activity ...
>
> (In Dafermos, 2018, p. 221)

References

Dafermos, M. (2018). *Rethinking cultural-historical theory: a dialectical perspective to Vygotsky*. Singapore: Springer.

Derry, J. (2013). *Vygotsky: Philosophy and education*. Chichester: Wiley Blackwell.

Lee, B. (1985). 'Intellectual origins of Vygotsky's semiotic analysis'. In Wertsch, J.V. (ed.). *Culture, communication, and cognition: Vygotskian perspectives*, pp. 66–93. Cambridge: Cambridge University Press.

Mecacci, L. (1992). 'Introduzione', in Vygotsky, L.S., *Pensiero e linguaggio* [1934], pp. v–x. Bari: Editori Laterza.

Mecacci, L. (2017). *Lev Vygotskii: Sviluppo, educazione e patologia della mente*. Florence: Giunti.

Miller, R. (2011). *Vygotsky in perspective*. Cambridge: Cambridge University Press.

Vygotsky, L.S. (1962). *Thought and language* [1934]. Trans. E. Hanfmann and G. Vakar. Cambridge, MA: MIT Press.

Vygotsky, L.S. (1971). *The psychology of art* [1925]. Intro. A.N. Leontiev; commentary V.V. Ivanov. Cambridge, MA: MIT Press.

Vygotsky, L.S. (1978). *Mind in society*. Cole, M., John-Steiner, V., Scribner, S. and Souberman, E. (eds). Cambridge, MA: Harvard University Press.

Vygotsky, L.S. (1986). *Thought and language* [1934]. Trans. A. Kozulin. Cambridge, MA: MIT Press.

Vygotsky, L.S. (1987). *The collected works of L.S. Vygotsky. Volume 1, Problems of general psychology*. Trans. and intro. N. Minick; Rieber, R.W. and Carton, A.S. (eds). New York: Plenum Press.

Vygotsky, L.S. (1987a). *Thinking and speech* [1934], in Vygotsky, L.S., *The collected works of L.S. Vygotsky. Volume 1, Problems of general psychology*, pp. 37–285. Trans. and intro. N. Minick; Rieber, R.W. and Carton, A.S. (eds). New York: Plenum Press.

Vygotsky, L.S. (1992). *Pensiero e linguaggio* [1934]. Trans. L. Mecacci. Bari: Editori Laterza.

Vygotsky, L.S. (1998). *The collected works of L.S. Vygotsky. Volume 5, Child psychology*. Rieber, R.W. (ed.). New York: Plenum Press.

Vygotsky, L.S. (1998a). 'Dynamics and structure of the adolescent's personality' [1931], in Vygotsky, L.S., *The collected works of L.S. Vygotsky. Volume 5, Child psychology*, pp. 167–184. New York: Plenum Press.

Vygotsky, L.S. (2017). 'The problem of teaching and mental development at school age' ['*Problema obučenija i umstvennogo razvitiya v škol'nom vozraste*'] [1935]. Trans. S. Mitchell. *Changing English*, 24 (4), pp. 359–371.

Vygotsky, L.S. (2019). *L.S. Vygotsky's pedological works. Volume 1, Foundations of pedology*. Trans. and with notes D. Kellogg and N. Veresov. Singapore: Springer Nature.

Wertsch, J.V. (ed.) (1985). *Culture, communication, and cognition: Vygotskian perspectives*. Cambridge: Cambridge University Press.

Zavershneva, E. and Van der Veer, R. (eds) (2018). *Vygotsky's notebooks: a selection*. Singapore: Springer Nature.

Chapter 1

Beginnings

The young Vygotsky

Lev Semyonovich Vygotsky was born in 1896 to a Jewish middle-class family living in Orsha, Belorussia, within the pale of settlement for Russian Jews. When he was only a few months old the family moved to Gomel, also in Belorussia, where Vygotsky's father became a manager at the Gomel branch of Union Bank. It was a highly literate family. Vygotsky's mother was a qualified teacher and fluent in several languages. There were eight children in the family and Lev was the second; like all the children, he was initially taught by his mother. Lev also grew up with his cousin David, who was only three years older than him.

Vygotsky's daughter Gita Vygodskaya, in her memoir, describes the household:

> A cult of the book literally reigned in the house. Regardless of how modestly the family lived, they nevertheless bought books. Works of the Russian classics and foreign literature were in the house … An interest in literature predominated perhaps above all else in the family, and a love of literature united them. Joint readings aloud of the classics and of new literature were a family practice. After new works were read, or after a visit to the theater, the family discussed together what they had read or seen, and each could state his own opinion and impressions about the book or the play.
>
> (Vygodskaya and Lifanova, 1999, p. 25)

Vygotsky's father was the president of the local branch of OPE, the Association for the Enlightenment of the Jews of Russia. He founded a public library, which was open to all, in the same building as the family apartment (Kotik-Friedgut and Friedgut, 2008, p. 18).

These were very problematic times for the Jews of Russia. Following the assassination of Tsar Alexander in 1881, blamed by some on the Jews, there was a series of violent anti-Semitic attacks and pogroms, which led to further

DOI: 10.4324/9780429203046-1

restrictions on Jewish rights. Jews were expelled from Moscow in 1891. Pogroms increased across various cities in the early 1900s. In Gomel there were two pogroms during Vygotsky's childhood, one in 1903 when he was seven. The Jewish community anticipated an attack, and trained and armed themselves beforehand; Lev's father was on the organising committee. This self-defence group repelled the invaders, but then had to resist an attack by the police, who tried to disarm them. Thirty-six Jewish defenders and 44 non-Jews were subsequently tried. Lev's father was a witness for the Jewish self-defence group; in his testimony he spoke about the suffering that Jews were experiencing for having sought equal rights (Kozulin, 1990).

After Vygotsky's early education with his mother, when he learnt German, English, Hebrew and other languages, Vygotsky had an outstanding home tutor, Solomon Markovich Aspiz, whose Socratic style of teaching was intellectually demanding. Vygotsky was taught always to look for the flaws in his own arguments. In due course he went on to study in the sixth form of a Jewish private secondary school. Semyon Dobkin, a school friend, remembers that Vygotsky's sister and his own sister formed a Jewish history study group and invited him to join it; Vygotsky was asked to chair the group. Under his leadership it soon became a study group on the philosophy of history, and its meetings went on for two years. Vygotsky had read both Hegel and Spinoza – his father had given him a copy of the *Ethics*, and he continued to refer to Spinoza throughout his life.

David Vygodsky, Vygotsky's cousin, was a great influence on Vygotsky as a student. He was a linguist, translator and poet with a strong interest in modern Jewish poetry, and was eventually a friend of Roman Jakobson and Victor Shklovsky. Dobkin reports that he was an enthusiast for Esperanto; under his influence Vygotsky learnt Esperanto and corresponded with an Icelandic penfriend in that language.

It is obviously intriguing that David Vygodsky and the rest of the family spelt their name with a 'd', whereas Vygotsky spelt it with a 't'. This name change was a deliberate decision by Vygotsky. Gita Vygodskaya explains it this way:

> Thus, in his youth he thought about the origin of his family, his name, and his kin. He studied this question and got to the truth. He showed his father that their family name was written incorrectly, that it did not come from the word *vygodu*, but from the name of a small village in Belarus from whence his kin came, and hence should be written with a "t", Vygotsky. From that time on, he began to write his last name accordingly, and that is how the whole world knows it today.
>
> The desire to 'get to the core' of things, to dig to the depths of everything he undertook, was typical of his character.
>
> (Vygodskaya and Lifanova, 1999, p. 21)

In 2013, Vygotsky passed the final school exams with honours, and was awarded a gold medal. He planned to go to university but there was a quota of three per cent of the intake for Jews seeking admission to higher education. His gold medal meant that in normal times he would have automatically qualified for admission to Moscow University. But that summer the rules were changed; Jewish applicants were now to be chosen by lot, not merit. Despite this extra hurdle Vygotsky was given a place in the University by the lottery draw. He was going to read for a medical degree; this would mean that he had a profession (Jews were not allowed to be government employees at that time) and enable him to work outside the pale of settlement.

When he went up to Moscow University he almost immediately transferred to the law department – law was also a permitted profession. And he enrolled as well for Shanyavsky University, a private mixed university with some celebrated scholars in its faculty and a more liberal atmosphere; here he studied philosophy, literature and psychology.

In 1915 his sister Zinaida joined him in Moscow and they shared a lodging. She was reading philosophy and languages and the topic of her dissertation was Spinoza. The topic of Vygotsky's final thesis for Shanyavsky University was Shakespeare's *Hamlet*, a play which had already been the topic of a long essay that he wrote in high school. While in Moscow both Vygotsky and his sister often went to the theatre; they knew the whole repertoire of the Moscow Arts Theatre and did not miss a single performance (Vygodskaya and Lifanova, 1999, p. 28).

During his last year in Moscow Vygotsky began to work for *Novyi put'*, a liberal Jewish periodical, for which he wrote articles on the Jewish people's situation in Russia, and on literary works by Lermontov and others. He also wrote theatrical reviews for the journal *Letopis*.

In 1917, after decades of unrest and uprisings, the February revolution began in Petrograd with mass demonstrations, extensive mutinies in the army, and the abdication of the Tsar. A provisional revolutionary government came into power in March with a manifesto proposing a plan of civic and political rights. Later in March the government, with Alexander Kerensky as Attorney General, passed a decree repealing anti-Semitic Tsarist laws, making all citizens equal before the law, and banning discrimination based on religion or ethnic origin. To mark this decree Vygotsky wrote an article for *Novyi put'* entitled 'We were slaves'.

Vygotsky graduated in the turbulent year of 1917, although he did not take his degree in law from Moscow University, presumably because of the chaos of the times. He may not have returned to Gomel immediately. Luciano Mecacci (2017) states that he accompanied his mother and younger brother Dodik, who was very ill with tuberculosis, to Samara and Kiev, possibly for medical care. It was still wartime and Gomel was under German occupation. Later in 1917 Dodik died, and a second brother died of typhoid fever (Vygodskaya, 1995).

There was now no law against Jews working in public service, so Vygotsky was finally able to work as a teacher in Gomel from about 1918. He taught

Russian language and literature, philosophy and logic at several institutions, including vocational schools for printers and metalworkers, and summer training courses for teachers. He taught logic and psychology to kindergarten teachers. At the same time he was writing regular theatre reviews for the local paper. In 1919 he became head of the theatre section of the Gomel Department of Public Education. In this role he worked with Israel Daniushevsky, who was to be his friend and supporter for the rest of his life.

Vygotsky's lifelong interest in literature had been developed partly through his close friendship with his cousin David Vygodsky (Kelner, 2006). During the Gomel period Vygotsky, his cousin and his friend Semyon Dobkin founded a small literary press to publish new poetry. All three shared a passion for literature and poetry; Vygotsky had a special admiration for the poetry of Heine, Blok and Tyutchev. The new press was able to publish only one book, Ilya Ehrenburg's *Fire*, before the government requisitioned all paper for official uses and the business was closed in 1919. Through David, Vygotsky came to know the works of Roman Jakobson, Viktor Shklovsky, Lev Jakubinsky and Osip Mandelstam (Dobkin, 1982).

Gita Vygodskaya provides a glimpse of his passion for poetry. She quotes Vygotsky's sister Maria telling the following story, which happened in 1919:

> Once I was washing the floors in the house when Lev Semenovich came in. He was happy and excited. 'Quick, finish scrubbing the floors and come with me. I have brought some very interesting poems by Mayakovsky and will read them.' I finished tidying up and hurried to him. Everyone was gathered around, and he began to read. I think it was ['The flutist']. At the time, it was difficult for me to understand Mayakovsky when I read him alone, but Lev Semenovich read so well that I immediately understood, and listened attentively. He read very simply, but drew out the main idea in such a way that it was very interesting and understandable to all.
>
> (Vygodskaya and Lifanova, 1999, p. 31)

Vygotsky gave popular literary lectures in Gomel on writers such as Shakespeare, Chekhov, Pushkin and Mayakovsky – but also general lectures on topics such as Einstein's theory of relativity (Blanck, 1990).

However, in 1920 Vygotsky suffered a severe attack of tuberculosis which he feared might be fatal. It was the first of a series of episodes of the disease that eventually killed him. When he did recover he began to teach again. He was reading omnivorously in poetry and literature and in linguistics, linguists like Potebnya and Humboldt as well as Jakobson and Jakubinsky. At this time he must have been writing his dissertation for Shanyavsky University, which became *The psychology of art* (Vygotsky, 1971). In addition, as always, he was reading philosophy, which now included, as well as Spinoza and Hegel, Feuerbach, Engels and Marx.

Before moving to Moscow in 1924, Vygotsky taught for several years at the teachers' college in Gomel, his home town. He taught Russian literature but also psychology. Alexander Luria, his friend and colleague in psychology, says that this experience was formative for Vygotsky:

> Vygotsky's work at the teachers' college brought him in contact with the problems of children who suffered from congenital defects – blindness, deafness, mental retardation – and with the need to discover ways to help such children fulfil their individual potentials. It was while searching for answers to these problems that he became interested in the work of academic psychologists.
>
> (Luria, 1979, p. 39)

Defectology and pedology

Books about Vygotsky, and there are many of them, have not, on the whole, given full weight to the fact that Vygotsky, although based at the Moscow Institute of Psychology, began his career in Moscow in 1924 primarily as a 'defectologist', that is to say, a specialist in the education of children with serious physical and mental impairments and severe developmental delays. Initially much of his work was with visually impaired and blind children, and those with deafness and impaired hearing. He continued to work in the field of defectology (which was a term in general use until the 1980s and not seen as negative) and in the allied field of pedology (the science of the child) for the rest of his life. Luciano Mecacci, a major Italian expert on Vygotsky's work, points out in the introduction to his translation of Vygotsky's *Thinking and speech* that Vygotsky never held a high-ranking post in psychology, only in defectology and pedology, although of course he taught on psychology courses, wrote about psychology and carried out psychological research (Mecacci, 1992, p. vi).

Part of the background to this story is the fact that there were about seven million street children in the USSR in the early 1920s. The end of the First World War, the civil war that followed the Revolution, and the famine of 1921–1922 had led to a situation where homeless children dressed in rags were wandering from city to city, with at least a thousand arriving in Moscow every week, to beg, rob and sleep rough. Only a fraction of them could be accommodated in orphanages and their education was sporadic or non-existent. Vygotsky would have been familiar with this horrifying situation and would have treated some of these children (Mecacci, 2019).

In this book there are separate chapters about Vygotsky's work in defectology (Chapter 3) and pedology (Chapter 7). It is apparent that his work in these areas influenced all his work in psychology. Vygotsky worked with both children and their teachers. He was a clinical psychologist at the Experimental Defectological Institute (EDI) Clinic in Moscow and at the Donskaya Clinic of the Pirogov Second Moscow Medical Institute – his notebooks contain case histories of some of the children he saw there. The Donskaya notebook shows that Vygotsky went on working there until May 1934, a month before his death. This notebook gives a good impression of the very difficult socio-economic circumstances and problematic backgrounds of several of these children, and reveals Vygotsky's acute and sympathetic style in clinical interviews. Boris Gindis observes:

> Vygotsky's socially, culturally, and developmentally oriented theory has the potential to unify, restructure, and promote special and remedial education as a science, profession, and social institution.
>
> (Gindis, 2003, p. 217)

Until recently Vygotsky was supposed to have started systematic work in psychology in 1924, when he gave an outstanding paper at a psychology conference in Moscow and was almost immediately invited to take up a post at the Moscow University Institute of Psychology. But in fact he had already been teaching psychology for some years before that. Nikolai Veresov says that Vygotsky himself pointed to 1917 as the year when he began his work in psychology (Veresov, 1999, p. 27).

One of Vygotsky's major commitments was his psychology course at Gomel's teachers' college. He had studied psychology at Shanyavsky University and had attended courses taught by the educational psychologist Pavel Blonsky, who was subsequently recruited by Krupskaya (in the Commissariat for Education) to draw up curricula for schools. He had also attended lectures on psychology by Shpet, the philosopher and psychologist, and by Chelpanov, the founder and Director of the Institute of Psychology. He had continued to read widely in psychology and to develop his own philosophy of pedagogy. His lectures at the Gomel teachers' college became the book *Educational psychology* – the first book, and one of the only books, published in his lifetime.

Educational psychology: psychology and learning

Educational psychology, the English edition of which was edited by Vassily V. Davydov and published in 1997 (Vygotsky, 1997a), is an unexpected and fascinating text. Nikolai Veresov sees it as 'almost a hymn to reflexology', the form of behaviourism that was dominating experimental psychology at the period when it was written, which Davydov (1997) places as between 1921 and 1923. It is true that in ch. 1 and ch. 2 Vygotsky writes as a reflexologist, or rather as a reactologist – since, as he points out, the term 'reflex' should really be used only for animals that possess a nervous system; it is a purely biological term. Human behaviour, which is infinitely more complex, is best described in terms of 'reactions'. At that point he sees no alternative to 'reactology' as a means of investigating behaviour.

The fascination of the book is that despite this relatively orthodox behaviourist opening, Vygotsky soon begins to push against the boundaries of behaviourism.

Throughout its pages we find, in ghost-like form, hints of the arguments that he will use in future articles and books, in future experiments and in later developments of his theory. In the course of reading this book it may be interesting for the reader to connect some of the statements in *Educational psychology* with statements in Vygotsky's later work:

In ch. 3, on the higher nervous system in man, Vygotsky writes:

> What constitutes the conscious aspect of human behaviour and what is the psychological nature of consciousness – these questions are very nearly the most difficult questions in all of psychology, about which we will speak later. But even now it is clear that consciousness must be considered as consisting of the most complex forms of organization of our behaviour, in particular, as Marx has shown, as a kind of doubling of experience that makes it possible to predict in advance the results of labour and to direct one's own reactions to this end ...
>
> Thus, the entire formula of human behaviour is not only the biological factor, but also the social factor, which brings with it entirely novel elements of behaviour.
>
> (Vygotsky, 1997a, p. 33)

Here already, in essence, are the arguments that we shall meet in Vygotsky's first conference papers in psychology, given in 1924. Here is the emphasis on the social factor in human development, which pervades his whole psychology. And here is the focus on the psychological nature of consciousness, the most difficult question in psychology, which is the theme that runs through his whole work and which he is determined to solve.

In ch. 6, on the education of emotional behaviour, Vygotsky writes:

> Emotion is no less important a tool than is thinking. The teacher must be concerned not only that students think about and learn geography, but also feel deeply about it. Such a thought usually does not come to mind and teaching that is emotionally felt is a rare visitor to our schools ...
>
> it is precisely the emotional reactions that have to serve as the foundation of the educational process ... of all the subjects taught in school, only in the teaching of literature, and there only to an insignificant extent, was the presence of an emotional component recognized as an essential element of the educational process in the classroom.
>
> (Vygotsky, 1997a, p. 107)

We shall find this focus on emotion growing in Vygotsky's psychology, most particularly in his work in pedology, and about play and the imagination. The central place of affect in thinking and in psychology was something that Vygotsky wanted to explore at length, although he was not able to finish his book about the emotions, begun towards the end of his life. The fundamental role that he sees affect and emotion as having in psychology is strongly emphasised in his last book, *Thinking and speech* (Vygotsky, 1987).

In ch. 9 of *Educational psychology*, on thinking as an especially complex form of human behaviour, Vygotsky writes:

> we are conscious of ourselves only to the extent that we are other for ourselves, i.e. somehow alien to ourselves. This is why language, this tool of social intercourse, is, in addition, also a tool of intercommunication between man and himself. The very consciousness of our thoughts and deeds must be understood as the very same mechanism responsible for the transmission of our reflexes to other systems or, speaking in terms of the traditional psychology, as the feedback reaction.
>
> (Vygotsky, 1997a, p. 172)

Here, Vygotsky's later ideas about the role of language in the construction of inner speech or thought are present – but clash with his fall-back mechanistic reflexological explanation.

Educational psychology: pedagogy

All of the above examples have great interest because of how they foreshadow Vygotsky's later psychology. But *Educational psychology* also has a wider scope, and is never so interesting as when Vygotsky is writing about teaching, as a person first and foremost interested in improving the quality of children's education and their ability to think and learn. Vygotsky was always a teacher and in this book we learn more about what kind of a teacher he was.

The early chapters in the book are about behaviourist psychology – reflex and reaction and 'higher nervous activity'. However from ch. 4 onwards most chapters contain a section on the educational implications of the subject of the chapter, on 'pedagogical applications' or 'pedagogical conclusions'. But perhaps to begin with, in order to gain an idea of the times in which Vygotsky was writing, we should look at a passage about the place of the school in the new society.

Vygotsky writes, in ch. 4, on biological and social factors in education:

> In the first year of the revolution, there were many people who saw the goal of education as a matter of demolishing the school. The path of revolution, the revolutionary avenue, is the best teacher, our children must become children of this avenue, the school must be demolished in the name of life – such were the slogans of the day ... However, this is not quite the way things work in more peaceable times, nor in the light of sober scientific reflection. It is true that we educate for life, that life is the highest judge ... that acculturation to life is our ultimate purpose ...
>
> (Vygotsky, 1997a, p. 51)

But Vygotsky is not in agreement with leaving the content of education to hazard:

> There is so much muck and mire along our way, together with the beautiful and the sublime that, were we to leave the outcome of the struggle for the child's motor field up to the free play of stimulation, we would be acting just as foolishly as a person who jumps into the ocean and yields to the free play of the waves out of a desire to get to America.
>
> (Vygotsky, 1997a, p. 51)

At the end of the same chapter he writes:

> Thus, education may be defined as a systematic, purposeful, intentional and conscious effort at intervening in and influencing all those processes that are part of the individual's natural growth. Consequently, only that formation of new reactions will be educational in nature which actually intervenes in growth processes to one degree or another, and steers those processes.
>
> (Vygotsky, 1997a, p. 58)

So Vygotsky has been through a period which has forced him to think about the kind of education that is essential in this new communist society. He is not a de-schooler, and though not an old-style Tsarist teacher, he is nevertheless a teacher who believes in intervening in, and steering, children's development.

In ch. 5, on the instincts as the subject, mechanism and means of education, Vygotsky writes:

> interest would appear to be the natural motive force of the child's behaviour, it is the true expression of instinctive striving, an indication that the child's activity coincides with his organic needs. That is why the fundamental rule demands that the entire education system, the entire structure of teaching, be constructed on the foundation of children's interests, taken into account in exact fashion.
>
> (Vygotsky, 1997a, p. 83)

> all the topics in a course must be interconnected, which is also the best way of ensuring that a common interest will be aroused and that this interest will collect around a single axis. Only then may we speak of a more or less prolonged, lasting, and deep interest, an interest that will not shatter into dozens of unrelated parts, making it impossible to grasp in a unified and general thought all the different subjects of study.
>
> (Vygotsky, 1997a, p. 86)

This was a theme that Vygotsky was committed to, and that in his later discussions of pedagogy he returned to (see ch. 1 of *Pedology of the adolescent* [Vygotsky, 1998]). He gives serious thought to how a teacher is to awaken children's interests – in this chapter he writes disapprovingly about a teacher who used cotton wool dipped in sulphur and placed in a pile of sand to simulate a volcanic eruption, and merely induced in her pupils a desire for the next teacher to show them more 'fireworks'. This chapter has some sensible rules of thumb, which it seems likely that Vygotsky had used in his own teaching – such as the undesirability of recourse to routine repetition in summarising what has been learned. Vygotsky's advice is:

> to review the same topic one more time in a more thorough and inclusive form, complemented with a wealth of new facts, generalisations and conclusions, so that topics students have already studied are repeated anew, though unfolded from a new perspective ... it is only a new view about what is old that may arouse our interest.
>
> (Vygotsky, 1997a, p. 86)

In ch. 8, on reinforcement and recollection of reactions, Vygotsky has a whole section on Functions of imagination, in which he writes:

> Everything we get to know out of what we have not experienced we get to know by means of imagination; specifically, if we study geography, history, physics or chemistry, astronomy, any science whatever, we are always dealing with the cognition of objects that are not given to us directly in our experience, but which constitute the most important achievement of mankind's collective social experience. If the study of the different subjects is not confined simply to relating anecdotes about the subjects, but strives to penetrate through this verbal shell of their description to their very essence, it must inevitably deal with the cognitive function of imagination ...
>
> (Vygotsky, 1997a, p. 150)

Giving us a glimpse of how he might achieve this use of the imagination in the teaching of physics, Vygotsky borrows an example from William James of how to convey to pupils the immensity of distance between earth and the sun.

> 'Suppose somebody shot at you from the sun, what would you do?' asks the teacher. When pupils said they would run or hide, the teacher reassures them; they would have time to grow up, learn a trade, reach the teacher's age – 'and only then will the bullet come close to you, and only then will you have to get out of the way. Thus you see how great is the distance of the earth from the sun.'
>
> (Vygotsky, 1997a, p. 152)

This anecdote illustrates a general rule: 'Imagination must always proceed on the basis of the known and familiar in order that we understand the unknown and unfamiliar' (ibid.).

Vygotsky was a memorable teacher and unquestionably some of the fascination of his teaching was his ability to stir the imagination and give his students graphic and sometimes humorous illustrations of the point he was trying to convey. We see this in his writing. In *The historical meaning of the crisis in psychology*, for instance, he illustrates the fact that in science the wrong questions can lead to meaningless answers:

> We can multiply the number of citizens of Paraguay with the number of kilometres from the earth to the sun and divide the product by the average life span of the elephant and carry out the whole operation irreproachably without a mistake in any number, and nevertheless the final outcome might mislead someone who is interested in the national income of this country.
>
> (Vygotsky, 1997b, p. 259)

In ch. 9 of *Educational psychology*, on Thinking, Vygotsky writes:

> what is pedagogically correct is to … let the child himself investigate the most complex and the most involved circumstances. If you would like a child to learn something well, take care to place obstacles in his path.
>
> It goes without saying that it is not a matter of constructing deliberately hopeless situations for the child, which would only lead to fruitless and unsystematic expenditure of the child's efforts. We are only concerned with organizing the child's life, and teaching, so that the child confront the two necessary elements for the development of thinking, as the highest forms of behaviour. These two elements are, first, the difficulty or, put differently, the problem which is to be solved, and, second, those elements and tools by means of which this problem may be solved.
>
> (Vygotsky, 1997a, p. 175)

So one of Vygotsky's main priorities as a teacher was to teach students to think, by not simplifying a problem. The teacher will, in this example, have made sure that the students have the tools they need to solve the problem, but not a blueprint of the answer. We are reminded of the Socratic method used by Vygotsky's home tutor, whose probing questions were designed to lead him to think for himself and defend his ideas. In the end, as Vygotsky makes clear throughout this book, the student must learn how to learn. The teacher's role is not to instruct, although it is to educate.

Despite his desire to shift the focus from the teacher to the learner, Vygotsky was obviously a magnetic and exciting teacher. D.B. El'konin remembered his lectures:

He held the entire audience captive from the first to the last minute …
The first thing that struck me and remained with me my whole life is how
Lev Semonovich presented his lectures and taught us how to think.
Although the lectures were for third-year students, everyone in education
and psychology attended them.

(Vygodskaya and Lifanova, 1999, p. 15)

One of his research students remembered him as a research tutor:

How did Lev Semonovich teach his fellow workers, pupils, and students?
He did not pontificate to them, but taught them by example how to
approach science and analyse children, through analytic examples given at
conferences, through his talks, by the way he did experiments, and
through the attention he devoted to people.

(Vygodskaya and Lifanova, 1999, p. 16)

His aim all along was to teach students to think, to look critically at their own
work, to 'be attentive to what was behind every fact and to explore every
psychological implication' (ibid.).

The glimpses of Vygotsky's philosophy of psychology and teaching, before he
moved to Moscow to begin (as it used to be thought) his career as a psychologist,
enable us to see that he had already formed firm views about both psychology
and pedagogy, which he would bring to the next phase of his work.

Two lifelong loves

Semyon Dobkin, Vygotsky's close friend in Gomel, maintained that there were
two main interests that dominated Vygotsky's life: 'What he really loved from
his youth and until his last days was theatre and poetry' (Dobkin, 1982, p. 27).
The next stage of this journey centres on Vygotsky's love of literature and on
his book *The psychology of art*. Here, Nikolai Veresov's account of the chron-
ology of Vygotsky's work before he moved to Moscow to take up his post in
the Institute of Psychology in 1924 is invaluable. He shows that the two books
that are usually dated 1925/26, *Educational psychology* and *The psychology of art*,
were probably both written during Vygotsky's years in Gomel, and he regards
them both as part of Vygotsky's 'intense search for a new psychological theory'
(Veresov, 1999, p. 77).

References

Blanck, G. (1990). 'Vygotsky: the man and his cause', in Moll, L.C. (ed.), *Vygotsky and
education*. Cambridge: Cambridge University Press, pp. 31–58.
Davydov, V.V. (1997). 'Lev Vygotsky and educational psychology', in Vygotsky, L.S.,
Educational psychology, pp. xiv–xxxix. Boca Raton, FL: CRC Press.

Dobkin, S. (1982). 'Ages and days', in Levitin, K., *One is not born a personality*, pp. 23–38. Moscow: Progress Publishers.

Gindis, B. (2003). 'Remediation through education', in Kozulin, A., Gindis, B., Ageyev, V.S. and Miller, S.M. (eds), *Vygotsky's educational theory in cultural context.* Cambridge: Cambridge University Press, pp. 200–222.

Kelner, V. E. (2006). 'David Vygodsky and his conception of the development of Jewish poetry'. Available online: http://judaica.spb.ru.

Kotik-Friedgut, B. and Friedgut, T.H. (2008). 'A man of his country and his time: Jewish influences on Lev Semionovich Vygotsky's world view'. *History of Psychology*, 11(1), pp. 15–39.

Kozulin, A. (1990). *Vygotsky's psychology: a biography of ideas.* Hemel Hempstead: Harvester Wheatsheaf.

Levitin, K. (1982). *One is not born a personality.* Moscow: Progress Publishers.

Luria, A.R. (1979). *The making of mind: a personal account of Soviet psychology.* Cole, M. and Cole, S. (eds). Cambridge, MA: Harvard University Press.

Mecacci, L. (1992). 'Introduzione', in Vygotsky, L.S., *Pensiero e linguaggio* [1934], pp. v–x. Bari: Editori Laterza.

Mecacci, L. (2017). *Lev Vygotskij: sviluppo, educazione e patologia della mente.* Florence: Giunti.

Mecacci, L. (2019). *Besprizornye: Bambini randagi nella Russia sovietica (1917–1935).* Milan: Adelphi.

Veresov, N. (1999). *Undiscovered Vygotsky: etudes on the pre-history of cultural-historical psychology.* Frankfurt am Main: Peter Lang.

Vygodskaya, G.L. (1995). 'His life'. *School Psychology International*, 16(2), pp. 105–116.

Vygodskaya, G.L. and Lifanova, T.M. (1999). 'Through the eyes of others'. *Journal of Russian and East European Psychology*, 37(4), pp. 3–40. doi:10.2753/RPO1061-040537043.

Vygotsky, L.S. (1971). *The psychology of art* [1925]. Intro. A.N. Leontiev; commentary V. V. Ivanov. Cambridge, MA: MIT Press.

Vygotsky, L.S. (1987). *Thinking and speech* [1934], in Vygotsky, L.S., *The collected works of L.S. Vygotsky. Volume 1, Problems of general psychology*, pp. 37–285. Trans. and intro. N. Minick; Rieber, R.W. and Carton, A.S. (eds.). New York: Plenum Press.

Vygotsky, L.S. (1992). *Pensiero e linguaggio* [1934]. Trans. L. Mecacci. Bari: Editori Laterza.

Vygotsky, L.S. (1997a). *Educational psychology* [1926]. Trans. R. Silverman. Davydov, V.V. (ed. and intro.). Boca Raton, FL: CRC Press.

Vygotsky, L.S. (1997b). *The historical meaning of the crisis in psychology: a methodological investigation* [1926–1927], in Vygotsky, L.S., *The collected works of L.S. Vygotsky. Volume 3, Problems of the theory and history of psychology*, pp. 233–343. Trans. and intro. R. Van der Veer; Rieber, R.W. and Wollock, J. (eds.). New York: Plenum Press.

Vygotsky, L.S. (1998). Chapter 1 of *Pedology of the adolescent* [1931], in Vygotsky, L.S., *The collected works of L.S. Vygotsky. Volume 5, Child psychology*, pp. 3–28. Rieber, R. W. (ed.). New York: Plenum Press.

Chapter 2

The psychology of art

> The melancholy of Chekhov's *Three Sisters*, presented on the stage by actresses of the Arts Theatre, becomes the emotion of the whole audience because it was to a large degree a crystallized formulation of the attitude of large social circles for whom its stage expression was a kind of means of realisation and artistic interpretation of themselves.
>
> (Vygotsky, 1999a, p. 241)

Introduction

Vygotsky's first major work in psychology was *The psychology of art*, [1] a study of how literature works, and works in us. This book signals his intention to include literature, drama, art and poetry within psychology, as valid evidence of human thinking and feeling.

As Veresov (1999) suggests, the book was perhaps written when Vygotsky was working in Gomel. It was presented in 1925 as his doctoral thesis. Vygotsky most definitely intended it as a work of psychology, but it also reflected his long-standing interest in literature, especially drama and poetry. It was not published until 1965 in Russia (1971 in the USA) and was not then given the place it deserved in Vygotsky's psychology. It was regarded as an early work, which had little significance for students of Vygotsky's psychological theory. This continued to be the case for many years.

However, the book shows Vygotsky already as a revolutionary psychologist who meant to alter the face of psychology so that it could address issues of the arts, and the relationship between the arts and emotion. His preface shows that he wants to look at art starting from Marxist principles, recognising that there is no contradiction between aesthetics and the Marxist sociological view of the arts. His aim is 'the achievement of a degree of scientific soundness and sobriety in the psychology of art, the most speculative and mystically unclear area of psychology' (Vygotsky, 1971, p. 6). In other words he wants to ensure that something as important as art is not excluded from psychology because it cannot yet be studied scientifically. This is obviously a hugely ambitious programme.

DOI: 10.4324/9780429203046-2

When we look at *The psychology of art* in the light of what came after, in the light of Vygotsky's later discussion (in *The historical meaning of the crisis in psychology*; Vygotsky, 1997) of the need for a properly scientific approach to methodology in psychology, and also in relation to his later work on play, creativity and the imagination, it is clear that the themes raised in this book run right through his work. Its very structure is strongly similar to the structure of his final book, *Thinking and speech* (Vygotsky, 1987b). From its epigraph, from Vygotsky's favourite philosopher, Spinoza, to its closing pages, which argue eloquently for the central place of art and literature in education, it is a considered and carefully structured work, entirely typical of his approach to the intellectual work of building a strong and well-evidenced theory.

The history of this book, and of its reception, tell us a lot about how Vygotskyan studies have changed and developed over the past fifty years. It shows how difficult it has been for some of his texts to find an understanding audience until comparatively recently. For teachers, this powerful argument for literature in education provides a particularly crucial insight into Vygotsky's educational psychology and philosophy.

Before *The psychology of art*

In Chapter 1, we saw the beginnings of Vygotsky's lifelong interest in literature, especially poetry and drama, both when he was at school and later as a university student. New evidence about his activities during that period has added to the picture we have from the commentaries of his friends and family.

From his youth, Vygotsky was enormously interested in the theatre. His sister Zinaida told Karl Levitin: 'I don't think there was any period in his life when he did not think or write about the theatre' (Levitin, 1982, p. 20).

While still at school, Vygotsky was involved in theatre and drama, from a practical point of view and as a theatregoer. According to his school friend Semyon Dobkin:

> He staged Gogol's play, *The marriage*, during a summer vacation. And he was something like a director, going over all the roles, male and female, with the participants.
>
> (Dobkin, 1982, p. 32)

The play that made the greatest impression on Vygotsky was Shakespeare's *Hamlet*. Dobkin tells us:

> I must note the profound impression *Hamlet* made on him while he was still a child. As a schoolboy, he began writing an essay on *Hamlet*, which as far as I remember, he did not show to anybody. It was his most closely

guarded secret. The essay was eventually published as a supplement to the
second edition of *The psychology of art*.

(Dobkin, 1982, p. 32)

While he was a student in Moscow he was 'a fervent admirer' (Veresov, 1999,
p. 61) of the Moscow Art Theatre where productions were always thought-
provoking. He would certainly have gone to see the famous production of
Hamlet, co-directed by Stanislavski and Gordon Craig, at the Art Theatre,
when Craig boldly dispensed with sets and focused on the mystery and myth of
the play, emphasising the central consciousness of Hamlet and using dramatic
lighting and surrealistic effects – Veresov says that there is no doubt that the
production and images 'made a deep impression on Vygotsky' (ibid.).

Theatre continued to be a major interest for Vygotsky, and he wrote extensively
for newspapers and magazines, in the form of theatre and book reviews and
magazine articles (Kotik-Freidgut, 2012; Marques, 2018; Sobkin, 2017).

Sobkin tells us that:

> Over almost a year and a half (from September 1922 through December
> 1923), Vygotsky published sixty-eight theater reviews and notices in
> Gomel newspapers. Since several of them covered not one production but
> two (and sometimes three or more), simple arithmetic shows that in those
> sixteen months he reviewed more than eighty performances in Gomel ...
>
> (Sobkin, 2017, p. 86)

This means that on average he went to at least six performances a month and
wrote reviews of them.

His comments are often trenchant and witty. About one actor's performance
as Raskolnikov, Vygotsky remarks:

> To play Dostoevsky at a normal temperature, say 36.6 or 36.8, is to undo
> him. But Sosin (Raskol'nikov) is before all else an actor whose temperature
> is normal. Dostoevsky's heroes are cut from a completely different spiritual
> cloth.
>
> (Sobkin, 2017, p. 89)

Dobkin suggested that Vygotsky became interested in the science of psychology
because 'the turn to that science was a natural corollary of his interest in fiction,
notably the psychological novel' (in Levitin, 1982, p. 17). That Vygotsky's first
major work was *The psychology of art* underlines his intention to include literature
within psychology as evidence of the importance of emotion in thinking.

Vygotsky read widely in philosophy, and among the philosophers he read he
reserved a special place for Spinoza, whose work offers a model of how to
build a new materialist and non-dualist philosophy. He also read in all branches
of psychology, including the works of psychologists such as William James and

Sigmund Freud. It is likely that psychology had been part of his philosophy course at Shanyavsky University (the study of psychology in Russia and the West originated in philosophy departments).

Until recently Vygotsky was supposed to have started systematic work in psychology only in 1924, when he gave an outstanding paper at a psychology conference in Moscow and was almost immediately invited to take up a post at the Institute of Psychology there. But in fact, as Nikolai Veresov (1999) has made clear, he had already been teaching psychology at Gomel teachers' college for some years before that.

The history of this text

As with many of Vygotsky's texts, this one has a particular story – and mystery – attached to it. We know that the text was essentially Vygotsky's doctoral thesis and that it was actually prepared for publication and delivered to a publisher (Van der Veer and Valsiner, 1991, p. 47). But the publisher's copy apparently went missing. There might be reasons for this related to the times – Vygotsky had, for instance, used quotations from Trotsky in the book, and by 1925 this would have been politically problematic. Even when a copy of *The psychology of art* was eventually found it was not published until 1965. However, Vygotsky had also given a copy of the book to the film director Eisenstein, who preserved it among his personal papers. (Eisenstein, Vygotsky and Luria were friends and regularly discussed questions of neurology and aesthetics together.) Eisenstein's copy included Vygotsky's own notes and the text of his early monograph on *Hamlet*. The 1971 text, however, is based on the Russian edition of 1965.

Leontiev's introduction

The book's introduction, by A.N. Leontiev (1971), is revealing because of the lukewarm nature of its evaluation. Leontiev, one of Vygotsky's colleagues, while describing the book as 'exceptional' and referring to its 'brilliant analysis', considers that Vygotsky outgrew the ideas in the book and 'clearly saw the incompleteness and imperfections of his work', putting it aside when he embarked on a career in psychology proper. This, he considers, was why the book was never published. He also refers to the content of the book as having been 'superseded'.

González Rey (2018) suggests that Leontiev's Introduction presented the book as a 'historical work with little theoretical value, considering the advances of Soviet psychology in the 40 years after the book had been written' (p. 344). He believes that the Introduction 'invalidated Vygotsky as a serious author' (ibid., p. 345) and was one reason why this work had so little impact either in the Soviet Union or in the West until quite recently. He also views the Introduction as an attempt to present Vygotsky's work as a forerunner of Leontiev's own Activity Theory 'which represented the new dominant official psychology of the Soviet Union in the 1960s' (ibid.). Leontiev may have wished to downplay Vygotsky's achievements for personal reasons; his own very successful career had built on his work with Vygotsky, from whom he had detached himself in 1932. A further likely explanation of Leontiev's attitude is that he was essentially out of sympathy with Vygotsky's introduction of ideas about literature and aesthetic development into psychology.

The reception of the book outside Russia

Leontiev's Introduction probably influenced the reception of the book outside Russia and psychologist commentators have certainly not paid much attention to it, or given it the status it merits, until relatively recently. They have tended to see it as a piece of juvenilia, not an integral part of Vygotsky's project. Joravsky comments:

> The Western psychologists who came to admire Vygotsky in the post-Stalin era have shown no more interest in his psychology of art than have his Soviet disciples.
>
> (Joravsky, 1989, p. 257)

Van der Veer and Valsiner, key commentators on Vygotsky, include their account of the book in an introductory section dealing with Vygotsky's childhood and youth; they do not include it in the study of his psychology proper, although they do say that:

> His work in art enabled him to tackle complex psychological problems and – the present authors would like to claim – far more rigorously than investigators trained as psychologists per se, in his time or ours. It was to Vygotsky's benefit – rather than detriment – that he moved to psychology from literary criticism and education.
>
> (Van der Veer and Valsiner, 1991, p. 35)

More recently, with the growing interest in Vygotsky's work before he moved to Moscow, more attention has begun to be paid to *The psychology of art*, and to the fact that some of his later ideas are clearly present in it, most particularly that of the development of emotions and of *perezhivanie* (often translated as 'emotional experience' or 'lived-through experience', or, in Italian, *vissuto*). González Rey (2016) makes a careful study of the use of the term *perezhivanie* in the book. He comments:

> Despite Vygotsky's *The psychology of art* having been largely ignored in both Soviet and Western psychology, this book has been one of the most important contributions of Vygotsky to the development of psychology.
>
> (González Rey, 2016, p. 2)

González Rey links the book to Vygotsky's 'late phase' in the early 1930s, when he was writing about imagination, creativity, and the emotions.

The construction of the book

The book is a complete argument addressing one subject, carefully planned and presented, with notes and references for every chapter. The most striking aspect of the book's construction is its symmetry. It is divided into four parts of which the first part is entitled 'On the methodology of the problem'. There follow three parts, two divided into three chapters and a third into four chapters.

In Vygotsky's own Preface to the book, he makes clear his belief that a work of art is 'a combination of aesthetic symbols aimed at arousing emotion in people' (Vygotsky, 1971, p. 5). His book will identify the psychological laws of works of art and the systems by which they work. His approach will be objective and analytic, and he will consider only the work of art itself, its form and material and its symbols, without any reference to the psychology of the author or his/her readers, which he does not believe would be either useful or possible.

'On the methodology of the problem' (part 1), reveals Vygotsky's thesis: 'Art systematises a very special sphere in the psyche of social man – his emotions' (Vygotsky, 1971, p. 13). Vygotsky makes the case for a Marxist psychological approach to the study of individual experience, arguing strongly that it is entirely legitimate to consider individual psychology as Marxist. He quotes a 'fundamental statement' by Marx, which says that 'man in the most literal sense is a *zoon politicon* (political animal), an animal to whom social intercourse is not only peculiar but necessary in order to stand out as a single individual' (ibid., p. 15). Vygotsky's method is going to be based firmly on Marxist and materialist principles.

This part provides a rationale for Vygotsky's approach in the book, and sets out in detail how he plans to tackle the problem. Vygotsky makes clear that his method will be like that of a historian who 'creates the object of his study by means of indirect, that is, analytic methods'. This strongly anticipates Vygotsky's approach in *The historical meaning of the crisis in psychology* (Vygotsky, 1997).

Part 2, 'Critique', is a review of three schools of art and literary criticism which have attempted, as Vygotsky intends to do, to give an objective explanation of the psychological basis of art. The three psychological theories of art Vygotsky deals with are:

- the school of 'art as perception';
- 'art as technique' – the theories of the Russian formalists; and finally,
- 'art and psychoanalysis' – the work of the Freudians.

All these theories have been chosen, says Vygotsky, because their analysis, like his own, starts from a consideration of the indirect evidence present in the work of art itself. But it is clear that these three schools have also been strategically chosen in order to prepare the way for Vygotsky's own argument, which has everything to do with the relationship between form and content.

Part 3, 'Analysis of the aesthetic reaction', is the core of the book and the one which probably holds most interest for general readers. Vygotsky is seen here as a subtle and responsive reader who engages closely with the detail of a text but is also constantly aware of its structure, its direction and its overall meaning. There are four chapters in part 3, the first of which is a general analysis of the fable, the earliest literary genre. In the remaining three chapters Vygotsky considers the construction and dynamic of three literary works, each representing a different type of literature, in increasing order of complexity. The works are: the Russian fables of Krylov (taken together), a short story by Bunin, and Shakespeare's *Hamlet*.

Finally, part 4, 'The psychology of art' (which has the same title as the book itself), consists of three chapters, in which Vygotsky, drawing the conclusions from his investigation, formulates his own psychology of art, and sets out his theory of the role of art in society and particularly in education.

Vygotsky's argument has been shaped carefully to advance his main thesis and this is apparent in the thoughtfully planned construction of the book. But the deliberate 'threeness' which is also apparent in the construction of this part represents another kind of shapeliness. It's an indication of Vygotsky's aesthetic pleasure in the beauty of the argument, with its balance and symmetry. It is the ease and grace of composition evident in this book that makes Stephen Toulmin's famous description of Vygotsky as 'the Mozart of psychology' (Toulmin, 1978) so particularly appropriate.

The construction of *The psychology of art* has much in common with that of Vygotsky's last book, *Thinking and speech* (Vygotsky, 1987b), which is equally a carefully planned complete argument, even though some of it was rapidly written and probably not revised (it was completed in 1934 as Vygotsky was dying). The two books also begin with a definition of the 'unit of analysis' to be used in their arguments, though they find this unit at opposite ends of the spectrum. In *The psychology of art*, Vygotsky's unit of analysis is the *complete work of literature*, while in *Thinking and speech* Vygotsky focuses on the *individual word* – or rather on '*word meaning*' (in the last chapter of this last book, 'the word' is often viewed in the context of works of literature). This deliberate emphasis on the centrality of language and of literature in the study of human psychology is one of the hallmarks of Vygotsky as a psychologist, but is also the aspect of his work that, until recently, has been taken least seriously.

In the remainder of this chapter we will look in more detail at the core of the book, part 3 – with its analysis of particular texts – and at Vygotsky's conclusions in part 4.

Part 3 – analysis of the aesthetic reaction

In the chapters that make up part 3, the progression in the three examples, from the elementary form of the fable to the problematic of *Hamlet*, the play that has probably generated more critical confusion and discussion than any other literary work, is deliberate. Vygotsky wants to show a certain principle at work in all three, and to show it at work in conditions of increasing complexity and subtlety.

This principle is the principle of contradiction, the collision between conflicting emotions, and the catharsis that resolves them. Vygotsky demonstrates that each of his literary examples contains this essential conflict or struggle.

Krylov's fables

The two chapters on fables, ch. 5 and ch. 6, are in fact longer than those on Bunin's short story or on *Hamlet*, and may have originated in a separate essay. Vygotsky finds in this popular folk form the seed of much later literature. In ch. 5, 'Analysis of the fable', he observes that: 'The fable is a basic, elementary form of poetry and therefore contains the seeds of lyric, epic and drama' (Vygotsky, 1971, p. 101).

This chapter is a prelude to Vygotsky's study, in ch. 6, of the fables of Krylov. What interests him particularly in these well-known fables is the 'subtle poison' infused there. Krylov had begun as a satirical writer, and was a frustrated dramatist. Vygotsky shows how in almost every one of his fables there is a double meaning, a second level, which 'turns his stories into real works of poetry' (Vygotsky, 1971, p. 137). For instance, in the fable 'The fox and the crow', the fox's flattering speech is not the speech of a supplicant; it is witty and mocking: 'each word he utters has for us a double meaning of adulation and mockery' (ibid., p. 120). Vygotsky finds this same 'second level' in each of the ten fables that he analyses. He suggests that for Krylov 'this double meaning overcame the narrow horizon of the prosaic fable which Krylov detested and helped him penetrate the wide field of dramatic poetry which was his passion.' (ibid., p. 137)

For instance, in 'The wolf in the kennel', which Vygotsky describes as 'the most noteworthy of Krylov's fables', a wolf has got into the hunting dogs' kennel by mistake, causing huge panic and confusion:

> And then all hell broke loose –
> Some ran around with guns;
> Some ran around with clubs.
> 'Light, give us light!' they screamed.
> (Vygotsky, 1971, p. 133)

But then the pace slows and the mood changes as the wolf is described:

> There was the wolf, pressed in a corner
> Gnashing his teeth, his hair abristle ...
> He saw that this was different from

the fields and woods. He saw
The reckoning before him for all the sheep
He'd killed, and he decided, cunningly,
To start discussions ...
                    (Vygotsky, 1971, p. 133)

The wolf speaks in a statesmanlike way, making a proposition:

I come to you in peace, not for a fight.
Let us forget the past and set up a joint order!
Not only will I henceforth not attack your herds,
But I shall fight for them against all common foes.
I am prepared to swear the oath of wolves ...
                    (Vygotsky, 1971, p. 134)

Vygotsky comments:

The exalted tone of the speech is in open contradiction to the actual situation ... his words ... say that he came to seek peace and graciously offer
protection for the herds, but in fact he is pressed into a corner, trembling. The
dogs are ready to tear him to pieces, yet his words offer them protection.
                    (Vygotsky, 1971, p. 134)

The catastrophe of the fable is reached when the huntsman announces his view:

'That peace with wolves is made in one way only –
After they have been stripped of hide and hair.'
This said, a pack of wolfhounds he unleashed.
                    (Vygotsky, 1971, p. 135)

So this fable too develops on two completely different emotional levels – we
expect the wolf's death at any moment, yet for a short time the wolf holds off
his enemies with his skilful and courageous speech. Initially it is the huntsman
and the dogs that are panic-stricken, but then they unleash their power.
Vygotsky suggests that the story works on two 'contrasting, and frequently
opposing, emotional levels', and that the combination of these two levels
'causes emotions characteristic of those provoked by a tragedy.' As readers we
are both impressed by the wolf and half believe that he has a chance of survival,
while also knowing that his death is inevitable.

From Vygotsky's point of view the doubleness of Krylov's fables also illustrates
in the simplest form his theory of catharsis:

If the two levels, or parallel themes, in the fable are supported and described
with all the skill of poetic technique, that is, if they exist not only as a logical

contradiction but also as an affective contradiction, the reader of the fable will experience contradictory feelings and emotions which evolve simultaneously with equal strength.

(Vygotsky, 1971, p. 139)

It is the form, the skill and organisation of the poetry, which makes this contradiction unignorable.

'Gentle breath'

Whereas in the simple form of the fable, the contradiction or struggle takes place within the action itself, in Bunin's short story 'Gentle breath' (1971) Vygotsky analyses the way in which form and content interact, or pull against one another. The material of the story is 'the insignificant and rather senseless life of a schoolgirl in a provincial Russian town'; her seduction by one lover and then her murder by another. All of the material, suggests Vygotsky, 'comes under the category "troubles of life". There is not one single bright spot in the entire story.' Yet this story leaves the reader with a sense of 'liberation, lightness, the crystal transparency of life, none of which can be derived from the literal events' (Vygotsky, 1971, p. 154). Vygotsky analyses the scheme of events in the story and shows how deliberately Bunin has changed the chronological path of events. The 1968 (Russian) edition showed how he actually *drew* the story, plotting its complicated sequence and recursive structure – how it seemingly begins at the end and then apparently 'drifts from one event to another, connecting the most remote events of the chronologically arranged material' (ibid., p. 152). It is this complex structure which moves the relatively banal material onto a different level:

> We recognise that the events are connected in such a way that they lose their turbidity. They are associated as in a melody ... Now we can formulate our idea and say that the author's reason for tracing such an extremely complex curve is his intent to undo life's turbidity and transform it into a crystal transparency.
>
> (Vygotsky, 1971, p. 154)

The main character, Olia, is a shallow and frivolous girl who is obsessed with her own appearance and her attractiveness to men. In the schoolyard one day she confides to her friend that she has read in one of her father's 'funny antique' books a description of what a woman's beauty should be – black eyes and eyelashes, a slender figure, long hands, a small foot, a moderately large bosom, a nice round calf ... 'and most important, you know what? A gentle breath! I have it, don't I? Listen, how I sigh. It's there, isn't it?' (ibid., p. 165).
   Bunin ends the story in the graveyard where Olia is buried:

And now this gentle breath is dissipated again in the world, in this cloud-covered sky in this cold spring wind ...

(Vygotsky, 1971, p. 165)

Vygotsky admired this story and used it in one of his psychological experiments in Gomel. He asked nine people to read it aloud and recorded their breathing with a pneumograph as they read it. He was interested to know how the author 'makes us breathe', and how the way we breathe creates an emotional mood in us.

Every poem or part of prose has its own system of breathing because of the immediate adaptation of breathing to speech. The writer creates not only the rhythm of words, but also rhythms of breathing. When we read Dostoevsky we read different from when we read Chekhov ...

(Quoted in Van der Veer and Valsiner, 1991, p. 30)

As so often Vygotsky was ahead of the game – there have been a number of research studies in recent years on the effects of reading or of experiencing live drama and or viewing films – especially as part of an audience – on our heart rate or breathing.

At the end of this chapter, Vygotsky is ready to state the main finding that he takes from his study of Bunin's text: its 'affective contradiction', the collision between two contrasting emotions that we experience in reading the story. The collision comes about because of a conflict between the content of the story and its form, the way its events are arranged and presented. Vygotsky describes this as an astonishing discovery:

Astonishing because traditional aesthetics prepared us for a diametrically opposed understanding of art. For centuries, scholars of aesthetics have told us of the harmony of form and content. They have told us that the form illustrates, completes or accompanies the content. And now we suddenly discover that this was an error, that the form may be in conflict with the content, struggle with it, overcome it. We discover in this dialectic contradiction between form and content the true psychological meaning of our own aesthetic reaction.

(Vygotsky, 1971, p. 160)

Hamlet

Vygotsky's analysis of *Hamlet* completes his thesis. This analysis is remarkable for the economy with which Vygotsky summarises and rejects a whole series of critical theories about *Hamlet* before proceeding to his own hypothesis. Vygotsky suggests that, in his source material:

Shakespeare had available to him ready-made logical and psychological motives. If he chose to process this material so as to ignore all the obvious ties which hold the original saga together, he must have had a special intention.

(Vygotsky, 1971, p. 181)

The tragedy continually draws our attention to the fact that Hamlet is delaying, while providing us with contradictory explanations of his procrastination. When he eventually comes to kill Claudius, it is at the point when the audience least expects it, and he does so to avenge not his father, but his mother.

Vygotsky again considers the 'interpretational curve' of this work – its topography. The plot – the basis of the tragedy – runs in a straight line, and 'if Hamlet had killed the king immediately after hearing the ghost's revelations he would cover the distance between these two points in the shortest possible way' (Vygotsky, 1971, p. 186). But as it is 'it appears as if Shakespeare had set himself the task of pushing the plot from its straight path onto a devious and twisted one.' The function of Hamlet's monologues is in fact to inform the audience 'in spurts, that the tragedy has left the pre-set track.' (ibid., p. 189) The structure of the tragedy is a double structure and can be expressed by:

two very simple formulas. The formula of the story is that Hamlet kills the king to avenge the death of his father; that of the plot is that he does not kill the king. If the material of the tragedy tells us how Hamlet kills the king to avenge the death of his father, then the plot of the tragedy show us how he fails to kill him and, when he finally does, that it is for reasons other than vengeance.

(Vygotsky, 1971, p. 189)

Vygotsky finds, then, in Shakespeare's play, the same emotional contradictions within the story itself that he found in Krylov's fables, and the same conflict between *form and content* that he found in Bunin's story, but there is now the added complexity of *character* – for in this play there is a clear 'incompatibility between protagonist and plot'. Hamlet the character becomes the 'supreme and ever-present embodiment of the contradictions inherent in the tragedy' (ibid., p. 195). Vygotsky sums up the progression between the texts he has studied in this way:

In the fable we discovered two meanings within one and the same action. In the short story we discovered one level for the story (subject) and one for the plot (material). In the tragedy we uncover yet another level, the psyche and the emotions of the hero.

(Vygotsky, 1971, pp. 192–193)

It is in the hero that the conflicts inherent in the structure of the play meet. The spectator is deceived: the different levels of the story and the plot converge in a scene which meets none of the expectations that have been built up in the course of the play. The final scene is a series of murders and deaths that culminate with that of Hamlet, on whom our attention and emotions have been focused throughout.

> This death makes the spectator at last aware of all the conflicts and contradictions that besieged his conscious and unconscious self during the play.
>
> (Vygotsky, 1971, pp. 192–193)

Part 4 – 'The psychology of art'

In the fourth and final part of the book, Vygotsky has two main purposes. One is to set out the psychological explanation of how the works he has considered affect the reader or theatregoer – to explore the nature of the aesthetic reaction – and also to relate his analysis to existing systems of psychology. Vygotsky's other major purpose in this part of the book is to consider the social and emotional significance of art in our lives; the part that it plays in education, in human development, and in the making of future societies.

'Art as a catharsis'

In the chapter 'Art as a catharsis', Vygotsky is intent on finding a theory of aesthetic response that will be adequate to explain how art works on us. In his habitual fashion he reviews a number of theories and schools of thought and finds them wanting:

> We realise that none of the existing theories of aesthetic emotion can explain the intimate connection between our feeling and the objects we perceive. To arrive at this explanation we must resort to psychological systems based on the association between fantasy and feeling.
>
> (Vygotsky, 1971, p. 209)

Vygotsky is interested in the association between emotion and imagination. He observes that it is a well-known fact that fantasies and imagined experiences can take place on a completely real emotional basis. Artistic feeling is the same as ordinary feeling but 'is released by extremely intensified activity of the imagination'. Instead of being acted out such feelings are expressed 'in images of fantasy'. In his search for a physiological explanation of the conflicting emotions that tragedy generates, Vygotsky resorts to Darwin's 'principle of antithesis', the tendency of every movement to call forth its opposite.

From his analysis of three types of text Vygotsky concludes that 'a work of art always includes an affective contradiction, causing conflicting feelings, and leads to the short-circuiting and destruction of these emotions. This is the true effect of a work of art' (ibid., p. 213). This leads him to Aristotle's theory of 'catharsis' which he acknowledges to be an enigmatic term, but which nevertheless fully expresses what he sees as the fundamental process at the heart of the aesthetic reaction.

> The law of aesthetic response is the same for a fable as for a tragedy: *it comprises an affect that develops into opposite directions but reaches annihilation at its point of termination.*
>
> (Vygotsky, 1971, p. 214)

What happens physiologically, in his view, is 'the discharge of nervous energy (which is the essence of any emotion)' (ibid.).

Later in the chapter he arrives at a law-like statement of this process:

> A work of art always contains an intimate conflict between its content and its form, and the artist achieves his effect by means of the form, which destroys the content.
>
> (Vygotsky, 1971, p. 215)

In this chapter we see Vygotsky the psychologist attempting to explain the most complex artistic experiences in relation to a developing theory of inner feelings and experiences, while also sometimes relating these inner events to physiological phenomena. As yet he has not gone beyond reactology (a development from reflexology) as a frame of reference, but he is intent on greatly widening its scope and including in its objects of study topics such as the arts and culture, emotion, imagination and consciousness.

It will not be till the early 1930s that Vygotsky returns to these issues and in a series of publications related to children's imaginative and emotional development focuses on imagination, the emotions, play and creativity.

'Art and life'

In the final chapter of the book, 'Art and life', Vygotsky draws the conclusions from the case he has made about the way literature works and about its psychological effects. Art cannot arise simply from the expression of strong feelings. Vygotsky emphasises the creative work involved in art and the way in which this work resolves the raw material of feeling:

> A sincere feeling taken per se cannot create art. It lacks more than technique or mastery, because a feeling expressed by a technique will never generate a lyric poem or a musical composition. To do this we require the creative act of overcoming the feeling, resolving it, conquering it. Only when this act has been performed – then and only then is art born.
>
> (Vygotsky, 1971, p. 248)

The act of catharsis has a function, in that it establishes an equilibrium between the organism and the environment in critical moments; it introduces order and harmony. But Vygotsky has more to say about the social significance of art. He sees this as being just as relevant to the single individual as to groups of people:

> It is quite naïve and inappropriate to take the social to be collective, as with a large crowd of persons. The social also exists where there is only one person with his individual experiences and tribulations. That is why the action of art, when it performs catharsis and pushes into this purifying flame the most intimate and important experiences, emotions and feelings of the soul, is a social action ... Art is the social technique of emotion, a tool of society which brings the most intimate and personal aspects of our being into the circle of social life.
>
> (Vygotsky, 1971, p. 249)

Some of Vygotsky's future psychological theory is already present in this passage, which introduces ideas of internalisation, and of the role of signs and symbols as 'psychological tools' in human development. It is true that Nikolai Veresov (1999) insists that the concept of psychological tools has yet to appear in Vygotsky's psychology; but this passage surely foreshadows its development.

Vygotsky realises that his complex picture of the workings of literature is not likely to be easy to implement in public education where, according to one critic, 'pupils are beaten with sticks to learn Pushkin as if they were cattle herded to the watering place' (Vygotsky, 1971, p. 255). Nevertheless Vygotsky feels that the study of literature is an essential part of the curriculum. 'A school that eliminates lessons in literature is bound to be a bad school' (ibid., p. 256).

At the end of his study, Vygotsky refers to art and young children, to the 'special kinship' that exists between art and play, and to the value of this kind of play for children in understanding reality. As in his later writing, he puts children's art in a special category and regards it as a form of playful self-expression. But his belief in the value of play is apparent here and will be expressed more fully in later writing.

At the end of the book comes a passage about the future of society. Vygotsky expresses his belief that art will have a key role to play in the development of society and the formation of 'the new man'. This phrase reminds us of the mood of the times, when there was so much discussion of 'the new Soviet man' and of the new society which was to be created under Communism. One of those who wrote about this was Leon Trotsky in his 1924 book *Literature and revolution*:

> Man will make it his purpose to master his own feelings, to raise his instincts to the heights of consciousness, to make them transparent, to extend the wires of his will into hidden recesses, and thereby to raise himself to a new plane, to create a higher social biologic type, or, if you please, a superman.
>
> (Trotsky, 2005, p. 207)

It is possible that Vygotsky had originally used a direct quotation from Trotsky, whom he admired, at the end of this last chapter; this has been suggested as one of the reasons why *The psychology of art* was never published in his lifetime. Trotsky was under attack; by 1925 he had been sidelined politically and in 1927 he was expelled from the Central Committee of the Communist Party.

The psychology of art is unique among Vygotsky's texts. In future his work was to be differently oriented; he was to become a working psychologist in a community which was confronting huge societal change. A.R. Luria, looking back on those times, said:

> The content and style of our lives changed almost immediately. Instead of cautiously groping for a foothold in life we were suddenly faced with many opportunities for action – action that went far beyond the confines of our own tiny circle of family and friends. The limits of our restricted, private world were broken down by the Revolution and new vistas opened before us. We were swept up in a great historical movement. Our private interests were consumed by the wider social goals of a new, collective society.
>
> (Luria, 1979, p. 19)

But despite the changes that were to come and the new pressures that he was under as a psychologist and a defectologist, working at the forefront of the development of psychology in Moscow, several of Vygotsky's concerns in *The psychology of art* remained priorities for him. Literature and theatre continued to be passionate interests, while in psychology he was always convinced of the importance of the role of the emotions in human development, and of the place of the imagination in thinking.

González Rey (2018) suggests that some of Vygotsky's later ideas first appeared in this book, and that its main concepts were taken up again only towards the end of his life, between 1932 and 1934. He particularly draws attention to Vygotsky's emphasis on the role of the imagination in feeling. Vygotsky's most explicit statement of the interrelationship between emotional processes and the imagination is this:

> This means that in essence, all our fantasy experiences take place on a completely real emotional basis. We see, therefore, that emotion and imagination are not two separate processes; on the contrary, they are the same process. We can regard a fantasy as the central expression of an emotional reaction.
>
> (Vygotsky, 1971, p. 210)

Vygotsky developed his psychology in these areas more fully in the early 1930s, when in the space of a short period he wrote the monograph *Imagination and creativity in childhood* (Vygotsky, 2004), the lecture 'Imagination and its development in childhood' (Vygotsky, 1987a) (as one of a series of lectures in psychology), and delivered a seminal lecture on play (Vygotsky, 2016). His long-projected book on the emotions (Vygotsky, 1999b) remained unfinished when he died.

Note

1 In *The psychology of art*, Vygotsky uses the word 'art' to include all the arts.

References

Bunin, I. (1971). 'Gentle breath', in Vygotsky, L.S., *The psychology of art*, pp. 161–165. Cambridge, MA: MIT Press.

Dobkin, S. (1982). 'Ages and days', in Levitin, K. (1982). *One is not born a personality*, pp. 23–38. Moscow: Progress Publishers.

González Rey, F.L. (2016). 'Vygotsky's concept of *perezhivanie* in *The psychology of art* and at the final moment of his work: advancing his legacy'. *Mind, Culture and Activity*, 23(4), pp. 1–10.

González Rey, F.L. (2018). 'Vygotsky's *The psychology of art*: a foundational and still unexplored text'. *Estudos de Psicologia*, 35(4), pp. 339–350. doi:10.1590/1982-02752018000400002

Joravsky, D. (1989). *Russian psychology: a critical history*. Oxford: Blackwell.

Kotik-Friedgut, B. (2012). 'Germinated seeds: the development of Vygotsky's *Psychology of art* in his early journalistic publications (1916–1923)'. *Education Circles* (Jerusalem), 3 November, pp. 133–144.

Leontiev, A.N. (1971). 'Introduction', in Vygotsky, L.S., *The psychology of art*, pp. v–xi. Cambridge, MA: MIT Press.

Levitin, K. (1982). *One is not born a personality*. Moscow: Progress Publishers.

Luria, A.R. (1979). *The making of mind: a personal account of Soviet psychology*. Cole, M. and Cole, S. (eds). Cambridge, MA: Harvard University Press.

Marques, P.N. (2018). '"Young" Vygotsky: unpublished works about art and the role of artistic creation in child development'. *Educação e Pesquisa*, 44. doi:10.1590/s1678-4634201844183267

Sobkin, V. (2017). 'Lev Vygotsky: from theater to psychology'. *Revue internationale du CRIRES: innover dans la tradition de Vygotsky*, 4(1), pp. 80–95.

Toulmin, S. (1978). 'The Mozart of psychology'. *The New York Review of Books*, 28 September, pp. 51–57.

Trotsky, L. (2005). *Literature and revolution* [1924]. Chicago, IL: Haymarket Books.

Van der Veer, R. and Valsiner, J. (1991). *Understanding Vygotsky: a quest for synthesis*. Oxford: Blackwell.

Veresov, N. (1999). *Undiscovered Vygotsky: etudes on pre-history of cultural-historical psychology*. New York: Peter Lang.

Vygotsky, L.S. (1971). *The psychology of art* [1925]. Intro. A.N. Leontiev; commentary V.V. Ivanov. Cambridge, MA: MIT Press.

Vygotsky, L.S. (1987a). 'Lecture 5. Imagination and its development in childhood' [1932], in Vygotsky, L.S., *The collected works of L.S. Vygotsky. Volume 1, Problems of general psychology*, pp. 339–349. Trans. and intro. N. Minick; Rieber, R.W. and Carton, A.S. (eds). New York: Plenum Press.

Vygotsky, L.S. (1987b). *Thinking and speech* [1934], in Vygotsky, L.S., *The collected works of L.S. Vygotsky. Volume 1, Problems of general psychology*, pp. 37–285. Trans. and intro. N. Minick; Rieber, R.W. and Carton, A.S. (eds). New York: Plenum Press.

Vygotsky, L.S. (1997). *The historical meaning of the crisis in psychology: a methodological investigation* [1926–1927], in Vygotsky, L.S., *The collected works of L.S. Vygotsky. Volume 3, Problems of the theory and history of psychology*, pp. 233–343. Trans. and intro. R. Van der Veer; Rieber, R.W. and Wollock, J. (eds.). New York: Plenum Press.

Vygotsky, L.S. (1999a). 'On the problem of the psychology of the actor's creative work' [1932], in Vygotsky, L.S., *The collected works of L.S. Vygotsky. Volume 6, Scientific legacy*, pp. 237–244. Trans. M.J. Hall; prologue D. Robbins; Rieber, R.W. (ed.). New York: Plenum Press.

Vygotsky, L.S. (1999b). *The teaching about emotions: historical-psychological studies* [1931–1933], in Vygotsky, L.S., *The collected works of L.S. Vygotsky. Volume 6. Scientific legacy*, pp. 71–235. Trans. M.J. Hall; prologue D. Robbins; Rieber, R.W. (ed.). New York: Plenum Press.

Vygotsky, L.S. (2004). 'Imagination and creativity in childhood' [1930]. *Journal of Russian and East European Psychology*, 42(1), pp. 7–97. Also available online in the Marxist Archive: www.marxists.org/archive/vygotsky/works/1927/imagination.pdf

Vygotsky, L.S. (2016). 'Play and its role in the mental development of the child' [1933]. Trans. N. Veresov and M. Barrs. *International Research in Early Childhood Education*, 7(2), pp. 3–25.

Chapter 3

Vygotsky and defectology

I am tired. Indifference, almost despair. My trip yesterday revealed to me its main contradiction. I am extremely tense (the language, the responsibilities, the suit, the foreign countries), on the other hand – I am outside time and space and free of everything as never before (aloof). The former pushes aside everything that yesterday was still dear to me and excited me (the flat and other things). The latter is a huge entrance to the basic undercurrents of life. A journey is a 'trial of oneself'.

(From *Vygotsky's notebooks*, Zavershneva and Van der Veer, 2018, p. 63)

Vygotsky in London

In July 1925 Vygotsky was sent as the delegate from the Soviet Union to the 8th International Conference on the Education of the Deaf, which took place in London. He had only been in post at the Moscow Institute of Psychology for a year. This nomination suggests that he was already highly regarded by the Commissariat of Enlightenment (Ministry of Education and Culture) and that his expertise in his field was respected.

Vygotsky did not participate in discussion at the conference, nor did he give a talk, although he did write a paper entitled 'Principles of social education for deaf and dumb children in Russia' which was added to the proceedings of the conference. The notebook that he kept during that period has now been deciphered. It is a uniquely personal document and it reveals that he was anxious and depressed during this time, missing his wife and new baby and feeling like a fish out of water at the conference with all its formal events, for which he had to wear a dinner suit.

He seemed unimpressed by the proceedings of the conference. His notes reveal some of his impatience and his pride in the work that was going on in defectology (special needs) in Russia:

In essence, Russia is the first country in the world. The Revolution is our supreme cause. In this room only 1 person knows the secret of the genuine education of the deafmutes. And that person is me. Not because I am

DOI: 10.4324/9780429203046-3

more educated than the others, but [because] I was sent by Russia and I speak on behalf of the Revolution.

(Zavershneva and Van der Veer, 2018, p. 63)

Vygotsky's position in defectology

A definition

Defectology was the discipline and occupation concerned with the study and care of children with developmental pathologies, disabilities and special needs. Its origins are to be found in late tsarist Russia, but it became fully institutionalised under this name only in the early Soviet period. The pioneers of the field were typically doctors, mostly those specialising in hygiene, psychiatry and neurology, who nevertheless strategically positioned their expertise across medicine's boundaries with education and psychology. In the Soviet Union defectology crystallised into the main disciplinary structure for special needs education, recruiting those with training in psychology and pedagogy even while retaining clinical approaches and therapeutic models deriving from medicine. During the 1920s, defectology was closely associated with the broader, multidisciplinary, field devoted to the study of child biopsychosocial development, which in the early Soviet Union thrived under the name 'paedology' (*pedologiia*).

(Byford, 2018, p. 68)

What had brought Vygotsky to this prominent position in the field of defectology and psychology in Russia? For a long time the myth persisted that his rapid advancement stemmed from a presentation he gave in 1924 at the 2nd Neuro-pyschological Congress. The topic of this paper was said to be Consciousness. This was incorrect – in fact the main psychological paper he gave on that occasion was about methods of reflexological and psychological investigation – but it is true that his presentation attracted widespread attention. The myth continues that Vygotsky was then simply a provincial teacher with no formal experience in psychology who, on the strength of this paper, was immediately recognised as being an impressive thinker and theorist. Soon after the conference he was invited to join the staff of the State Institute of Experimental Psychology in Moscow. His 'modest position', according to A.N. Leontiev (1971, p. v), was that of Staff Scientist, 2nd Class. Alexander Luria, who had also recently joined the Institute staff, was the head of his laboratory.

But it may not only have been Vygotsky's contribution at this conference which changed the course of his life. Richard Prawat (2000) speculates that he was already known to Anatoli Lunacharsky, the Director of the Commissariat of Enlightenment (Ministry of Education and Culture), through arts journalism and work in the arts field. As well as being a teacher Vygotsky was an organiser of the theatre section for the Gomel Department of People's Education and then Head of Art and Aesthetic Education in the town's Department of People's Education (Vygodskaya, 1995, p. 8). Vygotsky may also have been known to

Lunacharsky's Deputy (Nadezhda Krupskaya, Lenin's wife) since he had been selected as the best teacher in Gomel province; by 1919 he was lecturing at Gomel teachers' college in logic and psychology. Prawat suggests that Lunacharsky and Krupskaya might both have played a part in his move to Moscow.

However, Van der Veer and Valsiner (1991, p. 10) and other commentators identify the key figure in all this as Ivan Daniushevsky, who came from Gomel and who had worked with Vygotsky on the organisation of the theatre section of the Education Department. Daniushevsky left Gomel to take up a post in the Commissariat of Enlightenment in 1921–1922 and it seems likely that he initiated the invitation to Vygotsky to work in Moscow. Vygotsky would have been an obvious choice because of his considerable experience at Gomel teachers' college. Moreover a form that Vygotsky completed in July 1924, in an application for work in the Commissariat of Enlightenment, included the question: 'In what branch do you believe your employment would be most useful?', to which Vygotsky answered 'In the education of blind and deaf-blind children' (Yaroshevsky, 1989, p. 98, quoted in Prawat, 2000). Daniushevsky went on being a close friend and ally of Vygotsky's to the end of his life, and collaborated with him in some of his later papers on defectology.

So by the end of 1924 Vygotsky and his wife had moved to Moscow, and been given a lodging in the basement of the Institute of Experimental Psychology where the library archives were kept. But at the same time, probably on the instigation of Daniushevsky, he took up a position at the Commissariat of Enlightenment, where he was head of the sector for the education of physically handicapped and mentally retarded children (Veresov, 1999, p. 127). As a first step he compiled a short reader on defectology.

As for his previous experience in psychology, Vygotsky himself said that he started his scientific career in psychology in 1917 (ibid., p. 69). Veresov suggests that he did six years of intensive work in psychology in Gomel, teaching the psychology courses that formed the basis of his book *Educational psychology* (Vygotsky, 1997b).

It is important to stress that Vygotsky's focus on defectology dates from the beginning of his career in academic psychology and continued to be at the core of his work. It influenced everything he did. In 1925 he founded a laboratory for the study of 'abnormal children' and in 1927 became Head of the Medical Pedagogical Station in Moscow (Yasnitsky, 2018, p. 128). His fundamental commitment to defectology is not always highlighted in commentaries on his work; often the 'defectology chapter' comes towards the back of the book in general studies of his psychology. Yet if we look at the list of his publications from 1924 to 1927 (in Luciano Mecacci's invaluable bibliography: Mecacci, 2017) it is clear that they were predominantly in the field of defectology, even though during this period he was also producing important books and articles such as *The psychology of art* (Vygotsky, 1971), 'Consciousness as a problem for the psychology of behaviour' (Vygotsky, 1997a) and *The historical meaning of the crisis in psychology* (Vygotsky, 1997c).

Nikolai Veresov, in his book *Undiscovered Vygotsky*, which refers solely to the years from 1917 to 1927, sees Vygotsky's work in defectology as having had a profound effect on his development as a psychologist. He draws parallels between Vygotsky's defectological work and his writing on consciousness.

> The analysis of Vygotsky's defectological works shows that their theoretical basis was the programme of studying consciousness from the point of view of behaviour presented in the article 'Consciousness as a problem in the psychology of behaviour' in 1925.
>
> (Veresov, 1999, p. 135)

Vygotsky's main strategy for helping handicapped children to compensate for their difficulties was through 'the creation and incorporation of signs' (ibid., p. 136). Veresov concludes: 'the idea of *development of the structure of behaviour* which will be one of the basic theoretical ideas in cultural-historical theory originally appeared in defectological works of Vygotsky' (ibid.).

Towards the end of the 1920s Vygotsky became more closely identified with the practice of pedology (child science) than with defectology, although he retained a major working role at the Moscow Experimental-Defectological Institute (EDI). It is clear that the theories of learning he developed in his defectology studies influenced his better known studies of children's learning and thinking, carried out from 1927 to 1929 with Luria, Leontiev, and younger psychologists including Bozhovich, Levina, Morozova, Sakharov, Slavina and Zaporozhets. His psychological theory was always rooted in the practical, and he argued (in Marxist style) that practice (praxis) should always be the test of theory.

Vygotsky's vision

Vygotsky disapproved of much contemporary practice in special education, finding it dull, condescending, repetitive, mechanical, and negative. *The fundamentals of defectology* is volume 2 of Vygotsky's *Collected works*. On the first page of its Introduction (Vygotsky, 1993h, p. 29), he deplored the tendency to base practice on a 'purely quantitative conception of childhood development' and to use 'scale and measure as the basic categories of research'. He noted: 'In defectology, counting and measuring came before experimentation, observation, analysis, generalisation, description and qualitative diagnosis' (ibid.).

'Obsolete old-school defectology' looked only at a child's lacks and weaknesses, not at their strengths. Vygotsky's constant theme was:

> A child whose development is impeded by a defect is not simply a child less developed than his peers but a child who has developed differently.
>
> (Vygotsky, 1993h, p. 30)

In *The making of mind,* Luria describes Vygotsky's approach to evaluating children's abilities:

> Consistent with his overall approach, he rejected simple quantitative descriptions of such children in terms of unidimensional psychological traits reflected in test scores. Instead he relied on qualitative descriptions of the special organisation of their behaviour. His diagnostic protocols analysing children with various forms of deficiency were preserved by his collaborator L. Geshelina, but many were destroyed during the war and others were lost after Geshelina's death.
>
> (Luria, 1979, p. 53)

Vygotsky favoured this kind of qualitative assessment so that he could focus on children's positive abilities, which could be built on to develop their potential. The loss of his detailed diagnostic protocols has deprived us of a major source of illuminating information about his practice in this field. Vygotsky's general approach to work with children with special needs can be summarised under the following headings:

- overcoming social stigma; and
- ways round the handicap.

Overcoming social stigma

Vygotsky's daughter wrote:

> According to Vygotsky a special school should deal first and foremost with such tasks as bringing the abnormal child out of the state of isolation, providing him with broad possibilities for a genuinely human life, bringing him into contact with socially useful labour, and teaching him to be an active, conscious member of society.
>
>   Lev Semonovich refuted the false view that an abnormal child has diminished 'social impulses', and raised the question of the necessity of rearing him not as an invalid and a parasite or a socially neutral being, but as an active, conscious personality.
>
> (Vygodskaya and Lifanova, 1999, p. 12)

So Vygotsky believed that children with difficulties were struggling not only with their handicap but also with the *social difficulties deriving from it.* Consequently the first thing to deal with was children's confidence and self-worth; there would be no progress without a shift in attitude. Then the positive consequences of handicap might kick in as children strove, with strong motivation, to compensate for their handicap by taking ways to get round it. Vygotsky wrote:

Up to now we have … not taken into account the desire with which such a child struggles to be healthy and fully accepted socially.

(Vygotsky, 1993d, p. 57)

Vygotsky's vision was of an approach where psychologists and teachers would look at the positive aspects of children with difficulties, at their strengths and at indications of positive attitudes. Once they had identified these areas of strength they would offer children ways round their handicaps.

Ways round the handicap

Vygotsky returned constantly to the question of detours in development, noting their major importance for the process of compensation. In the process of cultural development, he writes, 'certain functions are replaced by others, detours are formed, and this opens up totally new possibilities for the development of the abnormal child. If such a child cannot achieve something directly, the development of detours becomes the basis on which compensation is achieved.' On the subject of compensation, Vygotsky pointed out that the entire practice of education of abnormal children consists in creating detours for the development of the abnormal child. To use Vygotsky's expression, this is the alpha and omega of special education.

(Vygodskaya and Lifanova, 1999, p. 10)

In relation to physically handicapped children, Vygotsky observed that biological compensation was not a realistic expectation for most conditions and that it was essential to look for ways of minimising the effect of handicaps on children's education and developing the '*enormous deposits and deep layers of psychological health within the child*' (Vygotsky, 1993i, p. 72) instead of focusing on their difficulties.

Developments in Vygotsky's approach to special education

Vygotsky's approach to the education of children with special needs, especially those with learning difficulties, was changing substantially in the course of the years 1924 to 1928. If we consider the development of his thought about the nature of the 'detours' that schools might offer children with special needs, especially those with physical handicaps, we can see that it parallels the development of his psychology in a very interesting way.

Between 1924 and 1926 the main features of Vygotsky's approach, mainly but not exclusively in relation to the education of blind and deaf children, were predominantly social. He was searingly critical of traditional approaches to the education of handicapped children, which he saw as condescending, philanthropic and pitying. Handicaps were often viewed as afflictions, and handicapped children as different and separate. Special schools were frequently organised so as to separate children off, which prevented them from socialising with normally developing children. The education in such separate schools was oriented towards deficiency; there was an excessive emphasis on children's 'defects'. The teaching was often pointless – involving exercises in 'the cultivation of the senses' such as 'studying smells, stringing and unstringing beads' (Vygotsky, 1993i, p. 73). Vygotsky remarks that such teaching 'will achieve nothing in our attempts to educate the retarded child, but instead only force him into greater retardation.'

Vygotsky was convinced, particularly in the early years of his work in defectology, by the ideas of Alfred Adler on compensation. Reading defectology through Adler's theory, it was clear that the social stigma resulting from the handicap created an *inferiority complex* in the child. For this reason, although it was usual to regard a child's *primary defect* as the organic impairment affecting them, Vygotsky regarded the effect of a child's actual handicap on their development as *secondary* (Knox and Stevens, 1993). The *primary* cause of their difficulties, in his view, was their treatment by society. Vygotsky observed that 'the task is not so much the education of blind children as it is the re-education of the sighted' (Vygotsky, 1993j, p. 86).

Consequently, during this earlier period Vygotsky advocated positive approaches to the education of handicapped children. For instance, '"special education" should lose its "special" character and became part of the general educational system' (ibid., p. 93). Only the socialisation of education could offer a solution – 'both psychologically and educationally this is a question of social education' (Vygotsky, 1993i, p. 67). For deaf children, for instance, 'speech makes communication possible between the deaf and the hearing and serves as a tool for developing thought and consciousness' (ibid., p. 69).

Speech and language at this stage of Vygotsky's thought were given great importance, but mainly as a route to communication and a path into normal social life:

> It remains to add that not only are the final goal and all developmental paths leading to it the same for blind and for a seeing person, but also the main source from which this development draws its contents is the same for both – language.
>
> (Vygotsky, 1993b, p. 105)

Vygotsky's psychological references in his writings of 1924–26 were mainly related to reflexology and the language and concepts of reflexology. And in one lecture, 'Defect and compensation', written in 1924, he referred approvingly to the work of Pavlov:

> Pavlov discovered a unique goal-oriented reflex ... Pavlov straightforwardly formulated the significance of this reflex for education.
>
> (Vygotsky, 1993d, p. 60)

This was Pavlov's suggestion that for a complete, true and fruitful manifestation of the goal reflex, it must be placed under a certain amount of stress, and that the main condition for achieving the goal might be 'the existence of obstacles'. Vygotsky used this example more than once and the idea that obstacles might be helpful to the achievement of a goal came to influence his later thinking and practice.

The role of language

However, by the time of his later work, for instance in the Introduction to *The fundamentals of defectology* (the text of which was originally published in 1929), Vygotsky had arrived at a new and well-developed position which drew on his experimental work and his recently formulated theory of the development of higher mental functions:

> the process of cultural development basically depends on acquiring cultural psychological tools, which were created by mankind during its historical development and which are analogous to language from a psychological perspective.
>
> (Vygotsky, 1993h, p. 44)

He quoted the psychologist Stern to make the case that language is the prime 'psychological tool':

> [It is] a tool of great power in the development of [the child's] life, his ideas, emotions and will; it alone ultimately makes possible any real thought, generalisation and comparison, synthesis and comprehension.
>
> (Vygotsky, 1993h, p. 44)

Vygotsky's approach to the education of children with disabilities had changed and broadened; he now placed great emphasis on language and other symbol systems as the route by which children could develop themselves and compensate for their 'deficits':

> The development of higher psychological functions is possible only along paths of cultural development, whether or not this development proceeds along lines which master external cultural means (speech, writing, arithmetic) or along the line of an internal perfection of psychological functions (the development of voluntary attention, logical memory, abstract thought, concept formations, volition and so forth) ... Cultural development, then, does not depend upon the organic deficit.
>
> (Vygotsky, 1993e, p. 169)

The education of blind and deaf children

Initially Vygotsky's work in defectology was predominantly focused on the education of blind, deaf, and deaf-blind children and of those they came into contact with. His approach to the education of the blind was straightforward – its main focus was the 're-education of the sighted'. The 'narrow, closed-off small worlds' created by many special schools for the blind were inadequate for preparing children for the normal world in which they would ultimately have to live.

> The environment nurtures the defect and fixes the child's attention on his blindness, 'traumatizing' him. Blindness is not overcome in such a school but is intensified.
>
> (Vygotsky, 1993j, p. 85)

But Vygotsky stressed that blind children acquired speech normally and were able to read and write – through the medium of Braille.

> A blind person reads, feeling the perforated dots with his fingers. What is important is that he reads in precisely the same way as we do; that he does this using different means, his fingers, not his eyes, cannot have any major significance ... meaning is what is important, not the signs in themselves.
>
> (Vygotsky, 1993j, p. 85)

Through this different form of written language blind children were able to develop their higher mental functions and have access to a world of knowledge.

Compensation then occurred 'not in the realm of elementary processes but in the realm of concepts, that is, in the higher functions' (Vygotsky, 1993c, p. 203). Vygotsky stressed that for children with 'defects' there might be no way of substituting directly for loss of sight, hearing, or other lacks. There were, however, other ways round the areas in which they had difficulties:

> the links, dependencies and relationships among things which are the content of our scientific knowledge are not the visually perceivable qualities of things; rather, they come to light through thought. This is also the way it works for a blind child. Thought is the basic area in which he compensates for the inadequacy of his visual perceptions.
>
> (Vygotsky, 1993c, p. 203)

Vygotsky's approach to the education of the deaf was less assured. He felt that the great handicap of deafness was that it isolated the deaf from social experiences, and therefore 'disrupts the social bonding of personality much more directly than does blindness' (Vygotsky, 1993j, p. 88). It was therefore a more profound defect than blindness. Like many educationalists of the time, Vygotsky was convinced that the most important task in the education of the deaf was to teach them oral speech. However, he was aware that this was often a very long and painful process, and that children were being drilled in the learning of single words or phrases, without the use of speech being made sufficiently clear. Vygotsky advocated approaches that made speech a real means of communication in natural language, so that it became necessary and interesting:

> In the old system, the oral method was murderous; in a new system it can become beneficial.
>
> (Vygotsky, 1993j, p. 90)

But of course an alternative to oral speech did exist in the sign language (known as 'mimicry') that deaf children used between themselves. Vygotsky thought that, although this was a deaf child's natural language, it could not be encouraged in education for several reasons:

> Mimicry very quickly degenerates into jargon, comprehensible only within one or another school and permits communication only with a small number of people. Mimicry allows one to convey only the crudest, tangible and concrete meanings. It never reaches a level of abstract concepts and ideas. In contrast, speech is not only an instrument for communication but also an instrument of thought; consciousness develops chiefly with the help of speech and arises out of social experience. Hence it is clear that mimicry dooms a deaf person to total underdevelopment.
>
> (Vygotsky, 1993j, p. 89)

However, over time Vygotsky's views on sign language changed, and he became convinced of the absolute necessity of using some variant of sign language with deaf-mute children:

> The deaf-mute child is taught to pronounce words but he is not taught to speak, that is to use speech as a means of communicating and thinking. Therefore, along with artificially inculcated speech, he more willingly uses his own language of mimicry, which fulfils for him the dynamic function of speech. The struggle between oral speech and mimicry (sign language), in spite of the good intentions on the part of the pedagogues, ends, as a rule, in the victory of sign language, not because mimicry is a psychologically natural speech for the deaf-mute, but because it is authentic speech with all the riches of functional meaning.
>
> (Vygotsky, 1993c, p. 206)

Vygotsky eventually came to accept that 'mimicry' was a deaf child's natural and first language and must be built on rather than ignored or extirpated:

> This means that in practice we must make use of all possibilities for speech activity for a deaf-mute child. We must not approach mimicry with condescension and scorn, treating it as an enemy. Rather we must understand that different forms of speech do not only compete with one another or disrupt one another's development, but that they can also serve as steps on which the deaf-mute child climbs to the mastery of speech.
>
> (Vygotsky, 1993c, p. 207)

He now recognised that deaf children were bilingual and that sign language was their mother tongue.

Vygotsky's work with blind-deaf children was groundbreaking, and informed by the same principles as his work with all children with physical handicaps. Building on the example of Helen Keller he insisted that the priority was to teach the child speech – primarily through the medium of touch – 'the hand alphabet' and eventually Braille (Vygotsky, 1993a, p. 181). This work was later continued by Alexander Meshcheryakov at the Zagorsk school (Bakhurst and Padden, 1991; and see Chapter 12).

Vygotsky was in two minds about *inclusion*, sometimes arguing for full inclusion and at other times for the need for children with particular defects to be in a homogeneous community so as to be given adequate individual attention. But even when he was arguing for a degree of separation for the purposes of teaching, he still argued that the facility for the children with defects should be close to and connected to a normal school.

He saw this connection as particularly important for the children known as 'mentally retarded', some of whom he described as 'socially delayed children' (Vygotsky, 1993j, p. 92). He suggested that pedagogical literature often pursued very negative goals for such children, seeing them as having 'inferior social instincts'. He argued that the social personality of a retarded child may well be impaired and underdeveloped, but that this was sometimes because '[a] retarded child is self-ostracised from peer ranks'. They might be branded as a fool or as handicapped by their peers, and this was damaging because '[a] defect is strengthened, nourished and reinforced by its social consequences' (ibid.).

For this reason he considers it very damaging for auxiliary schools, set up to assist regular schools with the education of handicapped children, to become separated off:

> The auxiliary school ... must *never in any way* sever ties with the [regular school]. This special school will often have to take in retarded children temporarily but then must return then again.
>
> (Vygotsky, 1993j, p. 93)

The discussion of integration or separate teaching in special education still, of course, continues.

The diagnostics of development

Vygotsky continued to publish in the overlapping fields of defectology and pedology until the end of his life, and the last item in *The fundamentals of defectology* is
the text of a pedology pamphlet written in 1931, entitled 'The diagnostics of
development and the pedological clinic for difficult children' (Vygotsky, 1993f). It
was published posthumously, in 1935, on the initiative of Ivan Daniushevsky, the
same person who had been a friend of Vygotsky's since their days together in
Gomel. Daniushevsky had replaced Vygotsky as director of the EDI in 1929,
although Vygotsky remained as research director. Daniushevsky had promoted
and defended Vygotsky's work throughout his life, and was determined that this
major treatise on diagnostics in pedology should be published. The text was prepared for publication by Vygotsky's collaborator Roza Levina.

This pamphlet is the best insight we have into Vygotsky's way of working as
a pedologist. Pedology was a young science at the time when Vygotsky was
writing; indeed he questioned whether as yet it was a science at all. He thought
that what it primarily lacked was research, and a clear taxonomy of ailments. In
this way it resembled medicine in the prescientific era, when:

> if a sick man came, complaining of a cough, the learned doctor probably
> gave the cough a Latin name and, with that diagnosis, let the patient go.
>
> (Vygotsky, 1993f, p. 245)

It was not enough to define diseases by their symptoms; the truly scientific
approach was to study what underlay the symptoms.

Similarly pedology, according to Vygotsky, must:

> study actual realities, identify and describe different mechanisms, forms and
> types of underdevelopment among children, and the educational problems of
> such children; we must accumulate these facts, check them, and draw general
> theoretical conclusions; and finally we must accustom ourselves to the fact
> that *retarded* as an expression means as little in contemporary pedology as *sick*
> means in contemporary medicine. Each of these expressions has a purely
> negative meaning ...
>
> (Vygotsky, 1993f, p. 250)

Vygotsky draws on his own research with colleagues in the remainder of the
paper. The first step was to reject traditional research methods, such as Binet's
scale of intelligence, as based on a vision of children's development that was
'purely quantitative':

> they are basically limited to characterising a child in an exclusively negative
> fashion. Child development, as this method envisions it, is considered to
> be a purely quantitative growth process ... one year's development is

always one year's development, whether one is referring to a child's movement between the sixth and seventh years or from the twelfth to the thirteenth ... This represents a fundamental failure to understand the issues of development and the new qualitative forms which appear during the developmental process.

(Vygotsky, 1993f, p. 253)

Vygotsky believed that these 'exclusively negative characterisations of the child ... represent practical reactions to the job of purely denying and excluding children from general schools which were deemed inappropriate for them' (ibid., p. 254).

Vygotsky thought that a system for studying development needed to take into account that it was *not* a homogeneous process and that in the process of development different psychological functions were integrated, through complex structural and functional links, relating to changes in the personality.

One fundamental proposition informing the work of his research team was that:

> In studying unmanageable and anomalous children one must observe a strict distinction between developmental delays, on the one hand, and primary and secondary deviations, on the other.

(Vygotsky, 1993f, p. 255)

'Deviations' in intellectual development were often linked to secondary complications, rather than to the original condition.

For instance, a secondary symptom in mental retardation was underdevelopment of the higher psychological functions. One of the reasons for this was that these children were often excluded from, or did not participate in, children's collectives. This could mean that both their social behaviour and their higher psychological functions were underdeveloped. However:

> Amazingly ... underdevelopment of the higher mental functions is not, in and of itself, necessarily connected to a mental retardation.

(Vygotsky, 1993f, p. 255)

The practical interest in this was that, despite their underlying condition, these children *could* respond to therapeutic pedagogical activity; they were educable.

Another example of a syndrome that affected children's development was that of 'primitive reactions' – outbursts, fits of passion and hysterical tensions, the consequence of a lack of inhibition because the personality was not fully developed. The analysis of such syndromes showed how complex the structure of mental retardation was.

The study of links, dependencies and relationships was part of the work of the researcher in this field. Vygotsky's view of the researcher's methodology is memorable:

The task of methodology is not only to learn to measure, but also to learn to see, think and associate. This means that our excessive fear of so-called subjective factors in interpretation ... [is] unfounded. Without subjective re-evaluation (that is, without thought and interpretation), the deciphering of results and evaluation of the data is not scientific research.

(Vygotsky, 1993f, p. 274)

By far the most interesting aspect of the pamphlet is the section in which Vygotsky, in considerable detail, sets out the scheme for pedological research. The elements to be included are as follows:

1   *The testimony of parents and children* – not only their opinions, but the evidence for their opinions. Subjective evidence must be collected, but checked against other evidence and evaluated. Vygotsky stresses that this was not just a question of listing events or grouping them – the work lay in 'penetrating to the deeper levels of the developmental processes by thoughtfully studying these external data' (Vygotsky, 1993f, p. 277).

Similarly, it is essential not to over-value 'mechanical and arithmetic analysis of external symptoms' (exemplified by Binet's scale). The result will be 'altogether lacking in reflective analysis' (ibid.).

Vygotsky drew an analogy with a doctor who measures temperature and pulse, looks at the result of chemical analyses and at X-rays and 'linking all this to the side of the picture he already knows, penetrates to the internal pathological process which has produced all the symptoms' (ibid.). *Reflective analysis* should be an essential part of diagnosis.

2   *The child's developmental history* – including, most importantly, a personal history of the child's education:

This most important influence from the environment ... is usually skipped altogether in a developmental history, while, at the same time, such things as the cubic footage of living space, the laundry routine, and other secondary details are transcribed in detail.

(Vygotsky, 1993f, pp. 277–278)

While family history was important, as were details of any inheritable illnesses, it was essential these were viewed in relation to the whole family. Similarly the living conditions of the family might be recorded but the analysis should not conclude that difficult living conditions provided a complete explanation; what was required was a scientific approach, not a gossipy one:

But any neighbour is capable of offering that kind of analysis; in such situations the neighbour might say 'But just look at how those people live!'.

(Vygotsky, 1993f, p. 281)

3   *The symptomatology of development* – including medical evidence, pedological evidence, educational evidence and so on. Vygotsky regretted that 'what is lacking in contemporary pedological research is precisely the scientific determination of symptoms'. Psychological measurement was only one of the elements to be taken into account:

> Diagnosis belongs to the final judgement of an occurrence as a whole, an occurrence which manifests itself in these symptoms, which is not sus-ceptible to direct perception and which must be evaluated on the basis of study, comparison, and in interpretation of the given symptoms.
>
> (Vygotsky, 1993f, p. 285)

Vygotsky maintained that establishing symptoms should never automatically lead to diagnosis. In arriving at a diagnosis a pedologist should take into account everything they knew from the evidence and use all of their previous experience. A knowledge of general patterns of development and how educa-tional difficulties are formed was part of a pedologist's growing conceptual system. If the diagnosis was correct it should help to explain the source of the child's symptoms. It should also be able to provide a prognosis, predicting how the next stage of growth would unfold.

4   And finally there came the *pedagogical recommendations* 'for the sake of which all pedological research is conducted' (Vygotsky, 1993f, p. 291). These recommendations must be concrete, have content, and offer 'complete, specific, detailed and clear indications' as to the measures to be applied in the education of the child.

This pamphlet, one of his last works, gives an insight into the rigour and detail of Vygotsky's methods in pedology, his encyclopaedic knowledge of pedological research, and the very high standards he brought to the training of pedologists.

Criticisms of Vygotsky's work in defectology

There are various criticisms of Vygotsky's work in defectology which may have contributed to the current neglect of his achievement in this area. Some are simply a reflection of the mental climate at that time – for instance his sense that *deaf children should be taught oral speech* in preference to sign language. Vygotsky changed his position on this issue in time.

More serious is the criticism, offered by Van der Veer and Valsiner and others, of Vygotsky's lack of concrete evidence in his writings in this area. But we have ample evidence that Vygotsky's experience of practical work in defectology was substantial and went on throughout his career as a psychologist.

It is clear that the completed diagnostic protocols that Vygotsky used to record his interviews with individual children, which were collected by Geshelina, would have provided rich detail of his clinical practice and of his ability to establish a dialogue with these children and interpret their responses. The fact that these protocols were lost or destroyed during the Second World War, when they were housed in Leningrad, has deprived us of a real insight into his practice.

Even though we do not have these written records as evidence of Vygotsky's way of working, we do have several first-person accounts of his approach to assessing children. Lev Zankov (a student of Vygotsky and a well-known child psychologist) recalled that:

> many observers were amazed how Vygotsky conversed with the child while examining him. These conversations were unique in comparison with the way the child was asked and answered questions during a regular evaluation. This was an involving, very personal converse with the little one, and always with an underlying theme: this child is not well, he needs to be helped. Vygotsky was always able to establish an atmosphere of trust in his rapport with the children, he always talked with them as though they were equals, always paid attention to their answers. In turn, the children opened up to him in a way they never did with other examiners.
>
> (Vygodskaya, 1995, pp. 112–113)

More recently published evidence can be found in *Vygotsky's notebooks* (Zavershneva and Van der Veer, 2018), which provides invaluable examples of Vygotsky's notes of clinical interviews with older children in pedology clinics. It cannot be over-emphasised that his work in defectology increasingly overlapped with his work in pedology, and that throughout his working life he was working (clinically) and publishing in defectology. *Vygotsky's notebooks* show that he kept detailed notes of individual interviews with children, some extremely revealing. As usual, his notes are acute and often include theoretical observations. We shall return to the *Notebooks* in Chapter 7, on pedology.

Vygotsky's legacy in defectology

Vygotsky's work in the practical fields of defectology and pedology lasted throughout his working life in Moscow – the ten years from 1924 to 1934. It is not an exaggeration to say that during that time he transformed defectology and gave it a new direction. In Russia he is still often described as the 'father of defectology', and he has had a huge influence on work in special needs education in many other countries. This includes the UK, where the significance of his work for special education was recognised at an early stage by Andrew Sutton (1980). But it is probably true to say that until recently his defectological work 'has remained in the shadow' (Gindis, 2003, p. 200) and 'has received limited attention in English translation' (Smagorinsky, 2012, p. 2).

The authors of the Afterword to *The fundamentals of defectology* (Bein et al., 1993), who include Roza Levina, Natalia Morozova and Zhozefina Shif, three of his former students and collaborators, identify the distinguishing feature of Vygotsky as a psychologist and defectologist: the fact that he was both a hugely influential theoretician, and a very experienced practitioner:

> It is impossible to understand Vygotsky's profound interest in the problems of child and age-group psychology without taking into account the fact that he was both a theoretician and, particularly importantly, a practitioner in the area of anomalous mental development. For many years he acted as the Scientific Director of a whole series of research projects undertaken at the Experimental Defectological Institute, and he systematically partici-pated in consultations about children, even here filling a directing role. Hundreds of children with the most varied of mental developmental anomalies passed through his consultations.
>
> For conferences organised by Vygotsky, children of all ages were selected and thoroughly studied. Their medical histories, the histories of their devel-opment, their studies and education, and the results of complex research were analysed in detail by Vygotsky ... through these studies, he showed how the well-timed and correctly organised teaching of anomalous children changes the appearance of a handicap, how possible additional consequences of han-dicap can be foreseen and forestalled, and how the higher psychological functions develop ...
>
> (Bein et al., 1993, p. 311)

An essential principle of Vygotsky's work with children with special needs was his emphasis on the role of the environment and of relationships in children's learning – how important it was for them not to be 'cut off from the world and excluded from social contact'. He insisted that '*Child development and character formulation are socially oriented processes*' (Vygotsky, 1993g, p. 161).

Of particular importance was his view that 'social activity, and pedagogical influences in particular, are an inexhaustible source of formations of the higher mental processes, both in normalcy and pathology' (Bein et al., 1993, p. 303). Note that pedagogy is particularly mentioned here as a source of mental development; Vygotsky believed that 'instruction always leads development' (ibid., p. 305) and that teaching is fundamental to learning.

Finding 'detours' around children's defects enabled Vygotsky to change the teaching of handicapped children by ensuring that they were offered alternative routes to the development of higher mental functions. The use of different symbol systems and signs in the education of the blind and deaf enabled them to gain access to language, spoken and written, as the 'main source of devel-opment'. This work paralleled Vygotsky's experimental work in psychology and reflects the role that he saw for language in the development of mind throughout his working life.

Similarly, the focus on the *positive* aspect of handicap and the stimulus created in the learner by *having to overcome obstacles* surely informed the experimental work carried out by Vygotsky, Luria and their colleagues in 1927–1929, when they deliberately devised challenging tasks for children to see how they would go about solving them, and at what stage they would be able to use various aids or tools.

Vygotsky always rejected the 'arithmetical concept of handicap' contained in standardised tests, and insisted that:

> Unusual qualities in this area cannot be understood through the traditional quantitative approach, which views the handicapped child under examination primarily from the negative side.
>
> (Bein et al., 1993, p. 304)

Our own age is obsessed with testing and with quantitative approaches to assessment; the negative view of children which this can lead to is unhelpful both to children with special needs and to normally developing children. Vygotsky's approach was 'always to look for the positive capacities for development' in children with special needs; 'What interested Vygotsky was a child's potential, not his handicap' (ibid.).

The development of the theory of the zone of proximal/proximate development[1] reflected his approach in defectology. Vygodskaya and Lifanova observe:

> Vygotsky thought that the 'zone of proximal development' acquired definition as a child goes about accomplishing tasks difficult for his age with the help of an adult. Hence, an evaluation of mental development must be based on two indices: receptivity to the help offered, and preparedness to acquire the capacity to solve similar tasks independently in the future … He came to believe that the idea of zones of development was very productive when applied to all categories of abnormal children.
>
> (Vygodskaya and Lifanova, 1999, pp. 13–14)

So alongside all Vygotsky's experimental and theoretical work in psychology he was deeply and practically involved, throughout his life, with children with special needs, their teachers, and other researchers. The understandings that he gained from his careful study of children with difficulties were of fundamental importance to his own development as a psychologist.

Note

1 See the discussion of the terms 'proximal' and 'proximate' in the Introduction.

References

Bakhurst, D. and Padden, C. (1991). 'The Meshcheryakov experiment: Soviet work on the education of blind-deaf children'. *Learning and Instruction*, 1(3), pp. 201–215.

Bein, E.S., Vlasova, T.A., Levina, R.E., Morozova, N.G. and Shif, Z.I. (1993). 'Afterword', in Vygotsky, L.S., *The collected works of L.S. Vygotsky. Volume 2, The fundamentals of defectology*, pp. 302–314. Trans. and intro. J.E. Knox and C.B. Stevens; Rieber, R.W. and Carton, A.S. (eds). New York: Plenum Press.

Byford, A. (2018). '*Lechebnaia pedagogika*: the concept and practice of therapy in Russian defectology, c.1880–1936'. *Medical History*, 62(1), pp. 67–90. doi:10.1017/mdh.2017.76.

Gindis, B. (2003). 'Remediation through education', in Kozulin, A., Gindis, B., Ageyev, V.S. and Miller, S.M. (eds), *Vygotsky's educational theory in cultural context*, pp. 200–221. Cambridge: Cambridge University Press.

Knox, J.E. and Stevens, C.B. (1993). 'Introduction', in Vygotsky, L.S., *The collected works of L.S. Vygotsky. Volume 2, The fundamentals of defectology*, pp. 1–25. Trans. and intro. J.E. Knox and C.B. Stevens; Rieber, R.W. and Carton, A.S. (eds). New York: Plenum Press.

Leontiev, A.N. (1971). 'Introduction', in Vygotsky, L.S., *The psychology of art*, pp. v–xi. Cambridge, MA: MIT Press.

Luria, A.R. (1979). *The making of mind: a personal account of Soviet psychology*. Cole, M. and Cole, S. (eds). Cambridge, MA: Harvard University Press.

Mecacci, L. (2017). *Lev Vygotskii: Sviluppo, educazione e patologia della mente*. Florence: Giunti.

Prawat, R. (2000). 'Dewey meets the "Mozart of psychology" in Moscow: the untold story'. *American Educational Research Journal*, 37(3), pp. 663–696.

Smagorinsky, P. (2012). 'Vygotsky, "Defectology", and the inclusion of people of difference in the broader cultural stream'. *Journal of Language and Literacy Education*, 8(1), pp. 1–25.

Sutton, A. (1980). 'Backward children in the USSR: an unfamiliar approach to a familiar problem', in Brine, J., Perrie, M. and Sutton, A. (eds), *Home, school and leisure in the Soviet Union*, pp. 160–189. London: George Allen and Unwin.

Van der Veer, R. and Valsiner, J. (1991). *Understanding Vygotsky: a quest for synthesis*. Oxford: Blackwell.

Veresov, N. (1999). *Undiscovered Vygotsky: etudes on the pre-history of cultural-historical psychology*. Frankfurt am Main: Peter Lang.

Vygodskaya, G.L. (1995). 'His life'. *School Psychology International*, 16(2), pp. 105–116.

Vygodskaya, G.L. and Lifanova, T.M. (1999). 'Life and works'. *Journal of Russian and East European Psychology*, 37(3), pp. 3–31. doi:10.2753/RPO1061-040537033

Vygotsky, L.S. (1971). *The psychology of art* [1925]. Intro. A.N. Leontiev; commentary V. V. Ivanov. Cambridge, MA: MIT Press.

Vygotsky, L.S. (1993a). 'Bases for working with mentally retarded and physically handicapped children' [1928], in Vygotsky, L.S., *The collected works of L.S. Vygotsky. Volume 2, The fundamentals of defectology*, pp. 178–183. Trans. and intro. J.E. Knox and C.B. Stevens; Rieber, R.W. and Carton, A.S. (eds). New York: Plenum Press.

Vygotsky, L.S. (1993b). 'The blind child' [early 1930s], in Vygotsky, L.S., *The collected works of L.S. Vygotsky. Volume 2, The fundamentals of defectology*, pp. 97–109. Trans. and intro. J.E. Knox and C.B. Stevens; Rieber, R.W. and Carton, A.S. (eds). New York: Plenum Press.

Vygotsky, L.S. (1993c). 'The collective as a factor in the development of the abnormal child' [1931], in Vygotsky, L.S., *The collected works of L.S. Vygotsky. Volume 2, The fundamentals of defectology*, pp. 191–208. Trans. and intro. J.E. Knox and C.B. Stevens; Rieber, R.W. and Carton, A.S. (eds). New York: Plenum Press.

Vygotsky, L.S. (1993d). 'Defect and compensation' [1927], in Vygotsky, L.S., *The collected works of L.S. Vygotsky. Volume 2, The fundamentals of defectology*, pp. 52–64. Trans. and intro. J.E. Knox and C.B. Stevens; Rieber, R.W. and Carton, A.S. (eds). New York: Plenum Press.

Vygotsky, L.S. (1993e). 'Defectology and the study of the development and education of abnormal children' [n.d.], in Vygotsky, L.S., *The collected works of L.S. Vygotsky. Volume 2, The fundamentals of defectology*, pp. 164–170. Trans. and intro. J.E. Knox and C.B. Stevens; Rieber, R.W. and Carton, A.S. (eds). New York: Plenum Press.

Vygotsky, L.S. (1993f). 'The diagnostics of development and the pedological clinic for difficult children' [1936], in Vygotsky, L.S., *The collected works of L.S. Vygotsky. Volume 2, The fundamentals of defectology*, pp. 241–291. Trans. and intro. J.E. Knox and C.B. Stevens; Rieber, R.W. and Carton, A.S. (eds). New York: Plenum Press.

Vygotsky, L.S. (1993g). 'The dynamics of child character' [1928], in Vygotsky, L.S., *The collected works of L.S. Vygotsky. Volume 2, The fundamentals of defectology*, pp. 153–163. Trans. and intro. J.E. Knox and C.B. Stevens; Rieber, R.W. and Carton, A.S. (eds). New York: Plenum Press.

Vygotsky, L.S. (1993h). 'Introduction: The fundamental problems of defectology' [1929], in Vygotsky, L.S., *The collected works of L.S. Vygotsky. Volume 2, The fundamentals of defectology*, pp. 29–51. Trans. and intro. J.E. Knox and C.B. Stevens; Rieber, R.W. and Carton, A.S. (eds). New York: Plenum Press.

Vygotsky, L.S. (1993i). 'Principles of education for physically handicapped children' [1924], in Vygotsky, L.S., *The collected works of L.S. Vygotsky. Volume 2, The fundamentals of defectology*, pp. 65–75. Trans. and intro. J.E. Knox and C.B. Stevens; Rieber, R.W. and Carton, A.S. (eds). New York: Plenum Press.

Vygotsky, L.S. (1993j). 'The psychology and pedagogy of children's handicaps' [1924], in Vygotsky, L.S., *The collected works of L.S. Vygotsky. Volume 2, The fundamentals of defectology*, pp. 76–93. Trans. and intro. J.E. Knox and C.B. Stevens; Rieber, R.W. and Carton, A.S. (eds). New York: Plenum Press.

Vygotsky, L.S. (1997a). 'Consciousness as a problem for the psychology of behaviour' [1925], in Vygotsky, L.S., *The collected works of L.S. Vygotsky. Volume 3, Problems of the theory and history of psychology*, pp. 63–79. Trans. and intro. R. Van der Veer; Rieber, R.W. and Wollock, J. (eds). New York: Plenum Press.

Vygotsky, L.S. (1997b). *Educational psychology* [1926]. Trans. R. Silverman. Davydov, V. V. (ed. and intro.). Boca Raton, FL: CRC Press.

Vygotsky, L.S. (1997c). *The historical meaning of the crisis in psychology: a methodological investigation* [1926–1927], in Vygotsky, L.S., *The collected works of L.S. Vygotsky. Volume 3, Problems of the theory and history of psychology*, pp. 233–343. Trans. and intro. R. Van der Veer; Rieber, R.W. and Wollock, J. (eds). New York: Plenum Press.

Yaroshevsky, M.G. (1989). *Lev Vygotsky*. Moscow: Progress Publishers.

Yasnitsky, A. (2018). *Vygotsky: an intellectual biography*. New York: Routledge.

Zavershneva, E. and Van der Veer, R. (eds) (2018). 'The trip to London', in Zavershneva, E. and Van der Veer, R. (eds), *Vygotsky's notebooks: a selection* (Perspectives in cultural-historical research 2). Singapore: Springer.

Chapter 4

The crisis in psychology

I have been [in the hospital] for a week now – in large wards with six seriously ill patients each, with noise and cries, without any table, and so on. The beds are arranged side by side with no space in between, as in a barracks. Moreover, I feel terrible physically and am depressed and disheartened psychologically.
(From Vygotsky's letter to Sakharov, 15 February 1926; Vygotsky, 2007, p. 15)

Vygotsky as a theoretical psychologist

Vygotsky returned to Moscow from the International Congress on the Education of the Deaf, held in London in July 1925. It is possible that the long journey to England and back, via Paris and Berlin, had been too much for his health, because he soon became ill and later that year was hospitalised with a serious recurrence of his tuberculosis. He was in hospital, and then in a sanatorium in Zakharino for six months, from November 1925 to May 1926. This long and gruelling bout of ill-ness was to be the prelude to a period of activity when he was intensely busy but constantly plagued with ill health.

While he was in the sanatorium and continuing his recovery afterwards, he began noting ideas for a book, *The historical meaning of the crisis in psychology: a methodological investigation* (Vygotsky, 1997c), usually referred to as *The crisis in psychology*. This book (which was not published until after his death) was to be a fundamental critique of existing schools of psychology, and an analysis of what would be required to create a general discipline of psychology, with a set of shared concepts and a clear approach to methodology. The work he did in this short book was to be crucial to the future development of his approach to psychology.

It was originally thought that Vygotsky had written some of the book while in the sanatorium, but Zavershneva's work on the manuscript in the Vygotsky family archive has established that, although one of the notebooks from Zakharino Sanatorium shows that Vygotsky was making notes for it, the book was in fact written after Vygotsky was discharged from the sanatorium (in May 1926). It was begun in approximately mid-1926, and probably completed in early 1927 (Zavershneva, 2012).

DOI: 10.4324/9780429203046-4

In this chapter we shall approach *The crisis in psychology* through a consideration of two of Vygotsky's earlier contributions to psychological theory: his paper 'The methods of reflexological and psychological investigation', which he gave at the 2nd Congress on Psycho-neurology in January 1924, and his paper on consciousness, given at an open conference in the Moscow Institute of Psychology later in 1924 and published in 1925.

Both of these papers contain powerful critiques of contemporary psychology, in particular of reflexology, and prepare the way for the larger argument of *The crisis in psychology*. So this chapter maps Vygotsky's intellectual journey towards the creation of a new psychology, one capable of including language and consciousness in its model of mind, and one different in kind from reflexology.

Early themes (1924–1925)

Vygotsky's famous 'entry into psychology' at the 2nd Pan-Russian Congress in Psycho-neurology in Petrograd (January 1924) came about when he presented a paper on reflexology which so impressed Kornilov, the new Director of the Moscow Institute of Psychology, that he offered him a post there. He was not, as was once thought, a novice in psychology; for some years he had taught psychology at the teachers' college in Gomel and later collected his lectures into a book, *Educational psychology* (Vygotsky, 1997b), discussed in Chapter 1. The book was described there as 'almost a hymn to conditioned reflexes' – but Vygotsky's contribution to the Congress was very far from being that.

The paper that made such an impression at the conference was about reflexology: 'The methods of reflexological and psychological investigation'. It was once thought that the paper that drew attention to him at the Congress was 'Consciousness as a problem for the psychology of behaviour' (Vygotsky, 1997a), but that was given later in 1924. However, the two papers related to two themes that continued to preoccupy Vygotsky for the rest of his life as a psychologist: methodology in psychology, and the subject of consciousness.

Reflexology

To understand Vygotsky's paper on reflexology we need to consider how psychology was being practised and taught at that time, and what prior experience Vygotsky had of reflexology.

In Russia, as elsewhere, the original academic home of psychology was in philosophy departments, where it was often studied in a theoretical and 'idealist' way, making use of self-observation and self-report. But there had been, for several years, two main traditions in psychology, one idealist and one scientific, experimental, and rooted in physiology. The work of the pioneer experimental psychologist Wilhelm Wundt in Germany had not been widely taken up in Russia, although some Russian scientists had visited Wundt's laboratory. One of these was Vladimir Bekhterev, a professor of nervous and psychiatric diseases at

Kazan University, who began to build a new psychology in Russia following Wundt's example. He originally named this new approach 'objective psychology' and was determined to turn it into an exact science on the model of neurology or physiology, with controlled experimental techniques. After 1917, Bekhterev began to call his psychology 'reflexology', borrowing this term and some of his experimental practices from Pavlov's approach to the study of animal physiology and behaviour (Joravsky, 1989).

Bekhterev set out to eliminate subjectivity in research. His researchers were thoroughly trained and provided with standard observational rubrics. Researchers were allowed to record only external movements; there was to be no hypothesis about subjects' responses; introspection had no role at all to play in experiment. Bekhterev wrote three books about his new version of reflexology in 1918, 1921 and 1923. He actually attended the 1924 2nd Pan-Russian Congress in Psycho-neurology at which Vygotsky gave his paper on reflexology.

In *Educational psychology*, Vygotsky did indeed give a full and faithful account of reflexology, its main findings and its methods, but he nevertheless made it quite clear that he did not consider that it could properly be applied to human behaviour, except in limited areas. He said that the term 'restricts us to the comparatively narrow circle of the physiology of the nervous system' and favoured instead the term 'reaction' (which was the term preferred by Kornilov) to describe the elements of human behaviour. He observed:

> Thus, the decisive factor of human behaviour is not only the biological factor but also the social factor, which brings with it entirely novel elements of behaviour. Man's experience is not just that of an animal that has assumed an upright position, but is a rather complex function of the entire social experience of mankind and of his individual groups.
>
> (Vygotsky, 1997b, p. 33)

Vygotsky's paper on reflexology

'The methods of reflexological and psychological investigation' (Vygotsky, 1997d) is a carefully argued paper that opens up a discussion of the methods of reflexology for studying human behaviour. It is clear from the outset that Vygotsky intends to engage in detail with the practice of reflexology and is thoroughly familiar with the language and concepts used in the discipline. One of the main purposes of his paper is to make a detailed case for the inclusion of a subject's verbal responses as acceptable evidence in a reflexological experiment. But from that Vygotsky moves on to a deeper purpose, which is to argue that reflexology has reached a dead end, that the study of human behaviour is incomplete without the study of mental activity, and that there needs to be a new psychology, one that is thoroughly scientific, but can broaden its scope to take in the question of the mind and consciousness.

Vygotsky builds his argument through a logical sequence, with obvious awareness of the traps that he is avoiding by the sophistication and cogency of his reasoning. Although apparently respectful of the reflexological approach, in the course of the paper Vygotsky increasingly exposes its limitations and questions its adequacy in relation to human subjects. Andy Blunden (2009) sees Vygotsky's approach here as an example of 'immanent critique'. This is a 'criticism from within' in which the critic, provisionally accepting the premises of a theory, tests out its claims and identifies its weak points and inner contradictions. The critique that is then made, starting entirely from the premises of the original theory and using its own terms, mounts a reasoned case against the theory by exposing its weaknesses and contradictions and developing the argument until the theory collapses. This is precisely the approach that Vygotsky adopts, and he does it brilliantly.

Reflexological investigations allowed for the 'interrogation of the subject' (i.e. the human subject of the experiment) through the study of 'complete speech reflexes' (words) but not 'inhibited reflexes', or thoughts. Vygotsky questions this:

> When I pronounce aloud, audible for the experimenter, the word 'evening', then this word that comes to my mind by association is taken into account as a verbal reaction = a conditional reflex. But when I pronounce it inaudibly, for myself, when I think it, does it really stop being a reflex and change its nature? And where is the boundary between the pronounced and the unpronounced word? When my lips started moving, when I whispered, but inaudibly for the experimenter, what then? Can he ask me to repeat this word aloud, or will that be a subjective method, self-observation and other forbidden things?
>
> (Vygotsky, 1997d, pp. 38–39)

There is a playful irony at work here in the teasing apart of the experimental rules of reflexology. Vygotsky concludes that thoughts, which are part of the study of human behaviour in its most essential forms, *must* be registered. 'Reflexology must study both thought and the whole mind if it wishes to understand behavior' (ibid., p. 39).

Vygotsky moves on to a discussion of the interrelatedness of reflexes, the links between them (producing conditional reflexes) and the relationship between internal reflexes (e.g. thoughts), which are not accessible to direct observation, and full reflexes (words). He suggests that the mind is a huge system of interacting reflexes, and that the only means of understanding these is through the interrogation of the subject:

> In such a conception the report of the subject is not at all an act of self-observation that, as it were, puts a spoke in the wheels of scientifically objective investigation. *No self-observation whatsoever* ... The subject *fully*

remains ... the *object* of the experiment, but in the experiment itself some changes, a transformation, are introduced through this interrogation.

(Vygotsky, 1997d, p. 40)

Vygotsky observes that the responses to interrogation during the experiment will merely become part of the experimental data. He suggests that awareness, or consciousness, is a system of transmissions between reflexes which is going on all the time:

The more correctly each internal reflex, as a stimulus, elicits a whole series of other reflexes from other systems, is transmitted to other systems – the better we are capable of *accounting* for ourselves and others for what is experienced, the more consciously it is experienced (felt, fixed in words, etc.) ... Consciousness is the experience of experiences in precisely the same way as experience is simply the experience of objects.

(Vygotsky, 1997d, pp. 40–41)

And from this Vygotsky argues for the existence of:

a group of reflexes that we might justifiably call the system of reflexes of social contact ... These reversible reflexes, which create the basis for consciousness (the interlacing of the reflexes), also serve as the basis of social interaction and the collective coordination of behaviour, which, incidentally, points to the social origin of consciousness ... The source of social behaviour and consciousness also lives in speech in the broad sense of the word.

(Vygotsky, 1997d, p. 42)

From an orthodox reflexological position Vygotsky has arrived, through a process of logical argument, using reflexological terminology, to a statement that foreshadows all his future psychology – the origins of mind/consciousness in social interaction and in human language.

Vygotsky points out that if reflexology aspires to explain the *whole* behaviour of man 'it will inevitably have to deal with the same material as psychology' (ibid., p. 44). He asks whether a scientific explanation of human behaviour is possible without the mind. Pavlov himself had suggested that his physiological reflexology could provide the foundations for the construction of the higher superstructure of human psychology. Bekhterev had suggested that in the future there might be a reflexology dealing entirely with 'subjective phenomena'. But Vygotsky says this would be dualism – a division of the study of man into two sciences:

Thus, two sciences with the *same* subject of investigation – the behaviour of man – and that use the *same methods*, nevertheless, despite everything, remain different sciences. What prevents them from merging? 'Subjective or mental phenomena' the reflexologists repeat in a thousand ways. What are these subjective phenomena, this mind? ... For Academician Pavlov they are nonspatial and noncausal phenomena. For Academician Bekhterev they have no objective existence *whatsoever* as they can only be studied on oneself. But both Bekhterev and Pavlov know that they rule our life ... *Mind without behaviour is as impossible as behaviour without mind*, if only because they are the same.

(Vygotsky, 1997d, p. 46)

Vygotsky has used the language of reflexology to call the discipline into question. Now, as he asserts that consciousness can and must be accommodated within one objective science, his words seem to be ambiguous:

In claiming that consciousness too has to be understood as a reaction of the organism to its own reactions, one must be a bigger reflexologist than Pavlov himself. So be it ...

(Vygotsky, 1997d, p. 47)

He believes that psychology is facing the same kind of crisis both in the West and in the USSR. To solve it the two sciences of reflexology and psychology must merge. Reflexology may have built the foundation, but it has now reached a dead end. It is isolating itself 'in the narrow circle of *physiological materialism*' (ibid., p. 48).

Towards the end of the paper his stance becomes openly radical:

We have to speak openly ... Psychologically speaking, consciousness is an indisputable fact, a primary reality, a fact of the greatest importance, and not a secondary or accidental one. About this there is no dispute.

(Vygotsky, 1997d, p. 47)

So a way must be found of studying the mind and taking into account self-observation. Vygotsky argues that just as in a lawsuit jurors listen to different testimonies and verify and compare them, so we can examine material evidence and documentation, evaluate the evidence and establish the facts. The ability to weigh evidence, discriminate and evaluate, must also be accepted in this area of science.

Vygotsky's paper found a way round the main objections to self-observation as evidence, and argued passionately for the place of mind in the study of behaviour. To some of the psychologists listening to this presentation, which makes such a powerful case for the inclusion of both non-verbal and verbal responses in reflexology, and of consciousness in psychology, it must have seemed a breakthrough.

'Consciousness as a problem for the psychology of behaviour'

The article on consciousness dealt with the subject that was to preoccupy Vygotsky for the rest of his life and was indeed the topic of the last pages of the last chapter in the last book that he wrote. For Vygotsky the problem of consciousness and how it was to be brought into mainstream psychology was a key problem. This paper was an early move towards making a case for the recognition of the fundamental role of consciousness in the working of the mind. He returned to this subject several times, particularly in the paper 'Mind, consciousness, the unconscious' (Vygotsky, 1997e).

'Consciousness as a problem for the psychology of behaviour' goes over some of the same ground as the paper on reflexology, but introduces some new points. It is very different from the reflexology paper. It is less rhetorical, less of a performance, and begins from further on in the argument. From its very first sentence, Vygotsky makes clear that he is intent on bringing the subject of consciousness into scientific discourse and that in this paper he is going to attempt to find a way of achieving this:

> The question of the psychological nature of consciousness is persistently and deliberately avoided in our scientific literature.
>
> (Vygotsky, 1997a, p. 63)

He argues that reflexology is incapable of explaining human behaviour because it cannot − will not − take into account 'internal reactions':

> To put it more simply; man always thinks to himself. This will always influence his behaviour ... But we have no idea how to take this influence into account.
>
> (Vygotsky, 1997a, p. 64)

Reflexology is unable to give more than the most basic account of human behaviour and refuses to investigate reactions that cannot be observed with the naked eye, such as internal movements, internal speech (thoughts), etc.

> Reflexology's basic assumption that it is possible to fully explain all of man's behaviour without resorting to subjective phenomena (to build a psychology without a mind) is the dualism of subjective psychology turned inside out.
>
> (Vygotsky, 1997a, p. 65)

The dualism that Vygotsky refers to is the idea that there can be two psychologies: one (reflexology) which deals with behaviour without mind, and the other ('subjective psychology' − or 'idealistic psychology') which deals with mind without behaviour. Vygotsky is arguing for a unified psychology and to do this he has to find a way of including consciousness and the mind within the ambit of a general monistic and materialist psychology. The argument for this is pursued in *The crisis in psychology*.

In this paper Vygotsky turns to the issue of what is to be done in order to *investigate* this most important problem: 'the *structure* of our behaviour, the analysis of its composition and form' (ibid., p. 66), without resorting to reflexology. He is fluent in reflexology, its terms and concepts – it is difficult for him to find a new language with which to talk about the workings of behaviour, but this is what he must now do. The rest of the paper is the *beginning* of an approach to the problem of how to construct a new psychology.

> Scientific psychology must not ignore the facts of consciousness but materialize them, translate them into the objective language of the objectively existing.
>
> (Vygotsky, 1997a, p. 67)

In the section that follows, Vygotsky considers the differences between animal and human behaviour. He thinks it is fair to describe animal behaviour in reflexological terms; it can be described as inherited reactions plus acquired reactions (unconditional reflexes plus acquired, or conditional, reflexes).

But human beings, in addition to their inherited experience and their personal experience, also inherit the experience of previous generations, which is handed down to them through history and culture. Vygotsky calls all of this *'historical experience'*.

And in addition they can share in the experience of other people through a multitude of connections. Because of this passed-on experience we can know about many aspects of the world that are not accessible to us personally. Vygotsky calls this *'social experience'*.

Finally, human beings don't simply have to adapt to their environment, they can also shape it to fit their needs. It's true that spiders can spin webs and birds can make nests, but as Marx[1] says, in the quotation that Vygotsky uses as an epigraph to this paper, unlike the spider an architect 'raises his structure *in imagination* [my italics] before he erects it in reality'. Vygotsky observes that all human work is like this; the worker thinks about what she is going to do, *imagines* the movements and materials she will use, before she starts work. This Vygotsky calls *'doubled experience'*. Human beings can be conscious of their own experience and plan their behaviour in their mind.

So any account of human psychology *must* take account of the much greater complexity of human behaviour, and the 'circular reactions' that provide feedback to the organism, in a way that enables the organism to adjust its reactions.

Vygotsky builds on the existence of the 'proprioceptive field' – the mechanisms that enable us to constantly monitor our physical movements. Our proprioceptive field is always helping the brain to monitor and adjust our muscular reactions. (Without this kind of feedback we wouldn't be able to carry a teacup across a room or walk downstairs easily.) He suggests that:

this experience is only accessible to one person – the one who is experiencing this experience. Only I, and I alone can observe and perceive my own secondary reactions, because only for me do my reflexes serve as new stimuli for the proprioceptive field.

(Vygotsky, 1997a, p. 73)

Consciousness, he says, is another such system that enables us to monitor our experiences and thoughts and adjust our responses accordingly. But he emphasizes that this awareness 'exists only for myself'. That is why psychology *must* admit self-observation as a necessary source of psychological knowledge.

He concludes:

taking into account the enormous and primary role that the mind, i.e. the non-manifest group of reflexes, plays in the system of behaviour, it would be suicidal to refrain from its exposure through the indirect path of its reflection on other systems of reflexes. After all, we are studying reflexes to stimuli that are internal and hidden from us.

(Vygotsky, 1997a, p. 73)

Vygotsky is still using the language and concepts of reflexology to outline the new psychology that he is intent on building. Perhaps it is appropriate for him to do that, since he is talking to fellow psychologists. Perhaps as yet he has no alternative terms to use. But in the last part of the paper he embarks on new territory in a discussion of 'the system of reversible reflexes', a concept that enables him to raise the topic of internalisation.

Vygotsky argues that these reversible reflexes create the basis of social behaviour; we very soon become able to reconstruct the 'social stimuli coming from people':

that is, they become reversible for me and thus determine my behaviour ... they make me comparable to another, identical to myself. The source of social behaviour and consciousness also lies in speech in the broad sense of the word.

(Vygotsky, 1997a, p. 77)

If this is so, he says,

then the mechanism of social behaviour (speech) and the mechanism of consciousness are one and the same. Speech is, on the one hand, the system of the 'reflexes of social contact' and, on the other hand, the system of the reflexes of consciousness ... i.e., an apparatus for the reflection of other systems.

(Vygotsky, 1997a, p. 77)

Vygotsky draws out the implications of this:

> The mechanism of knowledge of the self (self-consciousness) and knowledge of others is the same ... We are conscious of ourselves because we are conscious of others and by the same method as we are conscious of others, because we are the same vis-à-vis ourselves as others are vis-à-vis us. I am conscious of myself only to the extent that I am another to myself ...
>
> (Vygotsky, 1997a, p. 77)

Vygotsky describes this process as 'the sociologising of all consciousness'. Consciousness is developed through the internalisation of social interaction and through speech. With this statement he has arrived at his desired destination. And to support his argument, in the last pages of this paper he draws an example from his experience in defectology:

> In deaf-mutes, speech usually does not develop and gets stuck in the stage of the reflex cry, not because their speech centres are damaged, but because the possibility of the reversibility of the speech reflex is paralysed by the absence of hearing.
>
> (Vygotsky, 1997a, p. 78)

So alternative routes have to be found to enable the deaf to speak. Vygotsky, using the 'oralist' methods of the time, describes how deaf children learn language by lip reading and other ways of 'hearing' the sounds that are being made, e.g. by feeling the vibrations in the vocal cords. However, there is another development that accompanies learning language:

> Here the most remarkable thing is that conscious awareness of speech and social experience emerge simultaneously and completely in parallel ... The deaf-mute learns to become conscious of himself and his movements to the extent that he learns to become conscious of others.
>
> (Vygotsky, 1997a, p. 78)

Vygotsky regards this as 'a specially arranged experiment of nature' – a natural experiment – which confirms his basic thesis in the article. He has not yet developed a language or a conceptual structure for a new psychology. He is still reliant on the language of reflexology, while rejecting many of its assumptions. But this paper is an important staging post on the way to the construction of a psychology of mind.

In the final text that we will consider in this chapter, *The crisis in psychology*, Vygotsky undertook a much more comprehensive review of the fragmented state of psychology, preparatory to considering the language and methodology that will be needed to create a 'general psychology' within which specialist psychologies can be accommodated.

The historical meaning of the crisis in psychology

This book was never published during Vygotsky's lifetime, appearing for the first time in English in volume 3 of the *Collected works* (Vygotsky, 1997) and there has been speculation as to why this was so. Some have said that Vygotsky might have considered it unworthy of publication, but this seems a specious suggestion given the importance of its arguments to him at the time. He may have judged that the book would cause him political and professional difficulties, since he had referred to several well-known Russian psychologists (including some close colleagues such as Alexander Luria) often very critically. And in terms of politics, some of his most scathing remarks in the book referred to superficial approaches to Marxism. This might have offended some people in the field. Perhaps Vygotsky simply didn't have time to revise the book for publication, once he had started on a full work programme at the Moscow Institute, and returned to his other commitments in defectology.

But another reading might be that Vygotsky was using this opportunity to work things out for himself as well as for others. Veresov suggests that the methodological study in this book 'was necessary for Vygotsky himself' since 'the new ideas and concepts he came to in practical defectological work asked for such a kind of methodological analysis' (Veresov, 1999, p. 153). The book is often passionate and personal and it sometimes seems as if a struggle is going on, an inward struggle in which Vygotsky is engaging with ideas which it is important to him to defeat, or to justify. And possibly there was also another struggle involved, between different aspects of himself, since he is clearly pulled both ways in some parts of the argument.

The argument

The book is a thorough review of the state of psychology in Russia going back to the late 19th century. Alex Kozulin (2008) describes the Russian tradition in psychology as one of combining experimental activity with philosophical analysis. There was a pluralist tradition in pre-revolutionary psychology; psychologists tended to come either from philosophy or medicine. In fact this combination was also characteristic of psychology in America – the tradition of psychologist-philosophers was strong there.

Russian psychologists were in dialogue with psychologists in several European countries, especially Germany. European and American texts were translated into Russian in large numbers. But physiology was greatly expanding and was providing a clear, if limited, model of the study of behaviour. The increasingly urgent debate between philosopher-psychologists and psycho-physiologists, or idealists and materialists, had intensified with the Revolution. Many psychologists saw no possibility for their discipline to be both scientific and pluralistic at the same time.

So in *The crisis in psychology* Vygotsky set out to analyse this debate, examine the strengths and weaknesses of both traditions and identify the issues that divided them. He did so from the point of view of a concerned psychologist and a Marxist, pointing out that while academic psychology was indulging in this kind of intellectual debate, many applied psychologists, working in schools, factories, hospitals and institutions, needed more clarity and consensus in the discipline. The needs of *applied* psychology were particularly pressing in a period, after the Revolution, when so much was being demanded from psychology in the development of the new society. Towards the end of the book Vygotsky spends more time on the subject of applied psychology, and it becomes a major factor in his view of how the crisis can be resolved. Of course, he was himself directly involved in 'applied psychology' through his work in defectology.

The book is a firework display of erudition and cogent argument. Vygotsky had not only absorbed all of the critical ideas in this field; he was putting them to work. He began the book by talking about the crisis in psychology, the lack of consensus in the discipline, and the diversity of practice. Psychology needed to become more unified – to establish a 'general discipline'– in order to develop. This statement was not unusual; back in 1874 Franz Brentano had opened his major treatise on psychology 'with a lament on the unscientific clutter of psycholog*ies,* and starting more divisions with his project for a single united psychology' (Joravsky, 1989, p. 104).

Early in the book Vygotsky took on four major schools of psychology in order to reveal their inadequacies. These were: reflexology, Gestalt psychology, psychoanalysis and personal-ism. He argued that each of these systems starts with an empirical discovery, which becomes an explanatory principle, which then expands to include more and more aspects of psychology. For the reflexologists *all* behaviour turns out to be the sum of conditioned reflexes, for psychoanalysis it is the sum of unconscious drives, and so on. Vygotsky's major criticism was that these systems are circular; the concepts to be investigated are essentially the same as the explanatory principle that is being used to analyse them. Therefore none was at a level that would enable them to be the basis of a general psychology. What was needed was an explanatory principle *external* to the system under consideration. (Much later in the book Vygotsky identifies the explanatory principle for psychology as *praxis.*)

Vygotsky describes what constitutes a general discipline: it is an overarching discipline which relates to several sub-disciplines and integrates them. But even though it operates at a higher level of generalisation and abstraction, a general discipline never ceases to be a science or to refer to empirical data.

As an example of a general science Vygotsky offers general biology. It covers areas such as botany, zoology, physiology and so on – but its sphere is different from that of the subsidiary disciplines. General biology, for instance, deals in broad unifying higher-level concepts. But Vygotsky suggests that it is never divorced from facts.

It is a natural science, albeit of the highest level. Of course it does not deal with living concrete objects such as plants and animals, but with abstractions such as organism, evolution of species, natural selection and the like, but in the final analysis it nevertheless studies by means of these abstractions the same reality as zoology and botany.

(Vygotsky, 1997c, p. 247)

However, this does not mean that it becomes entirely abstract and detached from facts:

Every natural-scientific concept, however high the degree of its abstraction from the empirical fact, always contains a clot, a sediment of the concrete, real and scientifically known reality, albeit in a very weak solution.

(Vygotsky, 1997c, p. 248)

And Vygotsky suggests that, as well, 'even the most immediate, empirical, raw, singular natural scientific fact already contains a first abstraction' (ibid., p. 249) – i.e. it is a concept in embryo. So 'the difference between general and empirical sciences as regards the object of investigation is purely quantitative and not fundamental.' This is a difference of degree and not of kind; the subject matter of the general sciences is scientific concepts, but these concepts 'have their prototypes in reality' (ibid., p. 250). And of course over time these concepts change, they 'suffer wear and tear in their use, they become worn down, in need of revision and often of replacement' (ibid., p. 251). Finally, Vygotsky concludes, 'each discovery in science, each step forward in empirical science, is always at the same time an act of criticizing the concept' (ibid.).

Methodology

For me, the first question is the question of method; this, for me, is the question of truth, and hence of scientific discovery and invention.

(Vygotsky, 2007, p. 18)

In this argument for a new general psychology, Vygotsky gave central importance to the role of methodology. He knew that it was essential to develop a scientific methodology that was objective, and yet would be complex enough to explore the workings of the human mind. But he also knew that of all things this was the most difficult:

The subject matter of psychology is the most complicated of all things in the world and least accessible to investigation. Its methods must be full of special contrivances and precautions in order to yield what is expected of them.

(Vygotsky, 1997c, p. 328)

The creation of an adequate methodology had to take precedence even over the elaboration of theory.

Vygotsky wanted to study the mind, which was obviously not directly observable. He had already criticised reflexologists and behaviourists who had restricted themselves to examining only directly observable facts. He argued that very many interesting scientific investigations go beyond what is observable (for instance the rotation of the earth). In physics Max Planck had written of the need to liberate physics from the human eye, 'which only perceives the light beams within a small area of the spectrum' (ibid., p. 271). Vygotsky thought that psychology needed to 'emancipate itself from the tradition of narrow empirical naturalism' (Hyman, 2009, p. 2); it should be about explanation, not description.

In order to study what was not directly observable, Vygotsky argued that other disciplines, such as history or geology, do so by systematic analysis of documents, artefacts, and other traces (just as the jurors in a lawsuit examine the evidence). Ludmilla Hyman, a historian of science, suggests that Vygotsky was anticipating a shift which is now generally accepted towards 'interpretive methods that allow for the investigation of the invisible' (ibid., p. 5). She suggests that Vygotsky has a 'reliabilist' position; any specific claim can be wrong but the method of knowledge production must be reliable. 'In science we intensify control at all levels of perception and cognition to obtain reliable results' (ibid., p. 9). Hyman describes Vygotsky's view of the goal of science as:

> to arrive at essences rather than register perceptions ... Scientific understanding necessitates the explanation not the description of objects. Scientific understanding requires what Vygotsky called 'scientific concepts' – well-defined mental constructs that contain models of abstract relations between entities ... Scientific concepts are ways of understanding reality on a higher level of abstraction. They are logical and systemic (i.e. they are embedded in a network of concepts).
>
> (Hyman, 2009, pp. 5–6)

This definition of scientific concepts, as opposed to everyday concepts, supports Vygotsky's emphasis on analysis and abstraction as necessary elements of his methodology, but also prefigures his later work on the development of scientific concepts in children's learning.

Fundamentally, Vygotsky's argument in *The crisis in psychology* is an argument against making induction the main means of scientific thinking. He envisages an 'indirect method' in psychology where enquiry can proceed by the systematic analysis of psychological phenomena through the study of their effects. He also sees *theoretical analysis* as the key element in any experiment; with this approach it will be possible to infer the laws of what you are studying even from *one particular case*. He dismisses the idea that experiments should be realistic and natural; in his view 'the strength of analysis is in abstraction, just as the strength of experiment is in its artificiality' (Vygotsky, 1997c, p. 320) – the aim of the experiment is to isolate the phenomenon being studied.

In the course of the book, Vygotsky turns for support to two very different figures: Pavlov and Marx. Both had something in common when it came to thinking about the fundamentals of a new discipline. One was their clarity about what was to be investigated. Marx's approach in *Capital* is to analyse the 'cell' of bourgeois society – commodity value. He discerns the structure of the whole social order and all economic formations in this one cell. Vygotsky wrote:

> He who can decipher the meaning of the cell of psychology, the mechanism of one reaction, has found the key to all psychology.
>
> (Vygotsky, 1997c, p. 320)

Similarly Pavlov bases his whole psychology on the study of salivary reflexes in dogs, and from this derives a general biological principle of the functioning of the higher nervous system in animals. Here again, Vygotsky admires the clarity of the explanatory principle and he also draws attention to the fact that in his experiments Pavlov:

> *maximally abstracted* the phenomenon he studied from the specific conditions of the particular phenomenon. He brilliantly *perceived the general in the particular.*
>
> (Vygotsky, 1997c, p. 318)

In both these cases the investigators abstract a general principle from the study of a single phenomenon. Vygotsky admires the way that each of these very different thinkers has clearly defined what is to be investigated, and discovered a *unit of analysis* which will enable them to carry the investigation forward. This was part of his own approach in *The psychology of art* – arguing from a single work of literature – and will become a fundamental part of his methodology.

Vygotsky also considers the vocabulary of these two thinkers. Both succeeded in defining a set of terms, a scientific language, for their areas of investigation. Pavlov, indeed, introduced a penalty into his laboratory for the use of 'psychological' terms in talking about animals, which polluted the scientific discourse of the laboratory, thus threatening its foundations (Vygotsky, 1997c, p. 281). Marx's theory had its own vocabulary, its concepts of value, class, commodity, capital, interest, production forces, base, superstructure, etc. Vygotsky observed that:

> Psychology is in need of its own *Das Kapital* – its own concepts of class, basis, value et cetera – in which it might express and study its object.
>
> (Vygotsky, 1997c, p. 330)

He lamented the fact that psychological language was 'terminologically insufficient: this means that psychology does not yet have its *own* language.' (ibid., p. 281). This too was a necessary part of an adequate methodology.

Praxis

At the beginning of *The crisis in psychology* Vygotsky had named the main driving force of the crisis as applied psychology, which was in need of the support of a unified psychology. And towards the end of the book he also sees the solution to the crisis in applied psychology:

> the leading role in the development of our science belongs to applied psychology. It represents everything of psychology which is progressive, sound, which contains a germ of the future. It provides the best methodological work. It is only by studying this area that one can come to an understanding of what is going on and the possibility of genuine psychology.
>
> (Vygotsky, 1997c, p. 305)

This is essentially because the confrontation with applied psychology compels psychology to reform its principles so that they may withstand the highest test of practice, or praxis (practice that is reflective and grounded in Marxist theory).[2]

The principle and philosophy of practice has become 'the stone which the builders rejected and which became the headstone of the corner'[3] (ibid., p. 306). Through his substantial work with children with special needs Vygotsky has gained an important perspective on the needs of practice and how psychology can support it. He is grounded in this practical work, even as he discusses the most abstruse and detailed points of psychological theory:

> In his view, scientific psychology possesses enormous social significance because it can develop techniques to help people better manage themselves and maximize their natural endowments in society.
>
> (Hyman, 2011, p. 4)

The climax of the book comes when Vygotsky argues that there can be no further toleration of a blurred line between philosophical idealistic psychology and materialist experimental psychology. Only the second qualifies as a real science and can be the basis of research and it must therefore be severed from idealistic psychology. The reader gets the impression of a real tussle going on *within* Vygotsky as he reaches this point in the argument. As a person with a theoretical mind he had clearly felt the pull of the philosophical-psychological tradition and had learnt from some of its exponents, particularly William James, whose work he admired. His language here becomes dramatic and violent as he ventures 'to cut the living tissue of psychology, cutting it as it were into two heterogeneous bodies which grew together by mistake' (Vygotsky, 1997c, p. 323).

> Following Spinoza, we have compared our science to a mortally ill patient who looks for an unreliable medicine. Now we see that it is only

the surgeon's knife which can save the situation. A bloody operation is imminent.

(Vygotsky, 1997c, p. 324)

And what shall this new psychology be called? Vygotsky rejects many double-barrelled solutions: objective psychology, behavioural psychology, scientific psychology, even Marxist psychology. The new psychology will necessarily be both scientific and Marxist: 'That is why we will simply say: psychology' (ibid., p. 342).

Building the new psychology

In *The crisis in psychology* Vygotsky has been writing something into being. He is aware of the size of the task – psychology is not yet a fully developed science.

It is particularly difficult to study knowledge that has not yet become aware of itself and its own logos.

(Vygotsky, 1997c, p. 265)

When discussing the processes and phenomena that psychology must study, Vygotsky quite frequently employs the language of reflexology or reactology. He is not yet in a position to postulate a new vocabulary which will be part of the psychology to be developed. He has not yet, following Marx's example, found the cell which, once analysed, will give 'the key to all psychology' (ibid., p. 320), or arrived at a set of concepts that will define it. And although he has thought deeply about methodology, he has not yet developed a range of effective experimental methods.

It is remarkable to follow Vygotsky's thoughts in this book as he attempts to 'raise his structure in imagination' before 'erecting it in reality'. In building this new psychology he is starting from the top instead of from the foundations. Before he can put anything concrete in place he has to imagine a conceptual framework that it will fit into. But perhaps we should rather say that he is erecting a huge explanatory structure, within which all his future work will be done.

Notes

1 The quotation from Marx's *Capital* is in volume 1, part III, section 1, 'The labour-process or the production of use-values'.
2 Paulo Freire defines 'praxis' as 'reflection and action upon the world in order to transform it' (Freire, 1972, p. 52).
3 This is a quotation from Psalm 118.

References

Blunden, A. (2009). 'Vygotsky's critique of psychological science'. Available online: https://ethicalpolitics.org/ablunden/works/vygotskys-critique.htm

Freire, P. (1972). *Pedagogy of the oppressed*. Harmondsworth: Penguin Books.

Hyman, L. (2009). *Vygotsky on scientific observation*. Berlin: Max-Planck-Institut für Wissenschaftsgeschichte. Available online: www.mpiwg-berlin.mpg.de/sites/defa ult/files/Preprints/P375.pdf

Hyman, L. (2011). 'Vygotsky's crisis: Argument, context, relevance.' *Studies in History and Philosophy of Biological and Biomedical Sciences*, 43(2), pp. 473–482. doi:10.1016/j. shpsc.2011.11.007

Joravsky, D. (1989). *Russian psychology: a critical history*. Oxford: Blackwell.

Kozulin, A. (2008). *Psychology in utopia: towards a social history of Soviet psychology*. Cambridge, MA: MIT Press.

Veresov, N. (1999). *Undiscovered Vygotsky: etudes on the pre-history of cultural-historical psychology*. Frankfurt-am-Main: Peter Lang.

Vygotsky, L.S. (1997). *The collected works of L.S. Vygotsky. Volume 3, Problems of the theory and history of psychology*. Trans. and intro. R. Van der Veer; Rieber, R.W. and Wollock, J. (eds). New York: Plenum Press.

Vygotsky, L.S. (1997a). 'Consciousness as a problem for the psychology of behaviour' [1925], in Vygotsky, L.S., *The collected works of L.S. Vygotsky. Volume 3, Problems of the theory and history of psychology*, pp. 63–79. Trans. and intro. R. Van der Veer; Rieber, R.W. and Wollock, J. (eds). New York: Plenum Press.

Vygotsky, L.S. (1997b). *Educational psychology* [1926]. Trans. R. Silverman. Davydov, V.V. (ed. and intro.). Boca Raton, FL: CRC Press.

Vygotsky, L.S. (1997c). *The historical meaning of the crisis in psychology: a methodological investigation* [1926–1927], in Vygotsky, L.S., *The collected works of L.S. Vygotsky. Volume 3, Problems of the theory and history of psychology*, pp. 233–343. Trans. and intro. R. Van der Veer; Rieber, R.W. and Wollock, J. (eds). New York: Plenum Press.

Vygotsky, L.S. (1997d). 'The methods of reflexological and psychological investigation' [1924], in Vygotsky, L.S., *The collected works of L.S. Vygotsky. Volume 3, Problems of the theory and history of psychology*, pp. 35–49. Trans. and intro. R. Van der Veer; Rieber, R.W. and Wollock, J. (eds). New York: Plenum Press.

Vygotsky, L.S. (1997e). 'Mind, consciousness, the unconscious' [1930], in Vygotsky, L.S., *The collected works of L.S. Vygotsky. Volume 3, Problems of the theory and history of psychology*, pp. 109–122. Trans. and intro. R. Van der Veer; Rieber, R.W. and Wollock, J. (eds). New York: Plenum Press.

Vygotsky, L.S. (2007). 'In memory of L.S. Vygotsky (1896–1934): L.S. Vygotsky: Letters to students and colleagues'. Trans. M.E. Sharpe; Puzyrei, A.A. (ed.). *Journal of Russian and East European Psychology*, 45(2), pp. 11–60.

Zavershneva, E. (2012). 'Investigating L.S. Vygotsky's manuscript "The historical meaning of the crisis in psychology"', *Journal of Russian and East European Psychology*, 50(4), pp. 42–63.

Chapter 5

Tool and symbol

> The only serious comment is that everyone should work in his field according to the instrumental method. I am investing all the rest of my life and all my energy in this ... I firmly shake your hand and ask you to prepare yourself (mentally, of course) for our common endeavor. Always yours, LV
>
> (From letter to Luria, 26 July 1927; Vygotsky, 2007, p. 19)

The instrumental method

The 'instrumental method' (Vygotsky, 1997e) was one of the names that Vygotsky gave to an experimental approach also known as the 'method of double stimulation'. The series of experiments with children, using these methods, by the team of researchers working with Vygotsky and Luria in 1928–1930, is particularly well known to students of Vygotsky because some of them were taken from his and Luria's book *Tool and symbol in child development* (Vygotsky and Luria, 1994), selectively edited, and published in *Mind in society* (Vygotsky, 1978), a book that introduced Vygotsky's work to a wider public. The extracts taken from *Tool and symbol* form ch. 1–3 of *Mind in society*. (Ch. 4 was also stated to be from *Tool and symbol* but was actually taken from *The history of the development of higher mental functions* [Vygotsky, 1997d].)

Tool and symbol, the focus of this chapter, is an important and accessible short text. Joseph Glick, who wrote the Prologue to volume 4 of Vygotsky's *Collected works* (Vygotsky, 1997a) called it 'the epochal *Tool and symbol*' (Glick, 1997, p. vi). It is a relatively compact statement of the psychology that Vygotsky and his colleagues were developing in the late 1920s with the use of the 'instrumental method'. As in others of Vygotsky's major texts (*The history of the development of higher mental functions, Thinking and speech* [Vygotsky, 1987]) the focus is on language, which is, Glick notes: 'only a subordinate topic of *Mind in society*' (Glick, 1997, p. xiii). In this chapter I shall refer throughout to the translation of *Tool and symbol* by Teresa Prout that was published as ch. 7 of *The Vygotsky reader* (Van der Veer and Valsiner, 1994), and page references are to that chapter.

DOI: 10.4324/9780429203046-5

Vygotsky and Luria collaborated over the writing of *Tool and symbol* – the date of composition is thought to be 1930. Despite the title, tool use is actually given little prominence in the overall argument, appearing only in the first section. In this section – represented in *Mind and society* by ch. 1, 'Tool and symbol in child development' – Vygotsky and Luria focus on the differences between the 'practical intelligence' of young children and that of apes, as shown in tool use. The core of their argument concerns the role of language in these operations. Through a kind of research review of studies of child and animal behaviour, Vygotsky and Luria argue against the prevailing tendency in these studies: to view the development of practical intelligence in children and apes as fundamentally the same. On this topic they are sometimes scathing:

> Thus we see that the response of a three-year-old child in principle is equated to an ape's response, while speech which, by the way, is noted by all these authors as present in the process of solution of a practical problem, is treated as a secondary factor and is equated to the arm length of the ape.
>
> (Vygotsky and Luria, 1994, p. 104)

(This passage was omitted from *Mind in society*.)

In this first section of *Tool and symbol*, Vygotsky and Luria develop their argument that it is children's speech, combining with action 'into one structure' (ibid., p. 116), that helps them to solve tasks involving the practical use of tools and moves their behaviour up to another level, so that their problem-solving behaviour becomes qualitatively quite different from that of apes.

> We are witnessing the birth of those specifically human forms of behaviour that, breaking away from animal forms of behaviour, later create intellect and go on to become the base of labour: the specifically human form of the use of tools ...
>
> (Vygotsky and Luria, 1994, p. 109)

For instance, Vygotsky and Luria consider the development of perception as demonstrated through Kohl's 'non-verbal' tests, which require children to combine blocks with differently coloured sides in order to copy increasingly complex coloured models. These tests are known as 'non-verbal' because they are meant to focus on the development of perception, independently of language skills. However, referring to research conducted by Gueshelina with over 200 subjects, Vygotsky and Luria point out that, *though the tests take no account of speech, children do in fact engage in informal speech in approaching these problems, and this speech affects their responses* – they note that children in Gueshelina's sample made increasing use of speech to help them in solving the problems (ibid., p. 126).

Vygotsky and Luria refer to their own 'experimental genetic [i.e. developmental] research' for evidence of the way that children spontaneously make use of speech in problem-solving. In these experiments they set out to *provoke* development by introducing more difficulties and obstacles into children's tasks, and they observed that 'egocentric speech' increased as the problems to be solved became more intractable. Vygotsky and Luria used Piaget's own system for calculating this increase in the 'coefficient of egocentric speech' and found that this coefficient almost doubled during moments of difficulty:

Of Vygotsky's work on egocentric speech, Luria later wrote:

> Vygotsky stripped the appearance of egocentrism from the child's speech. His research was the first empirical attempt to identify the role of the child's early speech in his practical activity.
>
> (Luria, 1987, p. 361)

Just as speech helps to focus and direct perception, so Vygotsky and Luria see it as transforming children's ability to direct their own attention, perhaps the most important influence on their approach to problem-solving. In general they see speech as helping children to free themselves from their immediate perceptions and responses, and – by creating a 'time field' – enabling them to observe changes, learn from past experiences, plan future actions, and direct their own behaviour.

The examples given have in common the idea that children become increasingly able to form intentions and engage voluntarily in purposeful action because of their growing ability to represent their actions to themselves through language. In a valuable footnote (omitted from both the *Collected works* version of this text and from *Mind in society*) Vygotsky and Luria describe how the child moves towards a more purposeful and strategic approach to problem-solving:

> the child proves to be capable of breaking down the operation, trans-forming each of its separate parts into an independent problem which he formulates to himself with the help of speech.
>
> (Vygotsky and Luria, 1994, p. 173)

It is the analytic possibilities in speech that provide children with a way of breaking down problems into manageable chunks.

In the thesis that Vygotsky was developing about language and the develop-ment of mind, children's early monologuing speech provided him with a perfect window onto the formation of inner speech and thought. For a researcher looking for ways of surprising the mind at work, children's 'egocentric' speech – its appearance, its character, its content, its extent, its gradual disappearance/ internalisation – was invaluable evidence of how children learn to think. *Tool and symbol* is part of the long argument that Vygotsky was building throughout his work on the role of language in the development of mental processes, and the formation of consciousness.

The 'grand revision of psychology'

In his autobiography *The making of mind* (1979), Alexander Luria describes how Vygotsky and his colleagues at the Moscow Institute of Psychology embarked on their 'grand revision of psychology'.

> When we first began this work, the three of us – Vygotsky, Leontiev and I – used to meet at Vygotsky's apartment once or twice a week to plan the research that would be required to develop his ideas. We reviewed each of the major concepts in cognitive psychology – perception, memory, attention, speech, problem solving and motor activity. Within each of these areas we had to come up with new experimental arrangements which would incorporate the notion that, as higher processes take shape, the entire structure of behaviour is changed … Each of Vygotsky's students and colleagues undertook the task of inventing experimental models for the development of instrumental behaviour.
>
> (Luria, 1979, pp. 45–46)

The instrumental method consisted in providing children with what were called 'auxiliary stimuli' to help them to carry out difficult tasks. The experiments generally took the form of games. To help them with the problems they had to solve, which might be problems of attention or of memory, children might be provided with 'stimuli' or signs – for example colour cards or picture cards – which would serve as reminders and enable the children to direct their own behaviour. Each researcher was asked to invent model experiments of this kind, based on the instrumental method, which would help in studying the development of certain mental processes.

Most commentators place this work as having taken place from 1928 to 1930, after Vygotsky had moved his research team to Luria's psychology laboratory at the Krupskaya Institute of Communist Education. But the letter to Luria quoted at the head of this chapter, written in mid-1927, shows that both the term 'instrumental method', and the idea that 'everyone should work in his field' in accordance with this method, were already part of the common project that Vygotsky and Luria were planning. Stetsenko and Arievitch (2004) note that the project was 'profoundly collaborative'; all these researchers 'engaged in group discussions, developing many ideas in a truly collective dialogue' (p. 74).

These experiments were carried out, mainly during the years 1928–1930, by a group of colleagues, followers and students of Vygotsky and Luria, the original 'troika' of Vygotsky, Luria and Leontiev having been joined by the 'five' – Lydia Bozhovich, Roza Levina, Liva Slavina, Natalya Morozova and Alexander Zaporozhets. There were other researchers apart from this inner core. In the middle sections of *Tool and symbol* Vygotsky and Luria refer to about ten experiments carried out by them or their colleagues – sometimes, but not always, referring to the researcher by name. Researchers mentioned by name include Luria, Leontiev, Morozova, Sakharov, Yussevich and Zankov.

In *Tool and symbol*, detailed descriptions of the use of the 'instrumental method' do not appear until section 3 ('Sign operations and the organization of the psychological processes') and section 4 ('The analysis of sign operations in the child'). The whole of section 1 (Vygotsky and Luria, 1994, pp. 99–122), after the initial pages on practical intellect with their comparison of tool use in apes and children, is devoted to a discussion of the social behaviour of the child subjects in game-like experiments. The argument here hinges particularly on the role of speech in children's approach to the experiments.

The social nature of the experiments

Vygotsky emphatically asserted in his paper on reflexology that human subjects in psychological experiments sometimes exhibit unignorable behaviours, which *must* be taken into account in experimental observations. This view is repeated in the section of *Tool and symbol* where Vygotsky and Luria begin to look in more detail at what they learned from the experiments on the development of higher psychological processes in children. Over and again the children in these experiments demonstrate awareness of the *social* and *human* context of the experiments. This is one of the special challenges that the child subjects present to the psychological researchers.

Chief among these challenges is the fact that the 'subject' of the experiment is always changing; his/her development does not stand still. Vygotsky and Luria draw attention to a 'most important point ignored by psychologists': the fact that, unlike in experiments with apes,

> over the course of a series of experiments, the examined activity of the child changes, not only perfecting itself as is the case in the process of teaching, but undergoing such great qualitative changes as can only be regarded in their totality as development in the literal sense of the word.
>
> (Vygotsky and Luria, 1994, p. 114)

So the experimenters were faced with the fact that 'over a series of experiments, the object of the research changes'. The consequence of this, according to their way of thinking, was that the focus of the research had to change as well:

> This represented an unpleasant complication for all psychologists who at any cost endeavour to preserve the invariability of the examined activity; but for us it at once became central and we concentrated all our attention on its study.
>
> (Vygotsky and Luria, 1994, p. 114)

The *developments* in children's behaviour thus became the focus of these 'genetic experiments'; indeed the experimenters set out to provoke and stimulate development in children, often by presenting them with tasks beyond their capabilities.

All of this is the greatest interest for an understanding of Vygotsky's method, yet this important passage was completely omitted from *Mind in society*, perhaps because it reveals too frankly the unorthodox nature of Vygotsky's experimental methodology. As the editors of that book observed in their introduction:

> Those steeped in the methodology of experimental psychology as practised in most American laboratories may be inclined to withhold the term 'experiment' from Vygotsky's studies and consider them to be little more than interesting demonstrations or pilot studies. And so, in many respects, they were.
>
> (Vygotsky, 1978, p. 11)

Another major factor in these experiments that Vygotsky and Luria emphasise, again adopting a child's eye view, is that, for the child, the experiment is primarily a *social* situation and the experimental activities have a *social* meaning.

> The child views the situation as a problem posed by the experimentalist, and he senses that, present or not, a human being stands behind that problem.
>
> (Vygotsky and Luria, 1994, p. 116)

So the experiment is a social situation, in which the child enters into a relationship with the experimenter – and *this relationship is the source of development in the child*.

Vygotsky and Luria refute the suggestion that development is either a straightforward process of logical adaptation or the acquisition of complex habits. They see the process of development as a human and social process, and an interactive process. This powerful idea is underlined throughout this section (entitled 'Development in the light of the facts'). Vygotsky and Luria conclude:

> The entire history of the child's psychological development shows us that, from the very earliest days of development, its adaptation to the environment is achieved by social means, through the people surrounding him. The road from object to child and from child to object lies through another person.
>
> (Vygotsky and Luria, 1994, p. 116)

Nothing could be clearer than the message of these observations, which present the experimental situation as inescapably dyadic and children's development as fundamentally social. What Vygotsky and Luria clearly see is that *it isn't possible to do conventional psychology experiments with children who continually construe them as social situations, and in which the experimenter is necessarily a participant.*

Finally in this account of the social nature of development, and of developmental experiments, Vygotsky and Luria turn to the role of social speech in children's problem-solving, and in the relationship with the experimenter.

Reading *Tool and symbol* in its entirety draws attention to Vygotsky and Luria's emphasis on the *emotional* nature of children's speech. They report children as sometimes addressing the object they are trying to manipulate, talking to it and appealing to it.

Even more striking are the reports of children's speech to the experimenter. Vygotsky and Luria have already described the way in which a child sometimes, in the midst of attempts to solve a problem, suddenly: 'cuts short all attempts and turns for help to the experimentalist, asking him to move the object nearer' (Vygotsky and Luria, 1994, p. 117).

But they emphasise that children are also sharing their feelings with the experimenter:

> It would be a mistake to think that [a child's] social speech consists solely of appeals to the experimentalist for help: it always consists of emotional and expressive elements, communications as to what he intends to do and so on.
> (Vygotsky and Luria, 1994, p. 119)

Throughout this account of the social context of their experiments, Vygotsky and Luria stress the *affective* nature of the relationship between the child subject and the experimenter, and the emotional involvement of children in the problems.

The play experiments

In the long central part of *Tool and symbol* which deals with sign operations (sections 2, 3 and 4; Vygotsky and Luria, 1994, pp. 122–156), Vygotsky and Luria review in detail the development of higher forms of perception, memory and attention. Their detailed account of the formation of the 'higher mental processes' of *organised* perception, *voluntary* attention and *logical* memory centres both on the role of speech in the development of these processes, and on how they are united by their basis in the use of signs. Their account is based on findings drawn from all their observations, discussions and experiments in this area, but references to experimental evidence are often brief. However, enough detail is provided in some examples for us to get a picture of these 'formative experiments'.

In general these Vygotskyan experiments are always interested in the workings of mind, in the way in which children represent problems to themselves in language, in the stories they tell themselves, in how they play with a problem or use their imagination to go beyond it. The experimenters observe the intelligent, creative, resourceful mind at work – the children in Vygotskyan experiments are never passive. Similarly, the experiments referred to in *Tool and symbol* are creative in their design, inventive and imaginative, demanding of the subject, open-ended, capable of diverse solutions, and just as focused on process – how the child goes about the activity – as in producing solutions.

Morozova's experiments on choice processes

In order to see Vygotsky and Luria's thinking at work on the issues raised by these experiments we will look first at the 'choice experiments' conducted by Natalia Morozova. Morozova's experimental method was based on Luria's 'combined motor method', in which he had looked at motor reactions as an indication of thinking.

The concrete experimental situation initially required a small child to press one of five keys on a keyboard in response to specific stimuli:

> The task exceeds the natural capabilities of the child and, therefore, causes intensive difficulties and still more intensive efforts aimed at solving the problem ...
>
> (Vygotsky and Luria, 1994, p. 129)

This approach, of presenting children with problems to solve that are strictly beyond their capabilities, was an essential part of these experiments.

Morozova found that children's responses differ from adults' in that the 'entire process of selection by the child is not separate from the motor system but is externally placed and concentrated in the motoric sphere' (ibid.). Just as egocentric speech gave these researchers an essential window onto the development of children's thinking, so in the Morozova experiments children's tentative movements, their 'mass of diffused gropings and trials' provided evidence of the selection and decision processes. The researchers were even able to keep a graphic record of these 'gropings', through the use of a cyclograph, which can show the details of children's motor reactions.

But just as important as the technical recording equipment is the close and sympathetic observation of a child's vacillation between the keys:

> Thus the child solves its problem of selection not in perception, but in movement, hesitating between two stimuli, its fingers hovering above and moving from one key to another, going halfway and then coming back ...
>
> (Vygotsky and Luria, 1994, p. 130)

This delicate description of the child's hovering fingers gives an insight into the fine-grained quality of the researcher's observation and note-taking. Later, as in other experiments, a new element is introduced: each key is marked with a corresponding sign. This is the method of 'double stimulation' – and now, with the help of an additional sign, '*as early as five or six the child fulfils this task with the greatest ease*'. In this way, with the help of cultural signs, Vygotsky, Luria and their associates enable children to gain more control over their own behaviour. The aim is *both* to speed up development by giving children access to supportive signs, *and* to make the developmental process more accessible to observation.

Leontiev's game-experiments on attention and memory

A key feature of these experiments is that they are often explicitly framed as games. For instance, Leontiev was responsible for carrying out a whole series of experiments on attention and memory which, like the Morozova choice experiments, were designed to look at what happens when children are given access to 'auxiliary signs' in order to help them solve particular tasks. A number of these tasks were based on pre-existing children's games. In the game called 'Forbidden colours', for example, a young child had to name the colour of a number of objects without mentioning two 'forbidden colours' *and* without mentioning the same colour twice. This task, requiring highly concentrated attention, proved extremely difficult; only with the aid of 'auxiliary signs' – colour cards to help simplify the task – was the child able to complete it. An important feature of the experiments was that children were free to use the cards to help them in whatever way they chose; they were learning to use signs to organise their own behaviour and the experimenters were interested to see how they went about it.

Leontiev's experiments are referred to in *Tool and symbol,* but only in summary. However, Leontiev's paper 'The development of voluntary attention in the child' was published in English in full in *The Vygotsky reader* (Leontiev, 1994). In this paper he describes three different stages of development in mediated remembering:

1 the preschool stage where children are not able to make use of the coloured cards to help them with the task;
2 the second stage of development, where children's performance on the task improves dramatically through their use of the cards; and
3 the third stage, with adults or adolescents – whose performance with and without the cards hardly differs, because their memorising has ceased to rely on external aids, having become internalised.

These stages, when mapped in a graph and diagrammed, produce what has been termed the 'parallelogram of development', a striking visual summary of the internalisation process – from unmediated, to mediated, to unmediated-but-internalised memorisation (Figure 5.1).

[In this scheme,] 'P = performance, the number of correctly recalled words; solid line, memory recall with secondary stimuli; broken line, memory recall without secondary stimuli'.

(in Kaptelinin and Nardi, 2009, p. 45)

The numbers 1, 2 and 3 on the horizontal axis refer to the three different stages.

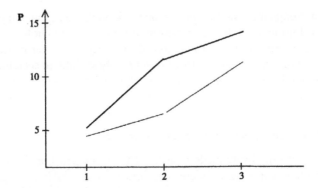

Figure 5.1 Leontiev's parallelogram of development.

Recent research by Meshcheryakov et al. (2008) has replicated this research with modern children and has confirmed the value of the 'parallelogram' model, which could potentially still have applications in Vygotskyan-type studies of the development of children's mental processes.

Internalisation

Leontiev's experiments on attention and memory lead to a section in which Vygotsky and Luria spell out the internalisation process that is part of the development of all higher mental functions. Through internalisation, or interiorisation, an external-instrumented operation becomes an inner-reconstructed operation. This process exactly mirrors the internalisation of speech, external speech passing through the stage of egocentric speech or 'speech-thinking', and becoming inner speech, that Vygotsky and Luria had identified at the beginning of *Tool and symbol*.

Therefore, although the higher functions do develop on the basis of lower, elementary functions, they also originate in the process of social intercourse, with the use of signs as an indispensable part of the development. So this development is not simply a continuation of earlier processes; it is a new development in which the child applies social behaviour to itself. This is 'voluntary behaviour', i.e. the child is learning to voluntarily regulate his/her own behaviour, and it clearly implies the involvement of the child's *will* in development. This emphasis on self-regulation and on the role of the will in the development of all psychological functions will become more marked in Vygotsky's work in pedology.

Vygotsky and Luria do not in this book say a great deal about the role of inner speech in these developments, but it seems clear that speech must also play a key part in self-regulation, both through children's external speech when they comment on their actions and give instructions to themselves in the experiments, and – as the functions become internalised – through unspoken instructions. Vygotsky and Luria stress that they regard speech as a system of auxiliary symbols that enable the child to direct its own behaviour. Thus, external and inner speech both necessarily have an important role in internalisation.

There is a strong emphasis throughout the book on the long and complex nature of these developments. In being transformed from inter-psychological to intra-psychological operations, mental functions do not become inner processes over-night. Some of the experiments in this chapter involved children aged from 7 up to adolescence, and Leontiev's experiments on voluntary attention went on to involve adults. There is a clear implication that full internalisation may take many years.

Sakharov's experiments on concept formation

Even where it is not always made clear from Vygotsky and Luria's summaries, it seems that other experiments were also presented to children as games. For instance the experiments on concept formation, carried out by Sakharov – which are referred to only briefly in *Tool and symbol* but at much more length in ch. 5 of *Thinking and speech* – were actually introduced to children as imaginative games. This is made clear in Sakharov's original paper, also available in *The Vygotsky reader* (Sakharov, 1994), where we can now see how the original experimental procedure (by Ach) was developed by Vygotsky and Sakharov.

Sakharov explained that, in their new version of the experiment, the experimenter would tell the child that the wooden blocks on the table were toys belonging to children from another country. Some toys were called 'bat' in the language of that country; others had different names. (The names were on the underside of the blocks.) If the child could think hard and, without looking, guess which other blocks were called 'bat', grouping them together in a special place on the board, he would receive a prize.

This element of 'pretending' was absent from the original Ach experiment. Under Vygotsky's leadership, the experiments were presented to children in a much more imaginative and playful way. (ibid., p. 94)

The natural history of the sign

Within these experiments, then, the experimenters and the children were involved in game-like activities and in playful relationships. In some of the memory experiments children were encouraged to choose their own 'auxiliary signs' and in some cases to *create* them – drawing their own cards to help their remembering, for instance.

But Vygotsky and Luria stress that the youngest children they worked with were not yet able to use signs unless they bore a concrete pictorial relation to the words to be remembered. Sometimes they rejected *all* the cards they were offered, saying that 'nothing works'. In other cases, as in some experiments by Zankov and Yussevich, children found a way of *changing* the offered signs in order to make them into more direct reflections of the word. For instance in Zankov's tests, which presented children with meaningless shapes as a means of remembering, children either rejected the cards or attempted to make the shapes into pictures of the word by turning them upside down or altering them in some way.

Only considerably later did children become able to use signs in more considered ways. Vygotsky and Luria (1994, p. 151) conclude: 'Sign operations are the result of a complex process of development in the full sense of the word.' Experiments which included older children, such as the Sakharov experiments with children between the ages of six and seventeen, traced the development of concepts with children of different ages through the gradual introduction of new elements in the experiment, so that the 'method of the double stimulation continually varies' (Sakharov, 1994, p. 96).

In this account of 'the natural history of the sign', Vygotsky and Luria put a particular emphasis on the role of play in development. The game-like nature of their play experiments is important: it engages children and involves them in playing and experimenting with signs and meanings. As a consequence:

> our experiments lead us to the conclusion that play constitutes the main avenue of the child's cultural development and in particular of the development of the child's symbolic activity.
>
> (Vygotsky and Luria, 1994, p. 151)

This is a strong statement and introduces a new factor into the accounts of these experiments on the development of higher mental functions. The emphasis on the leading role of play in development is familiar from Vygotsky's lecture 'Play and its role in the mental development of the child' (Vygotsky, 2016; see Chapter 8, this volume). But the emphasis on play as the *main avenue of the child's cultural development* is not nearly so familiar.

Methods for the study of higher psychological functions

Vygotsky was always deeply preoccupied by the problem of methodology. In *The crisis in psychology* he observed that 'methodology is the linchpin through which philosophy guides science' (Vygotsky, 1997c, p. 329). One key aim of Vygotsky's life project can reasonably be said to have been the resolution of the 'crisis' in psychology and the establishment of psychology as a science with an adequate methodology – a task which he said 'would take decades'. Methodology was at the heart of the matter:

> Whether psychology is possible as a science is, above all, a methodological problem. In no other science are there so many difficulties, insoluble controversies and combinations of incompatible things as in psychology. The subject matter of psychology is the most complicated of all things in the world and least accessible to investigation. Its methods must be full of special contrivances and precautions in order to yield what is expected of them.
>
> (Vygotsky, 1997c, p. 328)

The same issues that Vygotsky explores through a lengthy intellectual analysis in *The crisis in psychology* are touched on briefly in the methodology section (section 5) of *Tool and symbol*. This section begins with a critique of the research methods of both idealism and behaviourism. Idealism could rely only on description and self-observation for its psychological investigations, while behaviourism's reflexological methods were unsuitable for the study of complex psychological processes and were 'anti-genetic': unequal to the task of exploring new psychological phenomena in the process of development.

Vygotsky and Luria make clear that they want to look at 'the inner structure of the higher psychological processes' (Vygotsky and Luria, 1994, p. 159) and especially at their development – therefore their methodology is particularly aimed at studying the shift from elementary to higher processes. Their key method is the 'functional method of double stimulation' (ibid.) where sets of symbols or signs are introduced to enable a subject to organise their own behaviour in solving an experimental problem, thus enabling hidden/internal processes to be studied over the whole course of their development. This focus on development leads to Vygotsky and Luria's description of their research approach as 'an integral experimental-genetic method' (ibid., p. 160).

In the methodology section, Vygotsky and Luria also lay the foundation for the bigger argument about language, which they will present in their conclusions: signs and symbols have been shown by their research model to be fundamental to mental development. Psychological development is seen as a reconstruction of human behaviour through sign use. Language, as a particularly important and complex system of signs *and* as a window on children's thinking, is essential to their methodology and their theory.

The role of language in the development of consciousness

After a discussion of the importance of drawing a real distinction between the basic (or lower) and the higher psychological functions, Vygotsky and Luria move, in the final section of *Tool and symbol*, to their conclusions, which have to do with the relative roles of activity and language in the development of mind. This section must surely be seen in the context of the developing differences between Vygotsky and some of his associates, led by Leontiev, about the primacy of activity, on the one hand, and language, on the other, in the development of mental functions:

> In the system of concepts of Vygotsky and Leontiev the notions of activity occupy different positions, and, therefore, play different roles. For Leontiev activity is the central notion that itself predetermines the conceptual framework of the entire theory. Activity for Leontiev is the central notion of the conceptual system and the main explanatory principle. For Vygotsky,

activity – being an important notion – is not the foundational concept like it is for Leontiev and certainly it is not an explanatory principle.

(Veresov, n.d.)

In their conclusions to *Tool and symbol* Vygotsky and Luria acknowledge the role of activity – or, in Marxist terms, of labour – in the creation of the higher psychological functions. But their assessment of the place of labour in human development takes them straight back to their argument in section 1 of the book: human activity is only free and purposeful because human beings (unlike chimpanzees) can control and regulate their own behaviour. And this kind of freedom and self-regulation comes about through language: 'The history of labour and that of speech can scarcely be understood without each other' (Vygotsky and Luria, 1994, p. 164). The argument has already been well established in the course of the book, but here Vygotsky and Luria use it as a stepping stone to a closer examination of 'the relation between word and action, which lies at the beginnings of the formation of the child's will' (ibid., p. 166). Vygotsky's picture of development, particularly expressed through his pedological writings, will increasingly present it as a process of 'progressive freeing' where children, through their own volitional actions, with the aid of speech, develop greater freedom of action.

The last section of *Tool and symbol* is echoed in the last pages of *Thinking and speech*, and indeed there is a close relationship between the conclusions of these two texts. Vygotsky and Luria build their argument carefully. They agree with Leontiev that 'the word does not stand at the beginning of the development of the child's mind' and that 'action precedes the word', but they question the tendency, at the time of their writing, 'to overestimate action at the word's expense' (Vygotsky and Luria, 1994, p. 166).

Their investigations have shown that speech is intimately involved in the development of all higher mental functions and in children's growing mastery of their own behaviour. Now they argue that speech and action do become a unity – 'the source of their changes rests in their functional junction' – and that as they do, 'speech lifts action to its highest stage' (ibid., p. 169). This is a point of cardinal importance to their overall argument: 'as a matter of fact our entire article was devoted to this problem'. They conclude:

> If at the beginning of development there stands the act, independent of the word, then at the end of it there stands the word that becomes the act, the word which makes man's action free.

(Vygotsky and Luria, 1994, p. 170)

It is difficult not to see these final pages as a response to Leontiev's growing distancing of himself from Vygotsky's emphasis on the role of speech and signs in mental development. Leontiev was intent on developing a theory of psychology in which physical activity (labour) was the main means of human development.

This position, being more obviously grounded in Marxist theories of labour activity, was more tuned to the requirements of the times than Vygotsky's semiotic psychology. Van der Veer and Valsiner (1991, p. 290) comment that 'Leontiev aligned himself with the official ideology'.

In *Thinking and speech* Vygotsky will have more to say, in his conclusion, about the role of language in the creation of consciousness. *Tool and symbol* does not specifically enter this territory, although the work that Vygotsky and Luria report on, and the methodology that they describe, go a long way to answering some of the questions that Vygotsky had raised in his paper 'Consciousness as a problem for the psychology of behaviour' (Vygotsky, 1997b). *Tool and symbol*, despite its brevity, is a remarkably thorough summary of Vygotsky's and Luria's work in progress, and its final pages build a strong argument which Vygotsky was to go on developing in his subsequent work and writing.

The story of the text

The history of the text of *Tool and symbol*, as with many of Vygotsky's texts, is unusually complicated. The English manuscript of the article was prepared as a submission for the *Handbook of child psychology*, which was published in 1931 by Clark University Press (Van der Veer and Valsiner, 1991, p. 188). The best-known child psychologists of that time contributed to this handbook; they included Anna Freud, Charlotte Buhler, Susan Isaacs and Jean Piaget. But for whatever reason, the Vygotsky–Luria manuscript was not published, either in English or in Russian, in Vygotsky's lifetime. It did not appear in Russian until 1984 when it was published in volume 6 of Vygotsky's *Collected works* (*Sobranie Sočinenij*). Even this posthumous publication was complicated by problems: Van der Veer and Valsiner tell how the Russian editors of the *Collected works* 'found that the original Russian version had been lost and had the (English) text translated back into Russian' (ibid.).

By the time the version known as *Tool and sign in the development of the child* (Vygotsky and Luria, 1999) was published in volume 6 of the English edition of the *Collected works* (Vygotsky, 1999), the English language original version of *Tool and symbol* had already been published in *The Vygotsky reader*, edited by Van der Veer and Valsiner in 1994. It was taken from a manuscript obtained by Van der Veer and Valsiner from Michael Cole. There were discrepancies between the version published in the Russian *Collected works* and the text published in *The Vygotsky reader*, although the Russian version had been sup-posed to be a translation of that text. For instance, a number of accounts of Vygotsky's and Luria's experiments with children are removed from the places where they appear in *The Vygotsky reader* text and are placed, all together, into a much earlier part of *Tool and sign,* where they are not supported by the developing argument. Some passages are omitted altogether. The version in volume 6 of the English *Collected works* is a translation of the Russian version, with all its discrepancies.

Since then, these two English versions have been the subject of extensive study by Anton Yasnitsky and David Kellogg, who eventually disagreed about which they considered to be the preferable text (Kellogg and Yasnitsky, 2011). I am personally convinced, having compared the two texts closely, that *The Vygotsky reader* translation is a preferable and more readable version; some of the variants in the *Collected works* version are unhelpful to the sense.

1930 was a landmark year in the development of Vygotsky's psychology, and *Tool and symbol* is an essential text for understanding that development. I am in complete agreement with David Kellogg's belief that 'this book played a pivotal role in the evolution of Vygotsky's thinking … and that it remains a central work for us today' (Kellogg, 2011, p. 80).

In 1930 Vygotsky was deeply involved in several writing projects. He was co-writing, again with Luria, *Studies on the history of behaviour* (Vygotsky and Luria, 1993), a book that was in some ways complementary to *Tool and symbol*, but which was to be a source of considerable political difficulties for its authors. He was continuing to write and publish in the overlapping fields of defectology and pedology. He was also putting together a major volume: *The history of the development of higher mental functions* (Vygotsky, 1997d), which was to draw on some of the experimental evidence from *Tool and symbol* and was completed in 1931.

But by this time he was already moving on in his theory formation. He was proposing to his colleagues that the focus of their work ought to be not on higher mental functions, but on psychological *systems*, the way in which different functions interacted. Several colleagues of Vygotsky, led by Leontiev, were unhappy about this, as they were about his continuing emphasis on the central role of language in psychology.

References

Glick, J. (1997). 'Prologue', in Vygotsky, L.S., *The collected works of L.S. Vygotsky. Volume 4, The History of the development of higher mental functions*, pp. v–xvi. Trans. M.J. Hall; Rieber, R.W. (ed.). New York: Plenum Press.

Kaptelinin, V. and Nardi, B.A. (2009). *Acting with technology: activity theory and interaction design*. Cambridge, MA: MIT Press.

Kellogg, D. (2011). 'Which is (more) original and does either version really matter?' *PsyAnima, Dubna Psychological Journal*, 4 (4), pp. 80–81.

Kellogg, D. and Yasnitsky, A. (2011). 'The differences between the Russian and English texts of "Tool and sign in child development"'. *PsyAnima, Dubna Psychological Journal*, 4 (4), pp. 98–158.

Leontiev, A.N. (1994). 'The development of voluntary attention in the child' [1932], in Van der Veer, R. and Valsiner, J. (eds), *The Vygotsky reader*, pp. 288–312. Oxford: Blackwell.

Luria, A.R. (1979). *The making of mind: a personal account of Soviet psychology*. Cole, M. and Cole, S. (eds). Cambridge, MA: Harvard University Press.

Luria, A.R. (1987) 'Afterword to the Russian edition', in Vygotsky, L.S., *The collected works of L.S. Vygotsky. Volume 1, Problems of general psychology*, pp. 359–373. Trans. and intro. N. Minick; Rieber, R.W. and Carton, A.S. (eds). New York: Plenum Press.

Meshcheryakov, B. G., Moiseyenko, E. V. and Kontorina, V. K. (2008). '*Parallelogramm razvitiya pamyati: Ne mit, no trebuyet utochneniya*' ['The parallelogram of memory development: not a myth, but requires improvement']. *Psikhologicheskiy zhurnal Mezhdunarodnogo universiteta prirody obshchestva i cheloveka 'Dubna'*, 1, pp. 19–41.

Sakharov, L. (1994). 'Methods for investigating concepts' [1930]. Trans. M. Vale, in Van der Veer, R. and Valsiner, J. (eds), *The Vygotsky reader*, pp. 73–98. Oxford: Blackwell.

Stetsenko, A. and Arievitch, I.M. (2004). 'Vygotskian collaborative project of social transformation'. *International Journal of Critical Psychology*, 12 (4), pp. 58–80.

Van der Veer, R. and Valsiner, J. (1991). *Understanding Vygotsky: a quest for synthesis*. Oxford: Blackwell.

Van der Veer, R. and Valsiner, J. (eds) (1994). *The Vygotsky reader*. Oxford: Blackwell.

Veresov, N. (n.d.) 'Investigation of play from the perspective of cultural-historical psychology'. Unpublished manuscript.

Vygotsky, L.S. (1978). *Mind in society*. Cole, M., John-Steiner, V., Scribner, S. and Souberman, E. (eds). Cambridge, MA: Harvard University Press.

Vygotsky, L. S. (1987). *Thinking and speech* [1934], in Vygotsky, L.S., *The collected works of L.S. Vygotsky. Volume 1, Problems of general psychology*, pp. 37–285. Trans. and intro. N. Minick; Rieber, R.W. and Carton, A.S. (eds). New York: Plenum Press.

Vygotsky, L.S. (1997a). *The collected works of L.S. Vygotsky. Volume 4, The history of the development of higher mental functions*. Trans. M.J. Hall; Rieber, R.W. (ed.). New York: Plenum Press.

Vygotsky, L.S. (1997b). 'Consciousness as a problem for the psychology of behaviour' [1925], in Vygotsky, L.S., *The collected works of L.S. Vygotsky. Volume 3, Problems of the theory and history of psychology*, pp. 63–79. Trans. and intro. R. Van der Veer; Rieber, R.W. and Wollock, J. (eds). New York: Plenum Press.

Vygotsky, L.S. (1997c). *The historical meaning of the crisis in psychology: a methodological investigation* [1926–1927], in Vygotsky, L.S., *The collected works of L.S. Vygotsky. Volume 3, Problems of the theory and history of psychology*, pp. 233–343. Trans. and intro. R. Van der Veer; Rieber, R.W. and Wollock, J. (eds). New York: Plenum Press.

Vygotsky, L.S. (1997d). *The history of the development of higher mental functions* [1931], in Vygotsky, L.S., *The collected works of L.S. Vygotsky. Volume 4, The history of the development of higher mental functions*, pp. 1–251. Trans. M.J. Hall; Rieber, R.W. (ed.). New York: Plenum Press.

Vygotsky, L.S. (1997e). 'The instrumental method in psychology' [1930], in Vygotsky, L.S., *The collected works of L.S. Vygotsky. Volume 3, Problems of the theory and history of psychology*, pp. 85–89. Trans. and intro. R. Van der Veer; Rieber, R.W. and Wollock, J. (eds). New York: Plenum Press.

Vygotsky, L.S. (1999). *The collected works of L.S. Vygotsky. Volume 6, Scientific legacy*. Trans. M.J. Hall; prologue D. Robbins; Rieber, R.W. (ed.). New York: Plenum Press.

Vygotsky, L.S. (2007). 'In Memory of L.S. Vygotsky (1896–1934): L.S. Vygotsky: Letters to Students and Colleagues'. Trans. M.E. Sharpe; Puzyrei, A.A. (ed.). *Journal of Russian and East European Psychology*, 45(2), pp. 11–60.

Vygotsky, L.S. (2016). 'Play and its role in the mental development of the child' [1933]. Trans. N. Veresov and M. Barrs. *International Research in Early Childhood Education*, 7(2), pp. 3–25.

Vygotsky, L.S. and Luria, A.R. (1993). *Studies on the history of behaviour: ape, primitive, child* [1930]. Hillsdale, NJ: Lawrence Erlbaum Associates.

Vygotsky, L.S. and Luria, A.R. (1994). *Tool and symbol in child development* [1930], in Van der Veer, R. and Valsiner, J. (eds), *The Vygotsky reader*, pp. 99–174. Oxford: Blackwell.

Vygotsky, L.S. and Luria, A.R. (1999). *Tool and sign in the development of the child* [1930], in Vygotsky, L.S., *The collected works of L.S. Vygotsky. Volume 6, Scientific legacy*, pp. 3–68. Trans. M.J. Hall; prologue D. Robbins; Rieber, R.W. (ed.). New York: Plenum Press.

Chapter 6

The development of higher psychological functions

Vygotsky, as a thinker, was deeply involved in developments within psychological theory on a wide number of fronts, in many different languages, and in a number of different analytic traditions. As such, his theoretical frame of reference was broader than the theoretical frame of reference within the English-speaking world, and in a very real sense he represented not only a Marxist approach to theorizing development, but a broadly 'European' approach as well.

(Glick, 1997, p. xiv)

1930

1930 was a dangerous year in Stalinist Russia. In 1928 the first of Stalin's five-year plans was launched, the aim of which was to bootstrap the Soviet economy through rapid industrialisation to a position where it could compete with Western nations, and also increase its war production. The plan was extended in 1929 to the collectivisation of agriculture, with the movement of millions of peasants into collective farms and the destruction of the class of kulaks (the better-off peasants). By 1930, with the defeat and expulsion from the Politburo of Bukharin – a high-ranking popular Bolshevik who opposed Stalin's plans for collectivisation – Stalin had essentially become a dictator. There had also begun the suppression of liberal policies in the arts and education: in 1929 Lunacharsky, who with Krupskaya had been a supporter of Vygotsky's work in education, was effectively dismissed from his post as Commissar of Enlightenment. The changing times were going to affect the context for Vygotsky's work (Fitzpatrick, 1979, p. 133).

In around 1930 (for in the textual history of Vygotsky all dates are provisional), Vygotsky and Luria completed two co-written books on the development of what Vygotsky generally referred to as 'higher psychological functions': *Tool and symbol* (Vygotsky and Luria, 1994) and *Studies on the history of behaviour* (Vygotsky and Luria, 1993). At about the same time Vygotsky also wrote a third book, *The history of the development of higher mental functions* (Vygotsky, 1997a), which is also the title of volume 4 of the *Collected works* (Vygotsky, 1997). The idea of the evolution and

DOI: 10.4324/9780429203046-6

the historical development of mind was central to Vygotsky's psychology and each of these texts approaches it in a different way. It seems likely that some books were being written simultaneously.

We have already, in Chapter 5, explored *Tool and symbol*, which of all these texts is the most compact and accessible. Some of the same arguments, and some of the same experimental evidence, are present in the other two books, which are the subject of this chapter. There is an easy transition from *Tool and symbol* to the first book we shall look at now: *Studies on the history of behaviour: ape, primitive, child*. This was the only one of the three books that was published in Vygotsky's lifetime, in 1930. Its subtitle probably explains some of the problems that it ran into, both at the time and subsequently.

We shall conclude the chapter with a discussion of *The history of the development of higher mental functions*. The biological and historical arguments that were used in *Tool and symbol* are again referred to in this book, which provides additional information about the research methods used in the *Tool and symbol* experiments, and about the psychological theory that underpins all three books. And in that book we also come closer to questions of education and teaching.

Studies on the history of behaviour: ape, primitive, child

This book introduces the 'grand theory' of the development of mind. Vygotsky and Luria are setting out their theory that there are *three* strands in mental development: phylogeny (evolutionary development); socio-historical development; and ontogeny (individual development). The book is divided into three corresponding sections, described as 'essays'. The overall thesis refers back to Darwin and to Marx. It's well known that Marx greatly admired Darwin and sent him a personally inscribed copy of *Capital*. Marx saw Darwin's theory of evolution as a forerunner of his own theory; he wrote to Ferdinand Lassalle:

> Darwin's work is most important and suits my purpose in that it provides a basis in natural science for the historical class struggle.
>
> (Marx, 1861)

Vygotsky would have similarly seen the work of Darwin and Marx as providing 'a basis in natural science' *and* in Marxist theory for his own plan to build a scientific and Marxist psychology. The translator of *Studies on the history of behaviour*, Jane Knox, writes in her introduction:

> Vygotsky and Luria extend Darwin's theory of evolution to a theory of cultural and ontogenetic change, arguing for the existence of developmental historical stages of mental phenomena as the mind develops from ape to primitive man to cultural man. From Darwin comes the idea of development from lower to higher stages, whereby 'primitive people' for

example are at a lower, or in other words earlier stage in the historical evolution of man.

(Knox, 1993, p. 1)

So the shape of the book reflects the 'three lines of development' that Vygotsky and Luria see as determining the mental development of every human being. The first two sections, on biological and historical development, were written by Vygotsky, and the third, on ontogenetic development, by Luria.

Section 1: Behaviour of the anthropoid ape

The first section refers explicitly to Darwin and his theory of evolution, and draws on many studies of animal behaviour, particularly of the higher apes, which were going on at the time Vygotsky and Luria were writing. Some of these studies were examining the similarities/differences between the behaviour and the psychology of anthropoid apes and human children, in relation to tool use and problem-solving. Vygotsky refers to several studies but focuses particularly closely on the work of Köhler, whose book *Intelligenzprüfungen an Menschenaffen* (*The mentality of apes*) was published in German in 1921 and in English in 1925.

Köhler's work with chimpanzees took place on a German primate research facility in the Canary Islands. He studied the chimpanzees' reactions to various kinds of problem-solving tasks, which often involved ways of getting at food which was visible but not accessible. Vygotsky takes a particular interest in certain episodes which indicate that the chimpanzees involved are practising their strategies in play, or are inventing tools as well as using them, or appear sometimes to be deliberating when confronted with obstacles.

Play is, for Vygotsky, a major area of learning for children, so he is interested in the manifestation of 'child' play in animals. He calls it 'the young animal's natural school' (Vygotsky and Luria, 1993, p. 42). Köhler notes that the chimpanzees were keen to re-enact in play the problem-solving techniques they've been using in the experiments. For instance, he describes all the different ways that the chimpanzees use sticks in their play, so that they become a lever, a spoon, a shovel, or a weapon. They also 'dress up' a lot in their play, decorating themselves with 'a cord, a cabbage leaf, a twig or a scrap of wool' (ibid., p. 71). Objects can be turned to all kinds of uses. These examples bring to mind Vygotsky's famous example in 'Play and its role in the mental development of the child' (Vygotsky, 2016) of how, in play, a stick can become a horse.

Vygotsky is also interested in the signs of creative thinking that Köhler sees in some chimpanzees. Faced with the problem of reaching some out-of-reach fruit, the chimpanzees may use a stick to reach it, or make a tower structure with old crates to get nearer it, or pelt it with stones to bring the fruit down. But in one case a chimpanzee called Sultan, faced with the problem of reaching some fruit with a piece of reed which is too short, eventually takes a similar but thicker reed stick and inserts the first stick into the end of it, so that it will reach the fruit. Other apes then imitate his technique for lengthening sticks. This kind of generative behaviour seems to be approaching inventive thinking (Vygotsky and Luria, 1993, p. 49).

Whether chimpanzees can be said to be 'thinking', when they pause and seem to deliberate on being faced with an obstacle which they have not negotiated before, fascinates Vygotsky. It's easy to see why – this behaviour must have reminded him of Pavlov's 'goal-oriented reflex'. Vygotsky had referred to this idea in a conference paper from 1924 on 'Defect and compensation', where he reports Pavlov's idea that 'an obstacle might be an aid to the achievement of a goal' (quoted in Vygotsky, 1993, p. 60).

The main difference between chimpanzee behaviour and human behaviour in relation to tool use seems to be that the chimpanzees' actions in Köhler's experiments always relate to a given actual situation. They are inclined to become aware of solutions only if they are in the same 'visual field'. Köhler concludes that 'the lack of an invaluable technical aid (speech) and a great limitation to those very important components of thought, so-called "images", would thus constitute the causes that prevent the chimpanzee from attaining even the smallest beginnings of cultural development' (Köhler, 1925, p. 277, quoted in Vygotsky and Luria, 1993, p. 73). This conclusion, especially the reference to speech, is exactly the one that Vygotsky and Luria drew in *Tool and symbol*.

Vygotsky recalls that Darwin completely rejected the opinion that only man uses tools. But he disagrees with Darwin over this; chimpanzees use tools only to a very limited extent, and in a rudimentary form, and their tool use is not conjoined with labour, which is what enables man to change the environment. Vygotsky sees a qualitative shift in human tool use. He quotes Marx:

> 'The use and creation of means of labour,' wrote Marx, 'even if in embryos for certain animal species, makes up the special feature characteristic for the human processes of labour.'
>
> (Vygotsky and Luria, 1993, p. 77)

Section 2: Primitive man and his behaviour

This section concerns the second line of development, which is historical, and draws on the work of anthropologists of the late nineteenth and early twentieth centuries, and what they were discovering about the mind and behaviour of 'primitive peoples'. Vygotsky argues that whereas the *biological* development of the species had been extensively studied and that the work of Darwin and others had demonstrated the links between the anthropoid apes and early man, the *historical* development of human behaviour had been less amenable to study in its earlier (prehistoric) stages, because there was very little surviving material for scientists to study. Therefore it was legitimate to consider as evidence the cultural practices of so-called 'primitive people', and the findings of anthropologists working with remote under-developed peoples. Like Marx and Engels, Vygotsky thought that the lack of access to tools and technology was one of the main determining features of under-development.

Vygotsky focuses particularly on the work of the anthropologist Lévy-Bruhl and his writing about the thinking of 'primitives'. Lévy-Bruhl's book *Les fonctions mentales dans les sociétés inférieures* was published in English in 1926 as *How natives think*. As in *Tool and symbol*, Vygotsky concentrates particularly on the usage of sign among these peoples, and the lack of systems of abstract signs or symbolic systems, such as numerals. He is particularly interested in the concrete and detailed nature of primitive languages, and their concomitant lack of abstract concepts.

The term 'primitive'

From the beginning Vygotsky makes it quite clear that 'primitive' is a problematic term:

> these people cannot by full right be called primitive, because they all seem to possess a greater or lesser degree of civilisation. They all come from the prehistoric period of man's existence. Many of them possess very ancient traditions ... *In the strict sense of the word, primitive man now exists nowhere*, and the human type as he is represented among primaeval peoples may be called primitive only relatively speaking.
>
> (Vygotsky and Luria, 1993, p. 82)

Despite these considerations, he continues to use the word, as we shall have to do in discussing this section, but it is valuable to see the provisos he brings to its use. However, the problem that Vygotsky and Luria have in the book is larger than this. In their use of anthropological evidence they may be seen as aligning themselves with a view of less developed cultures as intrinsically inferior, and certainly the subtitle of their book implies that it may regard 'primitive' peoples as lower on the evolutionary ladder.

Nevertheless Vygotsky 'avoided ... the mistake of explaining cultural and mental differences by referring to biological or even racial differences ... In this respect his cultural-historical theory constituted a definite step forward in our understanding of people from different cultural backgrounds' (Van der Veer and Valsiner, 1991, p. 214). Vygotsky argues that the study of data about the comparative psychology of people at an early stage of cultural development provides a legitimate basis for the understanding of the psychology of prehistoric primitive humans, because of the close cultural and technological parallels. The aspects of behaviour that Vygotsky is most interested in exploring in anthropological evidence are those that relate to the psychological processes that are the subject of his experimental work with children. He looks particularly at memory, language and thinking, and numeric operations. In all cases he focuses on the use of signs and language.

Memory

The memory of primitive peoples was found by many anthropologists to be outstanding; messengers for instance could carry messages of considerable length over great distances and deliver them almost word for word. Their topographic memory was often incredibly detailed, enabling them to find their way unerringly through large wild forests. Lévy-Bruhl suggests that some of this direction-finding is down to observation and deduction just as much as to memory, and Vygotsky speculates that primitive peoples may have unusually well-developed eidetic (visual) memories.

Many primitive people did use artificial signs to aid memory and Vygotsky is particularly interested in this evidence of moves towards using 'instruments' to mediate remembering. He finds many (illustrated) examples of systems of 'writing' where meanings are communicated with the help of systems of knotted cords (used in both ancient and modern Peru and in ancient China), notched feathers, and other memory aids. This is the beginning of the art of mnemotechnics. Other aids to memory were examples of 'picture-writing' – for instance a remarkable love letter, written by a girl of the Objibwa tribe to her lover, on bark, with a map showing the district between two lakes where they live, and the girl's tent with her hand stretching out to make an Indian welcoming sign (Vygotsky and Luria, 1993, p. 106).

But these systems were also the beginning of writing – and once actual written language systems developed, an outstanding memory became less and less important.

It is worth noting here that Vygotsky himself was known to have an extraordinary memory – remembering whole pages of books as if they had been photographed. He would often lecture without notes and was completely fluent; his lectures, transcribed, frequently became publications. But he had also trained his memory and was very interested in mnemotechnics. On occasion he demonstrated to his students his mnemonic system, which enabled him to remember long lists of, for instance, 400 words without effort (Vygodskaya and Lifanova, 1999, pp. 15–16, paraphrasing El'konin, Vygotsky's pupil).

Thinking and language

'The first thing that strikes us is about the language of a primitive man is precisely the immense wealth of nomenclature that he has at his disposal' (Vygotsky and Luria, 1993, p. 108). Vygotsky gives many examples of these huge vocabularies from Lévy-Bruhl: for instance, Maoris had an immensely detailed word bank for flora in New Zealand – trees had individual names; leaves had different names at different points of their growth; there were separate words for the tails of birds, animals and fish; there were three words for a parrot's cry depending on whether it was calm, frightened or angry. Some peoples had different names for different types of rain, or ice, or snow, or forms of clouds, or for deer at different ages.

But in several languages with huge numbers of nouns there were few adjectives; instead things were described through the use of similes. In some languages there were very complicated verb constructions – Lévy-Bruhl mentions a language with more than seventy forms of the present indicative, while another anthropologist described the Aleutian language as being able to change a verb in more than 400 ways according to its tense, mood or person. In addition many primitive languages employed systems of gesture to supplement language.

However there are often no generic terms in such languages; instead they 'load thought down with endless details and particulars' (Vygotsky and Luria, 1993, p. 112). A lack of generic terms indicates a lack of true concepts in the thinking of the speakers of the language. At most, objects are sometimes grouped in complexes, a form of loose association. While seeing the fascination of the specificity and expressiveness of these languages with their immense word hoards, Vygotsky is interested to find that many of these peoples are using complexes as a grouping principle, which his experimenters – especially Sakharov – had shown to be an earlier form of conceptual development in older children and adolescents.

Numeric operations

This is a shorter subsection but it has a similar shape to the others. Vygotsky looks at calculation in primitive peoples and finds on the one hand extra-ordinary strengths in their numeric skills, but also some restrictions, which make certain kinds of operation impossible – the kinds of operation which require the mastery of sign systems.

The 'natural arithmetic', which Vygotsky finds evidence of in different anthropological accounts, is highly efficient for its purposes. It largely depends on concrete perception; there is often no counting system beyond low num-bers. In many cases, men can detect whether a single animal is absent in a herd of several hundred. Instead of asking, 'How many horses have you brought home?' a member of a tribe might ask, 'How much space will the herd of horses you brought home take up?' (Vygotsky and Luria, 1993, p. 123). Some primitive peoples make use of memory aids for counting, sometimes touching their own body parts in a particular order as a means of counting, but still without using number names. If they are faced with a task that is beyond the natural memory, they may use numeric aids.

Possible aids are tallies, notched sticks, or – as with memory aids – knots of varying complexity. So numeric operations don't all depend on percep-tion, but also on the help of concrete mnemotechnics. The more abstract numeric operations that rely on more developed systems of signs, e.g. for multiplying and dividing, are not part of their repertoire, and nor are sophisticated symbols, such as algebra. This may reflect the level of abstraction in their thinking.

Section 3: The child and its behaviour

The third section of the book was written by Luria and concerns the third line of development: ontogenetic or individual. It is a very long section, as long as the first two put together. It provides a very detailed picture of child development; it begins with babyhood and the development of early speech, and describes the changes that take place through early childhood. Many examples, especially those of 'egocentric speech', are taken from Piaget. Luria's tone is discursive and relaxed throughout and there are some vivid pictures of young children's 'primitive thinking' and fantasies; such as when a child asked his mother to give him a pine forest, or to cook spinach in such a way that it would become potatoes (Vygotsky and Luria, 1993, p. 155). Luria reproduces one or two children's drawings in order to examine what they show about child thinking.

In the part of the section which deals with children of school age, Luria revisits the experiments that he and Vygotsky had carried out with their colleagues at the Communist Institute of Education and that are detailed in *Tool and symbol*. These all focused on the differences observed in children's problem-solving when they were supported by the use of external signs, and by their own 'speech-thinking'. He describes 'the instrumental method' of providing children with external signs to use in experiments on memory and attention, and emphasises the role that speech played in children's ways of going about the experimental task. Like *Tool and symbol*, this whole book is an argument for the crucial role of language and 'psychological tools' in the development of mind.

Finally in this section, Luria looks at the way in which both retarded children and gifted children approach the same kinds of experimental tasks and finds that the differences lie not in natural memory, which turns out to be the same for both groups, but in 'cultural memory' – what the children are able to do with the help of auxiliary symbols or pictures.

Luria's expeditions to Central Asia

Studies on the history of behaviour was a comprehensive argument for a developed thesis, one which may now be seen to be ethnocentric and have serious flaws, but which was in line with the scientific thinking of its time. But the experimental work that followed, in the years after its publication, was to meet violent criticism. This experimental work was carried out in 1931 and 1932, in Uzbekistan, and it was Luria who led the expeditions, raising funds and undertaking the huge amount of organisation involved. Vygotsky was too ill with tuberculosis to take part.

The expeditions were carried out in the remote mountainous regions of Uzbekistan, in order to investigate the differences between the thinking of traditional peasants in small out-of-the-way communities in the area of Shakhimardan, and that of workers in a large collectivised farm in Fergana, a region 60 kilometres away, where there were schools and a teacher-training college. Luria expected to find some similarities between the thinking of the unschooled peasants and the 'primitive' peoples that he and Vygotsky had learnt about from their anthropological studies. He expected there to be a marked difference between the ability of these groups of people to use abstraction in thinking. Luria and Vygotsky thought of this as a 'natural experiment' – the rapid change in some parts of Soviet Russia as a result of industrialisation and the collectivisation of farms created conditions where it was possible to find peoples at different stages of development within the same region.

The research broadly supported Luria and Vygotsky's hypotheses, but their opponents used it as evidence for their political criticism of Luria and Vygotsky's work in psychology. When he returned from Uzbekistan Luria was met by the KGB and subsequently lost his job: 'I was accused of all mortal sins right down to racism, and I was forced to leave the Institute of Psychology' (L. Luria, 1991, p. 98, quoted in Knox, 1993, p. 15). In the early 1930s Vygotsky, Luria and their colleagues were all subject to political investigation and their work was criticised for being too European, too 'idealist' (as opposed to materialist), and insufficiently Marxist. The range of European sources quoted in *Studies on the history of behaviour* had made it suspect. Luria's assumption that the Uzbek peasants were the equivalent of 'primitive' peoples was seen as insulting to Soviet workers and as evidence of 'bourgeois nationalism'. In modern times *Studies on the history of behaviour* has also been suspect, particularly in relation to its subtitle which arouses immediate concerns. It is not included in Vygotsky's *Collected works*. Luria did not publish the results of his investigations until more than forty years after they were undertaken (Luria, 1976).

Ironically Luria and Vygotsky intended their work to demonstrate the positive change that was being brought about by socialism in their country through the radical restructuring of the system of production and the rapid elimination of illiteracy. Luria wrote, 'collectivisation was under way, illiteracy was being liquidated, all before our very eyes ... We could see to what degree culture was influencing the formation of the psychological processes' (L. Luria, 1991, quoted in Knox, 1993, p. 14).

Luria, in the preface to his book *Cognitive development*, justifies the research work in Uzbekistan in these terms:

> Our data indicate the decisive changes that can occur in going from graphic and functional – concrete and practical – methods of thinking to much more theoretical and abstract modes brought about by fundamental changes in social conditions, in this instance by the socialist transformation of an entire culture. Thus the experimental observations shed light on one aspect of human cognitive activity that has received little scientific study but that corroborates the dialectics of social development.
>
> (Luria, 1976, p. vi)

The history of the development of higher mental functions

The other book to be explored in this chapter is *The history of the development of higher mental functions* (Vygotsky, 1997a). At the time of its writing Vygotsky was becoming dissatisfied with the model of mind that was emerging from his experimental work. He wanted to explore the dialectical way in which mental functions interrelated, and the psychological systems that they were part of. It's already clear that Vygotsky's picture of child development doesn't regard it as a process of the 'gradual and slow accumulation of separate changes' or as a purely quantitative phenomenon, reflecting step changes in behaviour. Instead he describes it as:

> a complex dialectical process that is characterised by complex periodicity, disproportion in the development of separate functions, metamorphoses or qualitative transformation of certain forms into others, a complex merging of the process of evolution and involution, a complex crossing of external and internal factors, a complex process of overcoming difficulties and adapting.
>
> (Vygotsky, 1997a, p. 99)

In mapping the process of development in the chapter on the 'Genesis of higher mental functions', Vygotsky suggests – drawing on Werner – that the behaviour of a contemporary cultured adult person can be understood only 'geologically', 'since in behaviour different genetic strata have also been preserved that reflect all the stages through which man passed in his mental development' (ibid., p. 102). But he adds to this picture the fact that in the course of development children assimilate *social* forms of behaviour, which include language.

Initially, Vygotsky says, speech is a means of socialising and only later, in the form of internal speech, does it become a means of thinking.

> In general we could say that the relations between higher mental functions were at one time real relations between people. I relate to myself in the same way that people relate to me. As verbal thinking represents an internalisation of speech, as reflection is an internalisation of argument, precisely so the mental function of the word, according to Janet [the French psychologist] cannot be explained in any other way unless we bring into the explanation a system broader than man himself.
>
> (Vygotsky, 1997a, p. 103)

Vygotsky's psychology is both social and cultural.

The history of the development of higher mental functions sets out to describe those processes, to map the development of higher mental functions and to present this development as a process of mastering one's own behaviour. It gives a central place to human relationships in learning:

> Every higher mental function was external because it was social before it became an internal, strictly mental function; it was formerly a social relation of two people.
>
> (Vygotsky, 1997a, p. 105)

This book was written in about 1931 and was not published during Vygotsky's lifetime. A partial version (the first five chapters) was published in 1960 in Russian, but the full text was not published until 1983 in Russian and 1997 in English. Its first sentence is challenging:

> The history of the development of the higher mental functions is a field in psychology that has never been explored.
>
> (Vygotsky, 1997a, p. 1)

The subject matter of the book overlaps with that of *Tool and symbol* and *Studies on the history of behaviour*, but here the treatment is more comprehensive. The book seems to be directed at a different audience, an audience with considerable knowledge of psychology. Vygotsky is justifying his main thesis to a profession and is doing so in detail. He often uses the language of reflexology, which is absent from the other texts of this period. He adduces evidence from a whole range of fellow psychologists and experimenters. But he is critical of much psychology in this field, where psychologists take a naturalistic approach and forget that 'man acts upon nature' and changes it (ibid., p. 38). His main criticism is that 'the higher mental processes remain forever closed to experimental psychology' (ibid., p. 32).

In the first five chapters Vygotsky introduces the new theory of development of higher psychological functions, discusses the research methods his team employed, and considers the analysis, structure and genesis of higher mental functions. But after the first five chapters there is a shift and a major change in approach. Vygotsky introduces the revolutionary change in this way:

> The concept of the development of higher mental functions and the subject of our research encompass two groups of phenomena that seem, at first glance, to be completely unrelated, but in fact represent two basic branches, two streams of the development of higher forms of behaviour inseparably connected, but never merging into one. These are, first, processes of mastering external materials of cultural development and thinking: language, writing, arithmetic, drawing; second, the processes of development of special higher mental functions not delimited and not determined with any degree of precision and in traditional psychology termed voluntary attention, logical memory, formation of concepts, etc. Both of these taken together also form

that which we conditionally call the process of development of higher forms of the child's behaviour.

(Vygotsky, 1997a, p. 14)

So, in this book, Vygotsky is presenting psychological development as an intrinsic result of the acquisition of the 'higher mental functions' which are embedded in cultural means of thinking, especially language. And in this picture of development the other higher mental functions are placed after these cultural means of thinking.

Genetic, comparative and instrumental methods

Vygotsky suggests that most child psychology is concentrated round the first years in a child's life when biological development is rapid and observable and individual development is dependent on life experience. But no serious thought is given to 'cultural development', which is the 'third line of development' that merges with biological development. He acknowledges the exceptional difficulty of studying this very complex process, but lays out how it may be done:

> Research uses two basic methods ... first, genetic examination, and second, a comparative method of study.
>
> (Vygotsky, 1997a, p. 22)

Genetic (or developmental) examination was the method used in the 'genetic experiments' using the 'instrumental method', with which we are familiar from *Tool and symbol*, and some of those findings are detailed in this book. But Vygotsky is careful to note that these developmental advances are dependent on levels of biological maturity (there is a link with 'a new stage in brain development'; ibid., p. 17) and that development is not a 'single unbroken' (ibid., p. 23) smooth and continuous process, but one that is marked by discontinuities and metamorphoses.

Comparative methods of study are available to Vygotsky through his work in defectology, where he has frequently met 'deviations from the normal type' which have made it possible to study the process of development in more detail, because they provide:

> a kind of specially managed natural experiment that discloses and exposes, frequently with tremendous force, the true nature and structure of the process which interests us.
>
> (Vygotsky, 1997a, p. 23)

Vygotsky's experience in defectology was never a sideline. Throughout his work as a psychologist it provided him with a fund of experience in the observation and analysis of how children can, with support, develop higher mental functions despite great difficulties.

These two methods will both contribute to an understanding of how the biological and cultural lines of development come together in childhood, thus enabling the study of 'the central and greatest problem of all psychology, the problem of personality and its development' (ibid., p. 26). The problem of the personality will be the subject of much of Vygotsky's work in pedology. In his late work he will expand his model of mental development to include other aspects of the personality: *perezhivanie* (or lived-through experience); the emotions; imagination and creativity; sense and meaning; and language and consciousness.

In ch. 2, on 'Research method' (Vygotsky, 1997a, pp. 27–63), Vygotsky also presents the *instrumental method* as a 'tool and a result' of the research; it is both the method/tool invented to research the development of higher mental functions, and one of its most important results in terms of methodology. The experiments on the development of choice, memory and perception through the use of signs are described, and Vygotsky underlines what they have in common. Their *essence* consists of enabling a transition from one form of behaviour, the lower, via auxiliary stimuli/ signs, to higher forms of behaviour, which are more complex and developed and are characterised by the use of cultural tools or languages. The uniqueness of the process is that the children involved in the experiments learn, through their acquired skills in using signs, to control their own behaviour.

Finally Vygotsky makes very clear the relationship between tool and sign in this model (see Figure 6.1). Both are a means of mediation. Tools mediate work, enabling us to act on things in the world. They are *outwardly* directed. Signs mediate psychological operations, allowing us to direct our own mental activity, our thinking. They are *inwardly* directed. These two forms of mediating activity are connected through their effects, because 'when man changes nature he changes the nature of man himself' (ibid., p. 63).

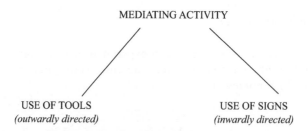

Figure 6.1 The relationship between tool and sign
Source: Vygotsky (1997a, fig.1, p. 62)

In the evolving model Vygotsky is describing, social interaction/communication through speech is basic to mental development. He explains why this is a fundamental point:

> Tracing the cultural development of mental functions, we trace the path of development of the personality of the child. The trend towards developing human psychology which drives all our research appears here. Psychology is humanised.
>
> (Vygotsky, 1997a, p. 58)

Following the general argument, chs. 6–15 focus on the 'cultural languages' that children learn and which are in themselves 'higher mental functions'; in that the acquisition of them changes thinking. The other chapters, on attention, memory and mnemonic techniques, and speech and thinking, all in one way or another relate to the process of mastering and planning one's own behaviour and thinking; the chapter on self-control sums up what Vygotsky thought was the main issue in the development of higher mental processes: the exercise of will.

The prehistory of the development of written language

The most interesting chapter in this section of the book, ch. 7, is already partly known to readers of *Mind in society* (Vygotsky, 1978) although it was truncated in that book. It is one of the most insightful and resonant texts in the whole literature of early literacy. It speaks to modern times just as powerfully as it spoke when it was written. It is an argument for children's learning of writing in school to be based on their experience of scribbling and drawing, of play and drama, of speech and reading. It also emphasises that it should be learned naturally and based on the 'naturally developing needs of the child'. 'Reading and writing must be needed by the child' (Vygotsky, 1997a, p. 145).

Yet Vygotsky is aware that most educational approaches to the teaching of writing fall short of these requirements.

> Pupils are not taught written language but writing of words and for this reason, to a significant degree, the teaching of written language has not yet been raised above the level of traditionally correct and neat writing.
>
> (Vygotsky, 1997a, p. 131)

The teaching of writing is 'presented to [the pupil] from outside, from the hands of the teacher, and it resembles the development of any technical habit' (ibid.). Vygotsky argues that learning to write is not a trainable skill but a long process of development, which is, like all development, not a smooth and continuous process but one that is marked by breaks and discontinuities. It is a revolutionary, not an evolutionary process.

Vygotsky tracks the development of writing from its beginnings in gesture, to the fixture of gesture in scribbles or pictures. These pictures are often amplified by gesture; for instance, he describes a child of four symbolising 'the sting of a mosquito by a stinging motion of the hand and by the point of the pencil' (ibid., p. 134). This is a form of enactment, and children's symbolic play also prefigures writing; play is basic to the development of all symbolising activity. In dramatic play children assign arbitrary meanings to objects, agreeing among themselves that 'This will be a house, that will be a plate', and discussing and explaining the games to themselves. Later, naming moves to the front of the process of all representation and children begin to name their constructions or drawings before they embark on them.

Vygotsky sees drawing above all as the preliminary stage of written language. A drawing is 'a unique graphic speech, a graphic story' (ibid., p. 138), and drawing is often accompanied by speech. But later there must come the realisation that writing is a way of *drawing speech*, not objects. This then is 'second order symbolism', a drawing of the word for the thing, rather than the thing itself. Of course, the experience of learning to read and reading accompanies and supports learning to write; reading is the other side of writing.

Vygotsky is interested in Montessori's teaching of reading and writing to four-year-old children in her kindergartens, but finds that what the children are writing is weak in content, and that too much attention is paid to the physical act of writing. For Montessori 'writing is a purely muscular activity and for this reason her children write letters that have no content' (ibid., p. 146). Vygotsky's belief is that content is all-important and so is the child's desire to write. 'The child must need reading and writing in his play' (ibid., p. 147).

He ends the chapter with a section on the teaching of writing with retarded, blind and deaf children. He acknowledges that for all these children learning to read and write is a more demanding and creative process than for normal children. However he suggests, quoting Delacroix, that as with normally developing children 'attention gradually transfers from the signs themselves to what they signify, and the processes of understanding are developed and established in exactly the same way' (ibid., p. 148). And deaf-mute children, 'if we teach [them] written language and not just calligraphy' (ibid.), may reach through books a level of development that they will not reach through social interaction.

Vygotsky brings to this short text not only a detailed first-hand experience of observing young children and their development, but also a concern for a meaningful pedagogy, which takes into account the fact that writing is both a way of talking and a way of thinking, and ensures that these powerful purposes are there from the beginning.

Cultivation of higher forms of behaviour

Three chapters in the latter half of this book deal with the 'higher mental functions' that we have grown familiar with from the experiments using the 'instrumental method'. These are the chapters on 'Mastering attention', 'The development of mnemonic and mnemotechnical functions' and 'The development of speech and thinking', the last of which includes a discussion of the development of concepts. All of these studies of development involve experiments based on the use of signs and language. Through internalisation, such 'psychological tools' enable us to master our own thinking and behaviour – basic to the discussion of mental development is the idea of self-control and self-mastery.

The chapter on 'Self-control' spells out the implications of these findings: in developing and internalising new intellectual functions, children are also developing the will, an essential factor in self-control. 'Will develops and is part of the cultural development of the child' (Vygotsky, 1997a, p. 218). In the rest of the chapter Vygotsky brings in philosophical arguments, drawing particularly on Spinoza but also on Marx and Engels. Jan Derry observes:

> Vygotsky follows Spinoza in taking the basis of freedom to be the human ability to separate ourselves from our passions, from the contingencies of nature, and to make for ourselves a space within which we can determine our passions.
>
> (Derry, 2013, p. 91)

For Spinoza, freedom arose from self-determination. Derry says he 'provided an argument to the effect that free will arises from the development of intellect. This is an insight from which Vygotsky benefits' (ibid., p. 89).

At the end of the chapter Vygotsky celebrates his belief that psychology has arrived at the resolution of a fundamental philosophical question:

> The philosophical perspective opens before us at this point of our study. For the first time in the process of psychological studies we can resolve essentially purely philosophical problems by means of a psychological experiment and demonstrate empirically the origin of the freedom of human will ... we cannot help but note that we have come to the same understanding of free-dom and self-control that Spinoza developed in his *Ethics*.
>
> (Vygotsky, 1997a, p. 219)

Jan Derry suggests that 'in the dominant, predominantly psychological research literature, the nature of the philosophical underpinnings of Vygotsky's work tends to receive little attention' (Derry, 2013, p. 1).

In this chapter of *The history of the development of higher mental functions*, Vygotsky's closing words make the philosophical foundations of his theory unignorable.

References

Derry, J. (2013). *Vygotsky: philosophy and education*. Chichester: Wiley-Blackwell.

Fitzpatrick, S. (1979). *Education and social mobility in the Soviet Union 1921–1934*. Cambridge: Cambridge University Press.

Glick, J. (1997). 'Prologue', in Vygotsky, L.S., *The collected works of L.S. Vygotsky. Volume 4, The history of the development of higher mental functions*, pp. v–xvi. Rieber, R. W. (ed.). New York: Plenum Press.

Knox, J.E. (1993). 'Translator's introduction', in Vygotsky, L.S. and Luria, A.R., *Studies on the history of behaviour: ape, primitive, child*, pp. 1–35. Hillsdale, NJ: Lawrence Erlbaum Associates.

Köhler, W. (1921). *Intelligenzprüfungen an Menschenaffen* [The mentality of apes]. Berlin: Springer.

Köhler, W. (1925). *The mentality of apes*. Trans. E. Winter. New York: Harcourt Brace and Co.

Lévy-Bruhl, L. (1926). *How natives think*. London: George Allen and Unwin.

Luria, A.R. (1976). *Cognitive development*. Cole, M. (ed.). Cambridge, MA: Harvard University Press.

Luria, L. (1991). 'Memories of her father's work and life'. Unpublished manuscript.

Marx, K. (1861) 'Letter to Ferdinand Lassalle', in *Marx–Engels collected works*, volume 41, p. 245. Available online in the Marxist Archive: https://marxists.catbull.com/archive/marx/works/1861/letters/61_01_16.htm.

Van der Veer, R. and Valsiner, J. (1991). *Understanding Vygotsky: a quest for synthesis*. Oxford: Blackwell.

Van der Veer, R. and Valsiner, J. (eds) (1994). *The Vygotsky reader*. Oxford: Blackwell.

Vygodskaya, G.L. and Lifanova, T.M. (1999). 'Through the eyes of others'. *Journal of Russian and East European Psychology*, 37(4), pp. 3–40. doi:10.2753/RPO1061-040537043.

Vygotsky, L.S. (1978). *Mind in society*. Cole, M., John-Steiner, V., Scribner, S. and Souberman, E. (eds). Cambridge, MA: Harvard University Press.

Vygotsky, L.S. (1993). 'Defect and compensation' [1924], in Vygotsky, L.S., *The collected works of L.S. Vygotsky. Volume 2, The fundamentals of defectology*, pp. 52–64. Trans. and intro. J.E. Knox and C.B. Stevens; Rieber, R.W. and Carton, A.S. (eds). New York: Plenum Press.

Vygotsky, L.S. (1997). *The collected works of L.S. Vygotsky. Volume 4, The history of the development of higher mental functions*. Rieber, R.W. (ed.). New York: Plenum Press.

Vygotsky, L.S. (1997a). *The history of the development of higher mental functions* [1931], in Vygotsky, L.S., *The collected works of L.S. Vygotsky. Volume 4, The history of the development of higher mental functions*, pp. 1–251. Rieber, R.W. (ed.). New York: Plenum Press.

Vygotsky, L.S. (2016). 'Play and its role in the mental development of the child' [1933]. Trans. N. Veresov and M. Barrs. *International Research in Early Childhood Education*, 7(2), pp. 3–25.

Vygotsky, L.S. and Luria, A.R. (1993). *Studies on the history of behaviour: ape, primitive, child* [1930]. Hillsdale, NJ: Lawrence Erlbaum Associates.

Vygotsky, L.S. and Luria, A.R. (1994). *Tool and symbol in child development* [1930], in Van der Veer, R. and Valsiner, J. (eds), *The Vygotsky reader*, pp. 99–174. Oxford: Blackwell.

Chapter 7

Vygotsky and pedology

[T]he central and greater problem of all psychology, the problem of the personality and its development, still remains closed. Child psychology, according to its best representatives, comes to the conclusion that describing the inner life of man as a whole belongs to the art of the poet or the historian … Only a decisive departure beyond the methodological limits of traditional child psychology can bring us to a study of the development of that same higher mental synthesis that, on a solid basis, must be called the personality of the child. The history of cultural development of the child brings us to the history of development of personality.

(Vygotsky, 1997b, p. 26)

'On psychological systems'

In October 1930, as well as summing up the work he and his collaborators had done in a series of publications on the development of higher psychological functions, Vygotsky was thinking about a new direction for their work. He presented this to them in a talk given at the Moscow State University Clinic of Nervous Diseases on 9 October 1930. The text of the talk was not published until it appeared in volume 1 of the Russian *Collected works* in 1982. The talk, 'On psychological systems' (Vygotsky, 1997a) is published in volume 3 of the English *Collected works* (Vygotsky, 1997) and is also available online in the Marxist Archive.

In fact, Vygotsky had for some time been thinking beyond the experimental work on the development of higher psychological functions. He had, in *The history of the development of higher mental functions* (Vygotsky, 1997b), which we discussed in the previous chapter, set these mental functions in a wider context, seeing them as part of the developing *personality*. Increasingly in that book Vygotsky explored how the higher mental functions are interrelated through the 'dynamics of development and growth' (ibid., p. 224). As the will develops, for instance, it becomes an essential part of children's ability to control and direct their own mental functions, their minds, themselves and their environment. Vygotsky's psychology was moving towards a more holistic view of mental development.

DOI: 10.4324/9780429203046-7

In 'On psychological systems' Vygotsky directly addresses these issues and proposes them as the subject of future organised enquiry. He wants to look more closely at 'the complex connections that develop between different functions in the process of development and that dissolve or undergo patholo- gical change in the process of development' (Vygotsky, 1997a, p. 92). He calls the interfunctional systems that he wants to study 'psychological systems'. In a disarmingly frank admission he says he has no real 'theoretical conception' to offer, only a 'certain ladder of facts' (ibid.) to present.

One of the first steps on the ladder is as follows: psychological functions can never operate in isolation. Vygotsky points out that it is nonsense to think that in an experiment on the memorisation of words by means of pictures, a child relies only on memory; he also relies 'on imagination and the ability to detect similarities and differences'. Vygotsky observes that 'not only memory changes when it marries, so to speak, thinking, but thinking itself changes its functions' (ibid., p. 95). So what is termed logical memory is 'a complex alloy of thinking and memory'. 'All structural connections, all relationships become changed and this … is the formation of a new system' (ibid.).

Another important step, bringing in new evidence, was from Vygotsky's studies of adolescence (Vygotsky, 1998b). He says he was 'surprised at the extent to which this stage contrasts with childhood … [it] is not that the connections increase in number, but that they change' (Vygotsky, 1997a, p. 98). The higher psychological functions had by adolescence been internalised and now thinking had the leading role in all other functions. In childhood for instance, memory plays a 'colossal role' in thinking: 'to think means to remember concrete events' (ibid.). For adolescents however 'to remember means to think', to 'search for what is needed in a certain logical order'. Thinking is a function 'which restructures and changes all other psychological processes' (ibid., p. 99).

The next step up the ladder leads to the system 'which form[s] the key to all processes of development and loss'. This is 'concept formation, a function which fully ripens and takes shape first in adolescence' (ibid.). To have devel- oped a mature concept means that a person also has a view of the whole system of which the concept is a part. To have a true concept of 'mammal', for instance, implies a view of the place of mammals in the animal world and in nature, a world-view. And adolescence is the age when a coherent world-view and a developed personality take shape.

The next step has to do with *dissolution* rather than development; Vygotsky believes that it is often possible to understand more about development by examining how systems break down in illness or old age. In schizophrenia, for instance, 'the first thing that is lost in the schizophrenic is the function of concept formation' (Vygotsky, 1997a, p. 102). This, Vygotsky says, is because 'the schizophrenic's thinking begins to be merely determined by his affect' (ibid.) and this leads to the breakdown of the complex system of intellectual thinking that had been built up, through social interaction, in normal development.

Finally, in a last huge step, Vygotsky asks 'what is it in the brain which physiologically corresponds to thinking in concepts?' (ibid., p. 104). He assumes that 'the brain contains enormous possibilities for the development of new systems' (ibid., p. 105). He also recognises that 'what we observe in mental processes is the joint activity of separate areas' (ibid.) which are linked by existing connections. But when new and more complex mental systems develop, which are not already connected in the brain, how are new connections between different parts of the brain established? It may, again, be possible to examine this by considering what happens in pathology, when there are lesions in the brain or when brain cells die off.

In people with Parkinson's disease, for instance, the motor system is disturbed so that they sometimes are unable to walk, even to take a step; a connection in the brain is broken. But this connection can be re-established through the use of external signs – placing pieces of paper on the floor can provide 'stepping stones' to enable Parkinson's patients to make their way across a room. 'The Parkinsonian patient establishes a connection between different points of his brain through a sign' (Vygotsky, 1997a, p. 106).

Vygotsky points out what his different examples had in common. Each system goes through three stages:

> First an inter-psychological stage – I order, you execute. Then an extra-psychological stage – I begin to speak to myself. Then an intra-psychological stage – two points of the brain which are excited from outside have the tendency to work in a unified system *and turn into an intracortical point.*
> (Vygotsky, 1997a, p. 106; my italics)

Tatiana Akhutina says that in this paper:

> Vygotsky developed two principles of neuropsychology: social genesis and the systemic structure of psychological functions. He also outlined the initial contours of the principle of the dynamic localisation of functions.
> (Akhutina, 2003, p. 168)

In her article she sees him as having arrived gradually at a 'comprehensive development of the principles of neuropsychology' (ibid., p. 159).

At the end of this talk, Vygotsky invites his colleagues to join him on his new voyage of discovery. His view was that the explorations of higher mental functions had gone as far as it could. The next task was to look at the interaction and the connections between them, the development of new syntheses and of psychological systems:

> Systems and their fate – it seems to me that for us the alpha and omega of our next work must reside in these four words.
> (Vygotsky, 1997a, p. 107)

The move to Kharkov

But the political context was becoming more problematic for Vygotsky and his colleagues. They were coming under increasing criticism for 'bourgeois', 'eclectic' and 'idealistic' views. In 1931 a resolution was published as part of an attack on Kornilov's Institute of Experimental Psychology, which declared that it was of the utmost importance to 'destroy and annihilate these remnants of bourgeois idealistic theories' at the Institute. To purge psychology of such elements it was suggested that textbooks should be scrutinised and the ideological commitments of the teaching personnel thoroughly examined (Van der Veer and Valsiner, 1991, p. 375). Also in 1931, at the First All-Union Congress on Psychotechnics and the Psychophysiology of Labour in Leningrad, one member criticised many psychologists, including Vygotsky and Luria, focusing particularly on their *Studies on the history of behaviour* (Vygotsky and Luria, 1993) for its uncritical importation of Western psychological theories, such as Gestalt psychology and Freudianism (Van der Veer and Valsiner, 1991, p. 377).

By the end of 1931 several of Vygotsky's former collaborators had moved to Kharkov in Soviet Ukraine, having been invited to work in the newly opened Ukrainian Psychoneurological Academy. At this time too some of Vygotsky's students (Morozova, Levina) were sent to work in different cities and were only able to return to Moscow for 'internal conferences' called by Vygotsky. This was a major disruption in the work of the old 'collective'.

The psychologists from Moscow who made the move to Kharkov included Luria, Leontiev, Lebedinskii, Bozhovich and Zaporozhets. The Moscow group joined a local group in Kharkov which included Gal'perin and Zinchenko. The group thus formed became known as the Kharkov school; although their work was initially derived from Vygotsky's, it later began to centre on Leontiev's more consciously materialist and Marxist 'theory of activity'. The psychological section of the Academy was initially headed by Luria, and then by Leontiev.

Zavershneva suggests that:

> By focusing on the ideologically more compliant theory of activity, A.N. Leontiev survived in the complex atmosphere of 'repressed science' … and later became not only the originator of a major movement but also the founder of the psychology department at Moscow State University.
>
> (Zavershneva, 2010, pp. 83–84)

She implies that Leontiev's dominant position in Soviet science may have been a reason why most of Vygotsky's works were not published in Russia until the 1980s.

Vygotsky meanwhile continued to work in Moscow at the EDI (Defectological Institute), with collaborators including Luria, Levina, Morozova, Shif, Zankov and Zeigarnik (Mecacci, 2017, p. 79). He travelled regularly to Kharkov to give lectures, and enrolled himself as a medical student there. Luria had done the same; both were preparing themselves for further work in neuroscience. Vygotsky also began to work with a new collective at the Herzen Institute of Education in Leningrad and in 1931 he became Professor of Pedology at the Moscow Medical Institute State University (Van der Veer and Valsiner, 1991, p. 307).

Pedology

Vygotsky's move towards a broader and more interdisciplinary approach to psychology was a natural development from his work in defectology. It enabled him to apply more widely the insights and theories of development that he was developing as a defectologist, which had already influenced his practice in experimental psychology. The move reflected his growing involvement with the pedology or 'child science' movement, which attracted widespread interest and support in Russia after 1918.

Pedology was an international movement, which arose in Europe and America in the late nineteenth century. It advocated the study of the whole child. Its membership was cross-disciplinary, a coming together of many groups involved in the care of children in order to map their physical and mental development, understand their emotional moods and attitudes, and discuss the best approaches to their care and teaching at home, in school and in other institutions. By 1927–1928, when the first congress devoted entirely to pedology was held in Russia, there was a well-established literature relating to the movement, including works by Baldwin, Piaget, Stern and Koffka. Vygotsky was on the editorial board of the journal *Pedology* from 1929 to 1931 and at the first Pedology Congress he was responsible for some of the congress organisation and contributed papers.

Vygotsky was intensely committed to pedology and wrote many pedological works. The 1934 edition of Vygotsky's *Thinking and speech* (Vygotsky, 1987), published posthumously, contained a full list of Vygotsky's works classified into categories. Psychology and pedology were treated as separate categories, with ten books being presented as belonging to psychology and eight books to pedology (Schneuwly and Leopoldoff-Martin, 2011, p. 41). Some of these works have still not been published in their entirety. Until they are all available, and also available in translation, we shall not have a full picture of Vygotsky's thought.

For many years Vygotsky's works in pedology were banned or censored. This reflects the state of psychology following Stalin's Pedology Decree of 1936, which continued to influence attitudes to pedology for many years afterwards.

The rise and fall of pedology

David Joravsky describes the rise and fall of pedology in his authoritative book *Russian psychology*:

> In 1931, after Lunacharsky had been dismissed, and ardent Stalinists had taken over the Commissariat of Education, it decreed support for

pedology, including the development of *testy* (tests) for placement and the establishment of special schools for children who would be found by testing and by the teachers' observation to be in need of special programs ... But fashions change in the public reputation of particular sciences ... In Stalin's Russia the decline [of pedology] came as an abrupt fall, by resolution of the Party's Central Committee on July 4 1936 ...

(Joravsky, 1989, p. 347)

Joravsky explains that the pedologists' '*testy*' were discovering more defects than merits and that special schools were growing at an alarming rate as more and more children were discovered to be unequal to normal schooling:

And it was largely the children of workers and peasants who were put out and down, in spite of the Party's efforts to 'push up' meritorious individuals of lower class origin. The Party's Central Committee therefore rebuked the Commissariat of Education for its 1931 endorsement of pedology and special schools. Most of the children labelled backward and unruly were immediately to be put back in regular classes.

(Joravsky, 1989, p. 348)

Elena Minkova describes what happened following the Pedology Decree:

[P]edology was declared to be reactionary bourgeois science. The Bolshevik Party set a number of tasks for the scientists – one of which was to criticize all of the works on the theory of pedology that had been released in the press up until year 1936.

Just one year after the publication of the new regulation, a large number of articles criticizing pedologists began to appear in the press ... [One article] called pedology 'the servant of the capitalists'.

(Minkova, 2012, p. 92)

Another critical paper asserted that 'the testing methods were developed and served as justification for the inequality of human beings and the human race' (ibid.).

Joravsky points out that pedologists by and large had been pursuing the very goals – the encouragement of working-class children, and the focus on raising their achievement – which they were accused of frustrating (Joravsky, 1989, p. 348). Many pedologists, like Vygotsky, had always been opposed to the blanket use of crude and questionable tests and had argued strongly for more qualitative and observation-based systems of assessment. But as a result of the Decree all pedologists and their works were criticized, whatever their views. All pedological institutes were closed and pedologists were dismissed. Many pedological publications were destroyed.

Vygotsky defined pedology as 'the science of the development of the child' (Van der Veer and Valsiner, 1991, p. 308) and was not prepared to distance himself from the growing science. He died in 1934, so did not experience the consequences of the Pedology Decree. It is doubtful whether he would ever have 'admitted his errors' in this area. Van der Veer and Valsiner sum up his position:

> Pedology afforded Vygotsky what he had been looking for during his career: a unification of his interest in the development of novel complex functions with that of the educational needs of normal and retarded children and he defended this new discipline against all criticism.
>
> (Van der Veer and Valsiner, 1991, p. 327)

Vygotsky's work in pedology

Only one volume of the *Collected works* (volume 5; Vygotsky, 1998) is devoted to pedological writing. There is no reference to pedology in the title and many references to pedology are omitted or changed to 'child science'. Certain key texts (such as those in *Foundations of pedology*; Vygotsky, 2019) are not included, and other texts are not published in their entirety but as excerpts. This makes it difficult to get a coherent picture of Vygotsky's work in this field. In addition, the editing of the texts is questionable, with numerous gaps and omissions. We can only sample Vygotsky's approach to pedology in this chapter, so I intend to consider his pedological works and concepts under three headings:

- the pedology of adolescence;
- *perezhivanie* (a term for 'experience' which has become a crux in translation); and
- periodisation and the 'crises' of different years/stages of development.

The pedology of adolescence

The chapters on adolescence in volume 5 of the *Collected works* come from the handbook *Pedology of the adolescent* (Vygotsky, 1998b), published in 1930–1931. But we are told in the notes that the editors of the *Collected works* included only those chapters that relate to psychological development proper; all chapters relating to other aspects of development in adolescence were omitted. As pedology was specifically concerned with children and young people as a whole, this editorial decision will have distorted the evidence. We will consider the first two chapters of this book.

Chapter 1: Development of interests at the transitional age

From the beginning of the book Vygotsky signals his strong intention to foreground what is of most importance to adolescents: their interests. Vygotsky saw these as the driving forces at this age. Many psychologists viewed development as essentially biological; a straightforward matter of growth without marked changes in direction. But for Vygotsky the driving forces of behaviour change at different phases of development (Vygotsky, 1998b, p. 4). He intends to consider the 'connectedness, orderliness, fusion and the mutual compatibility of separate processes of behavior' (ibid., p. 7).

Vygotsky emphasises that the transitional age is marked by 'a basic cluster of biological needs from which the development of interests begins' (ibid., p. 11). It is a phase marked by an 'extremely sharp acceleration of both the biological and the cultural wave of development' (ibid., p. 12). New formations appear, but other processes die off: evolution, but also involution. The death of childhood interests is a marker of adolescence, as is the rise of new interests.

Vygotsky describes adolescence as a disruptive, devastating phase, often marked by negativity, by discontent and rebellion against authority, rapid mood changes, pessimism and melancholy. He quotes Tolstoy who termed this period 'the desert of adolescence' (Vygotsky, 1998b, p. 17). The negativism of adolescence is often expressed in school, with school performance falling off, fatigue and a decrease in the ability to work, in both boys and girls.

Vygotsky underlines the importance of recognising and enabling adolescents' interests. He quotes a finding from Zagorovskii (who studied the negative phase of development in 104 adolescents) that adolescents may behave quite differently in different situations, showing negative attitudes at home but not in school, or vice versa. Zagorkovskii suggests that 'to a significant degree, a sharp exhibition of these symptoms may be due to inadequacies of the pedagogical approach' (ibid., p. 22). Building on interests is the key to successful pedagogy.

The positive aspects of adolescence often include a new orientation towards the future (which may seem to offer a way out of an unsatisfying present). Vygotsky is interested in Stern's theory of 'serious play' which includes both teenage erotic fantasy and 'playing at love', and the trying on of roles and personae in peer groups. This theory interests Vygotsky, but his main objection is that it doesn't take into account the 'complex synthesis' of biological and social influences involved. Play is *too* serious to be explained so simplistically. 'Play is self-education; what corresponds to it in the adolescent is a complex and long process of transforming tendencies into human needs and interests' (ibid., p. 28).

Chapter 2: Development of thinking and formation of concepts in the adolescent

For Vygotsky, the development of concepts was basic to the development of thought. He saw adolescence as a time of intensive intellectual development: a turning point. In this chapter he insists that this change does not happen through the simple maturation of elementary mental functions. It is only the theory of the development of higher psychological functions, developed by him and his colleagues, that will help bridge the gap between the elementary mental functions of young children and the more abstract thinking of adolescence. The qualitative change in children's thinking resulting from the development of higher psychological functions is an essential stepping-stone in the full picture of growth.

The central phenomenon of the 'transitional age' is the formation of concepts: a complex thought process involving substantial changes in both the content and the form of thinking. Certain thoughts can only be communicated properly in logical speech; mathematics and social sciences need to be presented through logical verbal thinking. Ach, the German psychologist who had published a book about concept formation in 1921, described the transitional age as a crucial boundary in the development of thinking. Vygotsky had used and refined Ach's experiments on concept formation in the psychological experiments he carried out with Sakharov. Like Vygotsky, Ach emphasised the role of speech in concept formation.

Sakharov's and Vygotsky's work on concept formation is described fully in ch. 5 of *Thinking and speech*, and is also the subject of an article by Sakharov (1994), included in *The Vygotsky reader* (Van der Veer and Valsiner, 1994). But in the current chapter Vygotsky makes a number of important observations that relate to concept formation.

The first concerns the methodology of pedological research. Vygotsky refers to the use of 'genetic sections' in studying the development of thinking. This holistic method aims to look at all aspects of the development of thinking. In his later lecture 'The characteristics of the method of pedology' (Vygotsky, 2019a) he describes it as a 'comparative-genetic' method – comparing the broad picture of thinking at different stages of development. The detailed observation of the *same* child at *different* stages provided a unique and specific picture of growth. Researchers looked not only for similarities but also 'the differences in the similarity' (Vygotsky, 1998b, p. 41). The Vygotsky/Sakharov experiments on concept formation, of course, enabled such changes in children's thinking to be tracked quite precisely.

The second observation refers to the 'deep and fundamental change' that occurs as the *content of thinking* is restructured by concepts. Vygotsky suggests that science, art, and all other branches of cultural life are adequately assimilated only in concepts. Concepts open up the deep structures of knowledge, revealing the connections between different phenomena. The formation of concepts is at the base of all intellectual growth; it takes place over long periods of time, sometimes years. But through this development 'the world becomes an environment for thinking' (ibid., p. 43).

Thirdly there is the role of language in all this. The word is 'the carrier of the concept' (ibid., p. 48), and language is in itself a categorising system, a way of 'ordering and generalizing reality' (ibid.). Since concepts are related and form systems, an understanding of concepts leads to a better understanding of the 'worlds of social consciousness'. Vygotsky quotes Humboldt's saying: 'to think in words is to join one's own thinking to thought in general' (ibid.). He suggests that 'Complete socialization of thought is contained in the function of concept formation' (ibid.).

For adolescents, thinking in concepts enables them to better understand and better order the *inner* world too, the world of their own experiences. It supports the development of self-consciousness:

> Thus understanding reality, understanding others, and understanding one-self – this is what thinking in concepts brings with itself. This is the kind of revolution in thinking and consciousness of the adolescent.
>
> (Vygotsky, 1998b, p. 49)

Thinking in concepts contributes to the development of logical thinking; it opens up the possibility of abstract thought, judgment, interpretation and reflection. In the remainder of the chapter Vygotsky reviews studies of concept formation by several researchers including Stern and Piaget. He particularly admires some of Piaget's work in this area, especially his ways of making children conscious of their thinking, such as by asking them 'how they arrived at their answers' in arithmetic problems. 'Introspection, perceiving one's own processes, is, therefore, a necessary factor for mastering them' (ibid., p. 65).

Perezhivanie

Words are 'carriers of the concept', and no word in Vygotsky's oeuvre, and especially in pedology, has aroused more discussion among Vygotsky commentators than the word '*perezhivanie*'. This word, usually translated as 'experience' or 'emotional experience', plays an important part in Vygotsky's pedology and in his developing theory of consciousness. The issues around *perezhivanie* are about translation, but also about conflicting interpretations of the *concept* that the word conveys. However, as David Bakhurst suggests:

> Elusive concepts that seemingly get at something deep can engender a kind of cultish fascination. As time goes on, they may gain a life of their own, people tire of explaining them, and it becomes accepted that they denote something of critical importance when in fact their meaning remains obscure ... In my view, we should avoid appropriating the Russian term and find ways that are natural in English to express what the Russian concept is so apt at revealing.
>
> (Bakhurst, 2019, p. 1)

The subtleties of meaning in *perezhivanie* are difficult to translate into English and there have been many attempts to define the term precisely. In Russian the two halves of the word: *pere-* (through) and *zhivat* (to live) suggest that 'a lived-through experience' would be a possible translation. There is an implication in this of an intense experience, and this suggestion is heightened if we know that '*perezhivat*' in Russian means to be upset, to experience trouble and come through it (Michell, 2016).

It's easier perhaps in Italian, where the translation '*vissuto*' means a lived experience, or in German, where '*Erlebnis*' also carries the overtone of a lived-through experience. (Yasnitsky suggests, without an exact reference, that when Vygotsky translated the word *Erlebnis* from the German, he used the Russian word *perezhivanie*; Yasnitsky, 2018, p. 210.) Among all the complex discussions of how *perezhivanie* should be expressed in English, a 'lived-though experience' or 'an emotional experience' suggest themselves as perhaps the best compromises, depending on the context. They at least avoid the use of the Russian word inserted in an English text; as just noted, Bakhurst suggests that the use of *perezhivanie* in this way is too exclusive (or excluding).

'The problem of the environment'

The lecture in which Vygotsky focuses on the concept of 'lived-through experience' is entitled 'The problem of the environment in pedology' (meaning the social rather than the physical environment; Vygotsky, 2019b). It was one of the lectures that made up *Foundations of pedology*, a course that Vygotsky taught at the Herzen Institute in Leningrad from 1932 until 1934, just before his death. These lectures are not included in volume 5 of the *Collected works* but are available, in a new translation by Kellogg and Veresov, in *Foundations of pedology* (Vygotsky, 2019). 'The problem of the environment' was also included in *The Vygotsky reader* (Van der Veer and Valsiner, 1994).

The main example of *perezhivanie*, or 'lived-through experience', that Vygotsky gives in 'The problem of the environment' is that of three children of an alcoholic, mentally ill and abusive mother who regularly beats them. 'In a word,' Vygotsky writes, 'the children live in a situation of terror and fear in connection with these conditions' (Vygotsky, 2019, p. 70).

All three children are brought to the Pedological Clinic but 'each of these children presents a completely different picture of developmental disorder due to the same situation' (ibid.). The youngest child had developed neurotic systems, terror attacks, enuresis and a stammer. He had become 'completely overwhelmed and helpless in this situation' (ibid.). The second child was developing a state of deep inner conflict, painfully attached to the mother but also regarding her as a source of terrible emotional experiences. This deep conflict produced 'acutely contradictory behaviour' in the child.

The third and eldest child, who was somewhat backward, was surprisingly stable. He understood the mother was ill and felt for her; he saw that the younger children were in danger; he had become the person who calmed the mother down and stopped her harming the others. 'He was, after all, the elder of the family, the one who had to take care of the rest' (ibid., p. 71).

So the same environment – the social situation of development – was experienced quite differently by the three children of different ages. And these emotional experiences (*perezhivaniya*) were dependent on the personality and attitude of the child experiencing them, and on their conscious realisation of the experience.

Interlude: Vygotsky at the EDI clinic

'The problem of the environment' provides one of the few detailed examples of the kind of concrete casework that went on in the EDI and in Vygotsky's other clinics. However, in the recently published *Vygotsky's notebooks* (Zavershneva and Van der Veer, 2018) we do find one or two examples of the notes he makes during case conferences about children. So before moving on to explore some of Vygotsky's other writing in pedology we will observe him at work *as* a pedologist in the EDI clinic, taking part in a long series of discussions about a ten-year-old boy, Kolya S. He makes detailed notes (as was his habit) in one of the hundreds of small notebooks he used.

These are brief glimpses, extracts from his notes on some meetings, in which Vygotsky asks himself questions about what he is seeing and hearing, listens to his colleagues, observes the child at work and play, and constantly analyses the evidence, relating it to the whole picture he is building and to theoretical frameworks. While remaining deeply attentive to the individual he is always considering him/her in a wider context. Vygotsky's great empathy with this difficult child is reflected in the vivid impression his notes give us of his ambivalent childish presence.

The case of Kolya S.

Conference with teachers

Kolya S., 10 years ... Mentally retarded. Mood changes: reticence and aggression ... Mendacity. Steals money for the cinema. In school he was silent. Answers only to questions he knows. Suddenly a change of mood: does not study, is pugnacious, behaves in an affected manner, does not control himself.

Around three years he began speaking two words. Until 5 to 6 years spoke little and badly (seven words). Irritability from the age of eight. Why? His grandfather beat him in the head. A caring family, but they punish him. The influence of the street. His younger brother began speaking earlier. His physical development is below the norm ...

What does he want? What motivates him? The mood changes are in which periods?

The most important is his age: a seven-year-old; this is the leitmotif ...

The inferiority is not an acute emotional experience but a character trait. Complexes. Mental retardation. Reflection, tries to improve himself, childish morals. Sensitivity to praise and reproof. 'I can do it' ... Three questions about his character: How does it function, how does it develop, what is its structure.

Conference with mother and child

The mother: K. behaves well in the group because the others are worse. Towards the end Kolya himself: Here I learned the easy things and now I can do the hard things as well.

Outbursts. Talks defiantly, rudely. Mischief on the quiet. Becomes very agitated. He behaves well and wants to be released as soon as possible. He behaves well and wants that everybody knows it. The sensitive traits diminish, the expansive traits appear – another side of his personality.

After an inconclusive (perhaps frustrating) discussion with colleagues

Why do we disagree? Methodologically: the facts and their interpretation; scientifically: the elucidation of the facts.

The main thing: primary and secondary infantilism. From the very beginning there is a delay in development. There is fixation, freezing because of the conflict in development, in childhood.

We did not cure the child: We did not remove the fixation in development or the secondary infantilism, but [we removed] the temporary reactions. We must evaluate the result of the pedagogical work: We did not cure but removed (symptom treatment) …

Following an observation

Yesterday's demonstration: acrobatics. There we saw in condensed experimental form Kolya's two faces (the schizo-silent one and the joyful-confident) separately. Today he guessed the course of the experiment: You are asking difficult things all the time. Today both faces together – in one moment – the ambivalence of his behavior here: he both wants and does not want. Reads poems (after we left). A preschool, superficial offense (he very rapidly forgot about it, schizo painful). But a childish radiance, ambition and pride with childish bashfulness, timidity …

(Zavershneva and Van der Veer, 2018, pp. 184–190)

Periodisation: 'The problem of age'

'The problem of age' (Vygotsky, 1998c), published for the first time as ch. 6 of volume 5 of the *Collected works*, was written as a chapter for a book that Vygotsky was preparing on developmental psychology in the last years of his life (1932–1934). In the first part of the chapter Vygotsky reviews some of the ways in which psychologists have attempted to divide childhood into different periods on the basis of physical characteristics (e.g. dentition or sexual development), or on 'changes in the rhythm of development related to age'. He suggests that a genuine periodicity can be based only on 'internal changes of development itself, only breaks and turning points in its flow can provide a reliable basis for determining the main periods of formation of the personality of the child' (ibid., p. 190). This model of development aims to identify the new developments – neoformations – that characterise the essence of new levels. Development in Vygotsky's model consists of a series of long stable periods with minor changes, interrupted by crises, which involve abrupt shifts, changes and discontinuities in behaviour. These are turning points in development.

Stable age periods have been fully studied, but crises have not – they are usually regarded as anomalies and deviations. Vygotsky says that the view he takes of them – as part of the normal pattern of development – is new. Crises are the opposite of stable periods and are marked by major shifts and discontinuities which are concentrated in a short time – a few months. 'Development takes on a stormy, impetuous and sometimes catastrophic character' (ibid., p. 191) during these periods. A crisis arises imperceptibly, it grows and reaches a culmination point before subsiding.

Vygotsky suggests that a significant number of children who go through major critical periods are difficult children; but *every* child during these crisis periods becomes markedly more difficult to manage and to teach than in stable periods. He suggests that inappropriate teaching may exacerbate the difficulty:

> At turning points of development, the child becomes relatively difficult due to the fact that the change in the pedagogical system applied to the child does not keep up with the rapid changes in his personality. Pedagogy during the critical ages is the least developed in practical and theoretical aspects.
>
> (Vygotsky, 1998c, pp. 193–194)

Many observers have spoken of crises in development as being solely negative and destructive. Vygotsky however sees them as an integral part of development; while it's true that children may become unstable and lose some of their usual interests, this is part of the change taking place. He suggests that the main critical periods are the crisis of the newborn, and the crises at age one, age three, age seven and age thirteen, and puberty (ages 14–18). Each of these crises includes processes of dying off, but also of development. 'The negative content of development at turning points is only the reverse or shadow side of positive changes of the personality ...' (ibid., p. 194).

These, then, are the key features of Vygotsky's theory of child development:

- there are longer stable periods interrupted by, and alternating in a dialectical pattern with ...
- disruptive 'crises' often marked by negative behaviour and the loss of old interests,
- but also leading to the emergence of new interests, new characteristics, and the reconstruction of the growing personality.
- The most important aspect of development at these ages is the appearance of 'neoformations' – which can appear both in stable or critical periods – and which are new and unique aspects of the personality.
- At each of these age periods the child's relation with the environment – with the social situation of development – changes.
- Vygotsky speaks of how 'the general structure of consciousness' also changes as a consequence of the child's changing relation with the environment.

The zone of proximal/proximate development[1]

Towards the end of 'The problem of age', Vygotsky – having laid out the features and the general dynamic of his model of development – turns to the model's implications for pedagogy. He believes that a basic task of the diagnostics of development is to determine a child's actual level of development. But by determining the actual level of development:

> we determine only the fruits of development, that is, that which has already matured and completed its cycle ... A genuine diagnosis of development must be able to catch, not only concluded cycles of development, not only the fruits, but also those processes that are in the period of maturation ... This task is accomplished by finding the zones of proximal development.
>
> (Vygotsky, 1998c, pp. 200–201)

This will involve identifying how far children can solve, with guidance from teachers or older students, problems that are more difficult than those they can solve independently. In these conditions, using their ability to imitate and collaborate, some 8-year-olds will be able to solve problems that are designed for 12-year-old children. Other 8-year-olds may be able to solve problems suitable for 9-year-olds. The first group of children is said to have a zone of proximal/proximate development of four years; this indicates their potential. The second group has a ZPD of one year.

Obviously this kind of information is of extreme interest to a teacher who wants to direct their teaching to a child's maturing functions rather than those that have already developed. Vygotsky makes the point that this development usually takes place in the presence of a teacher (or sometimes with another 'more developed' child). So it is a product of the social environment. All of children's *social* development, such as speech, comes from the presence of 'ideal' forms in the social environment, which provide examples of mature behaviour to imitate and learn from.

The ZPD is Vygotsky's best-known concept, perhaps because it resembles the kind of testing that educationalists are familiar with, and they can immediately see applications for it. Unfortunately it is generally taken out of the framing context – Vygotsky's work in pedology and the study of development – and this creates problems of interpretation.

'The crisis at age three'

This very short chapter in volume 5 of the *Collected works* is a stenographic transcript of a lecture Vygotsky gave during the 1933–1934 academic year (the last year of his life) at the Herzen Pedagogical Institute. It provides a vivid account of the kind of negativism that Vygotsky identified as marking critical periods. Vygotsky had already noted of the crisis at age 3 that 'during this period ... the personality of the child undergoes abrupt and unexpected changes. The child becomes a difficult child.' (ibid., p. 193) In this lecture he undertakes a close analysis of this process.

First he points out that the changes and events during a crisis period are 'grouped around some neoformation of a transitional type' (Vygotsky, 1998a, p. 283). It is the task of analysis to identify what is the new feature that appears at this time. Secondly he suggests that we need to consider how the crisis is affecting the child's development in general. And the third stage is to use the analysis to look forward to the child's subsequent growth. All of this analysis needs to take place in relation to factual materials (evidence) and include a consideration of the social situation of development.

The symptoms of the crisis

Vygotsky lists four major, sometimes overlapping, symptoms of the crisis at age 3. Top of the list is negativism, which is defined very specifically as being manifested 'when (a child) does not want to do something only because an adult told him to' (Vygotsky, 1998a, p. 283).

Vygotsky describes this as a unique shift in motivation. He gives an example from an observation in the clinic:

> A four year old girl with a lingering age-three crisis ... wants to be taken to a conference at which children are evaluated. The girl even prepares to go there. I invite the girl. But because I ask her, she will not go at all. She resists with all her might. 'Well, then go home.' She does not go. 'Well, come here.' She doesn't come. When she is left in the room, she begins to cry. She is hurt because she was not taken. Thus, negativism forces the child to act *against* her affective wishes. The girl wanted to go, but because she was asked to do so, she would never do it.
>
> (Vygotsky, 1998a, p. 284)

Vygotsky called this a unique shift in motivation because the girl is not responding under the influence of affect, but is acting *contrary* to her own affect. Social relations are at the forefront; the girl's behaviour is directed primarily to the person asking her, not to what she is being asked to do. The drive to contradict, to do the opposite, is negativism.

Stubbornness, the next symptom, is an active assertion of the child's will, against adults' wishes. Vygotsky suggests that this is different from persistence. In the case of stubbornness the child carries on insisting on something not necessarily because he really wants it very much, but *because he had demanded it*. He won't give in or go back on a previous decision.

The third symptom, obstinacy, differs from the other two because it is impersonal, it is a general rejection of the norms of family behaviour that the child is used to and that are expected. The child is rebellious and has a constantly discontented attitude, which is 'permeated with cryptic revolt' (Vygotsky, 1998a, p. 285).

The fourth symptom is self-will or wilfulness. 'It consists of a tendency of the child toward independence. This did not exist previously. Now the child wants to do everything himself' (ibid.).

Vygotsky sums up: 'The child acts as a difficult child.' All of these symptoms together denote a crisis and a reaction against the way the child has been reared: 'it is a kind of protest by the child who wants independence, who has outgrown the norms and forms of care that obtained in early childhood' (ibid., p. 286).

There have been changes in the child's relation to the close family environment, and the child has become unpredictable. Vygotsky notes: 'all the symptoms develop around the axis "I" and the people around him ... In general, the symptoms taken together create the impression of emancipation of the child' (ibid.). As a consequence of the crisis there is a restructuring of 'the social position of the child with respect to the people around him and to the authority of the mother and father' (ibid., p. 288).

So the child, through a display of negativism and protest, liberates her/himself from babyhood and acquires more agency. This model of development as a progressive freeing, and of *will* as a means of asserting selfhood and becoming a person, is a running thread through Vygotsky's work.

Coda: Asya

When Vygotsky went home from the EDI Clinic, he went to a small one-room flat in Serpukhova Street in Moscow, where he lived with his wife and two daughters. Asya, his younger daughter, was almost two in July 1932, when he made some observations of her, numbering the points, in another of his small notebooks. Some of these notes powerfully recall 'The crisis at age three', although Asya is younger:

> ... 3. When she says something to one of those present (mama), she repeats it for the other (papa) as if he had not heard it. Speech is a communicative function *à deux* ...
>
> 5. The questions about names are there. But they are questions about things and not about names ... To name a thing is to learn what it is. The proof: These questions are lost amidst the others: What is in the carafe, what in the box, where is he going, where has he been, etc.? The first period of questions is the natural continuation of the visible situation in questions that address what is not immediately given, not visible: Where does he go; where is the person who is usually with him; what is in the closed thing (a box), etc.? On the whole, as a rule: There is no perception of an object, there is perception of a moving situation. About everything: Where does it go? On the drawing there is a cockerel: Where does it go?

6. Marvelous attention (cf. memory). cf. Piaget's idea that children's direct attention is better than ours, like their memory: She herself looks for berries (strawberry), finds them, selects the green from the red, etc.

7. About the idea that negativism is the beginning of volition, differentiated from the affect and contradicting the affect ...

a   she found sugar, I take it away, bring other sugar, she lies on the floor, does not accept it, although she desperately wants it, later accepts it from the nanny;

b   is lying on the floor. Clearly does not want to do that, clearly wants what is used to tempt her to stand up, but only does it with rare exceptions, when the affect is very strong (+ or −). In addition: As in all genuine negativism, by suddenly changing our demands, we can cause a change of her attitude, and this clearly proves that the affect is not the core. For example: (1) You must go to sleep − I do not want to go nighty-night; (2) it is forbidden to sleep − I want to sleep, etc. The same when she throws herself on the ground: You must not stand up − she wants to stand up. A symptom that shows that the hypobulic reactions are negativistic. Negativism is the beginning of will, it is genuine hypobulia!

(Zavershneva and Van der Veer, 2018, pp. 238–239)

Vygotsky sums up:

In the crisis of the first year we clearly see negativism, stubbornness, and willfulness. Its meaning: the emancipation and development of the personality. Two reactions: goes (runs) away − a trait of a more mature age − and falls on the ground − regression.

(Zavershneva and Van der Veer, 2018, pp. 239)

Vygotsky's note-taking here shows how his mind moves easily between the detail of observation and the abstractions of theory. It offers another vivid insight into his approach to clinical work.

Note

1   See the discussion of the terms 'proximal' and 'proximate' in the Introduction. I shall use the abbreviation 'ZPD' frequently later in the book.

References

Akhutina, T. (2003). 'L.S. Vygotsky and A.R. Luria: foundations of neuropsychology'. *Journal of Russian and East European Psychology*, 41(3/4), pp. 159–190.

Bakhurst, D. (2019). '*Vygotsky's concept of perezhivanie: its philosophical and educational significance*'. Annual Conference of the Philosophy of Education Society of Great Britain, New College, Oxford University, 29–31 March.

Joravsky, D. (1989). *Russian psychology: a critical history*. Oxford: Blackwell.

Mecacci, L. (2017). *Lev Vygotskii: Sviluppo, educazione e patologia della mente*. Florence: Giunti.

Michell, M. (2016). 'Finding the "prism": understanding Vygotsky's *perezhivanie* as an ontogenetic unit of child consciousness'. *International Research in Early Childhood Education*, 7(1), pp. 5–33.

Minkova, E. (2012). 'Pedology as a complex science devoted to the study of children in Russia: the history of its origin and elimination'. *Psychological Thought*, 5(2), pp. 83–98. doi:10.5964/psyct.v5i2.23

Sakharov, L. (1994). 'Methods for investigating concepts' [1930]. Trans. M. Vale, in Van der Veer, R. and Valsiner, J. (eds), *The Vygotsky reader*, pp. 73–98. Oxford: Blackwell.

Schneuwly, B. and Leopoldoff-Martin, I. (2011). 'Vygotsky's "Lectures and articles on pedology". An interpretative adventure'. *Tätigkeitstheorie*, 4, pp. 37–52.

Van der Veer, R. and Valsiner, J. (1991). *Understanding Vygotsky: a quest for synthesis*. Oxford: Blackwell.

Van der Veer, R. and Valsiner, J. (eds) (1994). *The Vygotsky reader*. Oxford: Blackwell.

Vygotsky, L.S. (1987). *Thinking and speech* [1934], in Vygotsky, L.S., *The collected works of L.S. Vygotsky. Volume 1, Problems of general psychology*, pp. 37–285. New York: Plenum Press.

Vygotsky, L.S. (1994). 'The problem of the environment in pedology' [1935], in Van der Veer, R. and Valsiner, J. (eds), *The Vygotsky reader*, pp. 338–354. Oxford: Blackwell.

Vygotsky, L.S. (1997). *The collected works of L.S. Vygotsky. Volume 3, Problems of the theory and history of psychology*. Trans. and intro. R. Van der Veer. Rieber, R.W. and Wollock, J. (eds). New York: Plenum Press.

Vygotsky, L.S. (1997a). 'On psychological systems' [1930], in Vygotsky, L.S., *The collected works of L.S. Vygotsky. Volume 3, Problems of the theory and history of psychology*, pp. 91–107. Trans. and intro. R. Van der Veer. Rieber, R.W. and Wollock, J. (eds). New York: Plenum Press. Also available online in the Marxist Archive: www.marxists.org/archive/vygotsky/works/1930/psychological-systems.htm

Vygotsky, L.S. (1997b). *The history of the development of higher mental functions* [1931], in Vygotsky, L.S., *The collected works of L.S. Vygotsky. Volume 4, The history of the development of higher mental functions*, pp. 1–251. Trans. M.J. Hall; Rieber, R.W. (ed.). New York: Plenum Press.

Vygotsky, L.S. (1998). *The collected works of L.S. Vygotsky. Volume 5, Child psychology*. Rieber, R.W. (ed.). New York: Plenum Press.

Vygotsky, L.S. (1998a). 'The crisis at age three' [1932–1934], in Vygotsky, L.S., *The collected works of L.S. Vygotsky. Volume 5, Child psychology*, pp. 283–288. Rieber, R.W. (ed.). New York: Plenum Press.

Vygotsky, L.S. (1998b). 'Pedology of the adolescent' [1930–1931], in Vygotsky, L.S., *The collected works of L.S. Vygotsky. Volume 5, Child psychology*, pp. 3–184. Rieber, R.W. (ed.). New York: Plenum Press.

Vygotsky, L.S. (1998c). 'The problem of age' [1932–1934], in Vygotsky, L.S., *The collected works of L.S. Vygotsky. Volume 5, Child psychology*, pp. 187–205. Rieber, R.W. (ed.). New York: Plenum Press.

Vygotsky, L.S. (2019). *L.S. Vygotsky's pedological works. Volume 1, Foundations of pedology*. Trans. and notes D. Kellogg and N. Veresov. Singapore: Springer.

Vygotsky, L.S. (2019a). 'The characteristics of the method of pedology' [1934–1935], in Vygotsky, L.S., *L.S. Vygotsky's pedological works. Volume 1, Foundations of pedology*, pp. 23–42. Trans. and notes D. Kellogg and N. Veresov. Singapore: Springer.

Vygotsky, L.S. (2019b). 'The problem of the environment in pedology' [1935], in Vygotsky, L.S., *L.S. Vygotsky's pedological works. Volume 1, Foundations of pedology*, pp. 65–84. Trans. and notes D. Kellogg and N. Veresov. Singapore: Springer.

Vygotsky, L.S. and Luria, A.R. (1993). *Studies on the history of behaviour: ape, primitive, child* [1930]. Hillsdale, NJ: Lawrence Erlbaum Associates.

Yasnitsky, A. (2018). *Vygotsky: an intellectual biography*. Abingdon: Routledge.

Zavershneva, E. (2010). '"The way to freedom" (on the publication of documents from the family archive of Lev Vygotsky)'. *Journal of Russian and East European Psychology*, 48(1), pp. 61–90.

Zavershneva, E. and Van der Veer, R. (eds) (2018). *Vygotsky's notebooks: a selection* (Perspectives in cultural-historical research). Singapore: Springer.

Chapter 8

Play, imagination and creativity

Serious play

Vygotsky's recorded observations of his daughter Asya, quoted at the end of the previous chapter, show him attentively noting the details of her behaviour, her playfulness, and her attempts to get her own way. These observations reflect Vygotsky's pleasure in watching, studying and playing with children, and his serious interest in the part that play has in their development.

Vygotsky's work in pedology had enabled him to take a much wider view of child development, giving greater weight to children's emotional experiences and their response to their social environment in addition to their mental development. In the period 1930–1933, as well as several pedological publications, Vygotsky wrote four texts which give us a very full picture of his interest in play and the imagination: the lecture 'Play and its role in the mental development of the child' (Vygotsky, 2016), the lecture 'Imagination and its development in childhood' (Vygotsky, 1987), 'Imagination and creativity in the adolescent' (Vygotsky, 1998b) and *Imagination and creativity in childhood* (Vygotsky, 2004).

This can be seen as a return to a field that had deeply engaged Vygotsky when he was younger, and to the themes found in *The psychology of art* (Vygotsky, 1971) – the connections between art, the emotions, and the imagination. These are aspects of mind that he had always intended to include in an overall model of human psychology. Now he viewed them from a new perspective – through the contribution that they make to children's creative development and involvement in cultural life, and to their thinking. In this chapter I have chosen to begin with the text that relates to very young children: his celebrated lecture 'Play and its role in the mental development of the child'. In this text Vygotsky expressed all of his fascination with play and his conviction of its importance.

'Play and its role in the mental development of the child'

Vygotsky's seminal text on play was originally given as a lecture at the Herzen Pedagogical Institute in Leningrad in 1933, and is consequently a relatively late work. It is thanks to a stenographic record of the lecture that this text, a key

DOI: 10.4324/9780429203046-8

influence on research on play despite its brevity, survived. It has continued to resonate in all discussions of play ever since its publication, but it was not published until 1966, and not translated into English until 1968, more than thirty years after it was originally delivered. The first translation, by Catherine Mulholland, was used in the anthology *Play: its role in development and evolution* (Bruner et al., 1976), and also (in an abridged form) in *Mind in society* (Vygotsky, 1978), but in 2015 Nikolai Veresov asked me to assist him with a new translation, intended to correct some points in the first translation that needed amendment. The new translation was published in the *International Review of Early Childhood Education* (Vygotsky, 2016). I shall refer to it throughout this chapter.

It is important to note that this lecture is about *make-believe* play, which creates a *freedom from realistic thinking*. In another lecture given at the Herzen Institute in 1933, Vygotsky stressed that young children's play in the true sense of the word was always *imaginative* play. Other activities, such as tending to dolls or experimenting with objects, could not properly be termed play. In his words from his pedological text on early childhood, 'Play is a unique relation to reality that is characterised by creating imaginary situations or transferring the properties of some objects to others' (Vygotsky, 1998a, p. 267).

In 'Play and its role in the mental development of the child' Vygotsky makes clear that he regards play, not as the predominant form of activity, but as the 'leading line of development in the preschool years' (Vygotsky, 2016, p. 6). It appears in response to certain needs and incentives which must be taken into account in any theory of play. Vygotsky argues that 'to refuse to approach the problem of play from the standpoint of fulfilment of the child's needs, his incentives to act, and his affective aspirations would result in a terrible intellectualisation of play' (ibid.).

In Vygotsky's view, many 'age-based theories' of development disregard children's needs and motives; psychologists often consider development only in terms of the development of intellectual functions. But for Vygotsky, an analysis of play needs to start with affect. He suggests that 'play is invented at the point in development where unrealisable tendencies begin to appear. This is the way a very young child behaves: he wants a thing and must have it at once' (ibid.).

The description that follows of how young children can behave when thwarted – throwing themselves to the ground and having a temper tantrum – is very reminiscent of Vygotsky's description in his pedology work of the 'crisis' at age three. But here, in contrast, Vygotsky suggests that a child over the age of three experiences conflicting tendencies, a clash between the knowledge that certain desires cannot be met at once, and yet the strong urge to realise them:

> Henceforth play appears which – in answer to the question why the child plays – must always be understood as the imaginary, illusory realisation of unrealisable desires.
>
> (Vygotsky, 2016, p. 7)

Play is essentially wish fulfilment – not 'isolated wishes', Vygotsky says, but 'generalised affects'. The child does not play consciously, or with an awareness of the motives of the play. Vygotsky suggests that it is only in adolescence that young people become conscious of their feelings and motives. But play is always an expression of affect.

Because this text comes from a stenographic transcript, it is likely that Vygotsky had not written it down, but was speaking from notes. Daniel El'konin (1998) suggests that Vygotsky's lectures always had the character of thinking aloud, and it is most likely that this one was at least partly improvised. The stream of brilliant thoughts in the text follow one another so fast that it is hard to reflect on them. The whole text is now a classic, but the long central section is particularly dense and full of generative ideas.

Vygotsky begins the section by rejecting the idea that play is a symbolic activity – he sees this as an 'intellectualistic' approach. Play is not algebra in action, the child is not an unsuccessful algebrist, play is never symbolic in the proper sense of the term. To discuss it in this way is to regard play as a cognitive process and dismiss the affective aspect 'but also the fact that play *is* the child's activity' (Vygotsky, 2016, p. 9) – and is indeed what he called a 'leading activity'. So what is the meaning of this activity – what is it for? and what does it do for development?

Vygotsky dismisses another argument – that play is related to games with rules and that play in an imaginary situation is 'rule-based play'. He doesn't deny this last fact at all – it seems obvious that there *are* rules of behaviour in play – but he insists that it is not the whole explanation of play. In the course of this part of the argument he gives an amusing example of rule-based play observed by the psychologist James Sully, in which two sisters played at being sisters – the rules of the play meant that they had to *try* to be sisters and so went about dressed alike, always holding hands and so on. Vygotsky comments: 'What passes unnoticed by the child in real life becomes a rule of behaviour in play' (ibid., p. 10).

The core of play is that is *imaginative*:

> I think that play with an imaginative situation is something essentially new, impossible for a child under three, it is a novel form of behaviour in which the child's activity in an imaginary situation liberates him from situational constraints.
>
> (Vygotsky, 2016, p. 11)

This participation in a situation which is 'only conceived mentally in an imaginary field' (ibid., p. 12) enables the child to step outside his normal perceptions and assign different meanings to objects which have become part of the imaginary world. This creates 'a divergence between the field of meaning and the visual field' (ibid., p. 13), the possibilities of which are far-reaching.

> Thought is separated from objects because a piece of wood begins to play the role of a doll and a stick becomes a horse. Action according to rules begins to be determined by thought, not by objects themselves. This is such a reversal of the child's relationship to the real, immediate, concrete situation that it is hard to evaluate its full significance.
>
> (Vygotsky, 2016, p. 13)

One of the main possibilities opened up by this new behaviour is that there is now the possibility of splitting off the meaning of a word from its referent, making it possible to play with language and meanings. Vygotsky says indeed that with this shift 'one of the basic psychological structures determining the child's relationship to reality is radically altered' (ibid.).

This shift doesn't happen all at once. Play is a move towards the separation of a word from its object and Vygotsky stresses that it involves finding another object to act as a 'pivot' – a way of severing the meaning of 'horse' from a real horse. In the famous example he uses, this is the stick that becomes a horse. But it only does so when the child is physically playing at riding it; it is the *action* that makes the stick into the horse. For this reason not everything can be a horse – a match, for instance, is not acceptable to the child as a horse.

Vygotsky emphasises that in the play situation the child can never 'sever meaning from an object, or a word from an object, except by finding a pivot in something else, i.e. by the power of one object to steal another's name' (ibid., p. 14). He offers several descriptions of this process, some particularly suggestive:

> To separate the meaning of horse from a real horse and to transfer it to a stick (which is the necessary material pivot to keep the meaning from evaporating), and then to act with the stick as if it really were a horse, is a vital transitional stage to operating with meanings alone … In play a child unconsciously and spontaneously makes use of the fact that he can separate meaning from an object, without knowing he is doing it …
>
> (Vygotsky, 2016, p. 15)

If we look back at *Tool and symbol* (Vygotsky and Luria, 1994) we remember that some of the play experiments encouraged children to treat words as arbitrary signs, which they could then use to help them in tasks involving choosing, or remembering. Those experiments showed children becoming familiar with the possibility of detaching the meaning of words from their objects. It was the beginning of sign use, the beginning of symbolism. In *Tool and symbol* Vygotsky and Luria had suggested that the history of the development of sign use was a long one. They also observed in that monograph that 'In contrast to naturalistic theories of games, our experiments lead us to the conclusion that play constitutes the main avenue of the child's cultural development and, in particular, of the development of the child's symbolic activity' (ibid., p. 151). But of course the children in those experiments were at least two or three years older than the young children that Vygotsky is talking about in the play lecture. This explains Vygotsky's strong emphasis on the great significance of a young child splitting off the meaning of the word from its referent in the stick-horse example.

After this example Vygotsky observes, as if in passing:

> Hence we come to a functional definition of concepts, i.e. objects, and to a word as part of a thing.
>
> (Vygotsky, 2016, p. 15)

This shows Vygotsky making connections between the stick-horse, sign use, symbolisation, concepts, and (later in the lecture) abstraction:

> the movement in the field of meaning is the most important movement in play. On the one hand it is movement in an abstract field ... but the method of movement is situational and concrete.
>
> (Vygotsky, 2016, p. 17)

The other main way in which Vygotsky sees play influencing development is through children learning to control their immediate impulses in play. The rules of play may oblige them to act against their instincts. For instance in the game of 'sorcerer' children must run away from the sorcerer so as not to be caught – but need to stay and help their companions, who have to be disenchanted.

> In the game he acts counter to what he wants ... Ordinarily a child experiences subordination to rule in the renunciation of something he wants, but here subordination to a rule, and renunciation of acting on immediate impulse, are the way to maximum pleasure.
>
> (Vygotsky, 2016, p. 17)

This shows that 'a child's greatest self-control occurs in play'. Vygotsky points out that this is a Spinozan ideal, self-control leading to self-determination. It is a step on the path to freedom.

The child's ability to behave, in play, against their own desires and according to play rules, leads, Vygotsky suggests, to another development:

> thus play creates the zone of proximal[1] development of the child. In play a child is always above his average age, above his daily behaviour; in play it is as though he were a head taller than himself. As in the focus of a magnifying glass, play contains all developmental tendencies in condensed form; in play it is as though the child is trying to jump above the level of his normal behaviour.
>
> (Vygotsky, 2016, p. 18)

This is the most striking statement in the whole lecture. Vygotsky compares play with teaching in the way in which it advances development:

> The play–development relationship can be compared with the instruction-development relationship, but play provides changes in needs and in consciousness of a much wider nature. Play is the source of development and creates the zone of proximal development. Action in the imaginative field, in an imaginary situation, the creation of voluntary intentions and the formation of real-life plans and volitional motives – all appear in the play and make it the highest level of preschool development.
>
> The child moves forward essentially through play activity. It is in this way that play can be termed a leading activity that determines the child's development.
>
> (Vygotsky, 2016, p. 18)

Most other statements about the zone of proximal/proximate development relate to school-age children, and their ability to go beyond their normal solo performance when they are working with the teacher or more experienced peers. But here we are talking about a preschool child playing, by him/herself, in an informal context. Essentially Vygotsky's statement suggests that in imaginative dramatic play a child can access a much wider range of behaviour, can behave in a more mature way, and, in Vygotsky's marvellous metaphor, can become 'a head taller' than in his ordinary life. Teachers who have worked with children through drama will easily recognise this description of the changes that can appear when children take on different roles in a drama, and begin to speak and behave like adults, doctors, engineers, experts of all kinds.

The zone of proximal/proximate development (ZPD) is here completely detached from its usual association with testing and school performance. This is a much more open vision of the concept, and although it sits oddly with our usual understandings, it does suggest that the ZPD potentially has a wider range of meanings and applications than it is generally associated with.

The lecture on play is dense with thoughts and theories; unpacking it is challenging. But it probably gives us, more powerfully than any other text, a sense of what it would have been like to be at one of Vygotsky's lectures, watching him think aloud as he made his way through a complex argument. There is no doubt that many of his talks were extemporised; he was always improvising on sets of themes and ideas that were part of his mental life, continually revised and renewed.

The end of this lecture is somewhat disappointing in that Vygotsky turns to a rather conventional Piagetian explanation of what happens to imaginative play:

> At school age play does not die away, but permeates the attitude toward reality. It has its own continuation in school instruction and work (compulsory activity based on rules).
>
> (Vygotsky, 2016, p. 20)

This contradicts some of his other statements about the development of the imagination. In fact, earlier in the lecture, he had suggested:

> The old adage that children's play is imagination in action can be reversed: we can say that imagination in adolescents and schoolchildren is play without action.
>
> (Vygotsky, 2016, p. 7)

In the three texts that follow we shall find Vygotsky's most concentrated statements on the imagination, and on creativity.

Imagination and its development in childhood

The lecture on imagination forms part of a series of six lectures in psychology which Vygotsky gave at the Leningrad Pedagogical Institute in 1932, but which were not published until 1960. It's a usefully concise summary of his thinking about the imagination in psychology.

Vygotsky begins by rejecting the views of the imagination put forward by the 'old' psychologies, both the atomistic (or associative) psychology of Wundt and Ribot, who viewed imagination as an aspect of memory, and the idealistic (or metaphysical) psychology of Bergson and James, who saw imagination as a primal characteristic of mind. Neither school, Vygotsky saw, was thinking about this subject developmentally; both were presenting imagination either as a basic constituent of mind, or as the sum of other basic constituents.

Vygotsky links the development of the imagination to the development of language, which allows children to begin to represent and think about objects that are not present, and which frees them from immediate impressions. (This argument counters Piaget's presentation of the imagination as an essentially autistic, non-verbal and subconscious process.) Vygotsky argues that speech development plays a major role in the development of the imagination. He notes that, by contrast, the development of the imagination is delayed in deaf children and those who speech is retarded.

As in the lecture on play, Vygotsky underlines the importance of speech which *'frees the child from the immediate impression of an object'*, and thus enables children to think about objects they have not seen, and imagined forms.

As Vygotsky suggests in this lecture:

> Speech gives the child the power to free himself from the force of the immediate impressions and go beyond their limits. The child can express in words something that does not coincide with the precise arrangement of objects or representations. This provides him with the power to move with extraordinary freedom in the sphere of impressions, designating them with words.
>
> (Vygotsky, 1987, p. 346)

This continues the theme of the central importance of *increasing freedom of action* in development.

So far from imagination being non-verbal, Vygotsky thinks that its development 'like the development of other higher mental functions, is linked in an essential way with speech.' (ibid.) It is speech that allows a child to go beyond the limits of reality. And its development is also linked to the child's growing social interaction with other children, and their joint creative play activities.

Vygotsky's picture of children's joint 'world-making' activities – surely based on observation – shows them as being very far from autistic or subconscious fantasies:

> Consider, for example, what are commonly called utopian constructions. These are deliberate representations of a fantasy, representations that are clearly different in consciousness from realistic planes of thought. Clearly these representations are developed not subconsciously but consciously ... We could also consider the domain of artistic creativity in this connection. This domain of activity is available to the child at a young age. If we consider the projects of this creativity in drawing or storytelling, it quickly becomes apparent that this imagination has a directed nature. It is not a subconscious activity. Finally, if we consider the child's constructive imagination, the creative activity of consciousness associated with technical-constructive or building activity, we see consistently that real inventive imagination is among the basic functions underlying this activity. In this activity fantasy is highly directed. It is directed toward a goal that the individual is pursuing.'
>
> (Vygotsky, 1987, p. 346)

Vygotsky denies that imaginative activity is ruled by emotion, while realistic thinking is relatively unaffected by affect. Of course, in 'autistic thought' or daydreaming thinking is in a subordinate role to emotional impulses. But in realistic thinking the connections between logic and emotion are 'often infinitely deeper, stronger, more impelling, and more significant'. He concludes that there is no simple opposition to be set up between directed, realistic, cognitive thinking and autistic, emotional, imaginative thinking. Both imaginative thinking and realistic thinking can be directed and conscious, both can be characterised by high levels of emotion. The opposition that has sometimes been set up between them is 'both fictive and false'. He emphasises the 'extraordinary kinship that exists between thinking and imagination – in brief, the two processes develop as a unity' (ibid., p. 348).

Vygotsky suggests that the role that the imagination plays in thinking confirms that it is a psychological function, one which can take part in very different forms of complex activity. It also unifies several other functions, including emotion, in a unique relationship, and therefore goes beyond the boundaries of a psychological function to the extent that it can be termed *a psychological system.* This must be the first time that Vygotsky has included imagination and the emotions in a psychological system.

Vygotsky pinpoints the essential feature of imaginative thinking – that in this kind of thinking 'consciousness departs from reality'. But he regards this capacity to think about things that are not, to imagine other realities, as important to the development of thinking in general:

> By recognising this we can begin to understand the complex relationship between the activity of realistic thinking and the activity of advanced forms of the imagination ... A more profound penetration of reality demands that consciousness attain a freer relationship to the elements of that reality, that consciousness depart from the external and apparent aspect of reality that is given directly in perception.
>
> (Vygotsky, 1987, p. 349)

So imaginative thinking has the capacity to greatly enrich realistic thinking by liberating it from too close a dependence on immediate perception and reality, and enabling it to achieve a freer and more speculative character.

This view of imaginative thought as a no less important way of thinking than cognitive thought, like it in some respects, but also independent of it and able to interact with it in positive ways, is characteristic of Vygotsky's ability to integrate aspects of mind that are frequently viewed as separate. Moreover his way of bringing these independent aspects together means that imaginative thinking is not simply assimilated into a theory of cognitive development.

In some important respects Vygotsky's account of the role of imaginative thinking views it as *primary* in all advanced thinking – but in a different and less metaphysical way than in the arguments of the idealists. He stresses the social and linguistic origins of imaginative thinking, and as in all his arguments about the creative aspects of mind he refuses to see creativity and imagination as belonging mainly to the emotional sphere. In the course of the lecture he has turned the tables on conventional views of the relative importance of these two kinds of thinking. He has built a case for seeing imaginative thinking as paradigmatic of advanced thinking generally, and necessary for intellectual development.

Imagination and the turn to pedology

> Imagination is as necessary in geometry as it is in poetry.
>
> (Pushkin, quoted in Vygotsky, 1998b, p. 153)

Vygotsky at this stage of his life was thinking as a pedologist, with a view of child development much broader than that found in his psychological work – less focused on mental development and more interested in children's needs, motives and feelings. His view of the development of children and young people took all these aspects, including imagination and creativity, into account. In 'Imagination and creativity in the adolescent' (from which the Pushkin quotation above is taken), a pedological text written as a chapter in a teachers' handbook and published in 1931, Vygotsky continued to stress the central role of imagination in creative thinking.

> Everything that requires creative recreation of reality, everything that is connected with the interpretation and construction of something new, needs the indispensable participation of fantasy.
>
> (Vygotsky, 1998b, p. 153)

It's apparent that at this time Vygotsky was deeply engaged with the question of the role of play, the imagination and emotion in the development of personality. Perhaps this focus was part of his turn to pedology; perhaps it was linked to his exploration of essential elements in two of the major books he was then planning to write. In 1931–1933 he was drafting a book, which was never completed, about the emotions. At the same time his notebooks show that in 1932 he was actively planning a book on the problem of consciousness, which had long been his deepest preoccupation (Zavershneva and Van der Veer, 2018).

In writing about imagination, creativity and the emotions, Vygotsky was also returning to some of the ideas and themes that had preoccupied, indeed obsessed him, when he was in his teens and early twenties. His lifelong interest in the theatre and poetry was evidence that he had never abandoned his commitment to the belief that art and literature are an essential part of our emotional lives and contribute to our psychological development. He continued to think that it should be possible to include these issues in the study of development.

Possibly by the early 1930s Vygotsky, who was now less involved with psychological research, and was working more independently of his former colleagues, was drawn to some of the larger subjects that he wanted to explore. The colleagues who had left Moscow for Kharkov were less interested in these subjects; indeed they may have regarded them as dangerous. Zavershneva observes in relation to Vygotsky's larger vision of psychology: 'But that was what was dangerous about Vygotsky's ideas: he was always focused on studying the "internal"' (Zavershneva, 2010, p. 70).

Leontiev and others of Vygotsky's colleagues were dubious about the place that he was giving to consciousness and emotion in his later papers. Their attitude towards some of his later work was ambivalent or uncomprehending and they distanced themselves from it.

For by then Vygotsky and Luria had been accused of having 'constantly been captive [to] … "fashionable" bourgeois psychological movements and perverting the tenets of Marxism' (quoted in Zavershneva, 2010, p. 80) for their *Studies on the history of behaviour* (Vygotsky and Luria, 1993). An article in the journal

Pedology in 1932 by a writer named Feofanov attacked Vygotsky directly and at length, distorting his statements and misunderstanding his theories. Van der Veer and Valsiner sum up:

> Vygotsky's views were deemed to be 'abstract' and Feofanov concluded that they gave 'an incorrect view of the development of the Soviet child' and had 'a harmful influence on the practice of our education'.
>
> (Van der Veer and Valsiner, 1991, p. 380)

In 1933 Vygotsky wrote in a letter to Luria that a commission was investigating his work, but that he believed that there would be a chance to continue it. In another letter to Luria he reported: 'I am endlessly being interrogated and pulled about' (ibid., p. 381).

These external pressures explain the context in which Vygotsky was writing his papers on play, the imagination and creativity. His deep commitment to these themes was partly due to his conviction that they should be given a proper place in a theory of mental and emotional development. But it was also a reflection of his priorities as the teacher that he had never ceased to be. The work on play and imagination had direct implications for teaching; Vygotsky envisaged a school curriculum in which the arts and the imagination were central to learning. This is particularly so in the next text that we shall consider.

Imagination and creativity in childhood

This text is longer than the others we have been considering in this chapter. It's really an accessible short book, or monograph, with chapters. It was published during Vygotsky's lifetime by GIZ, a state publisher, and as a journal article in 2004 (Vygotsky, 2004). It is also available in the Marxist Archive (see reference list).

Imagination and creativity in childhood is an accessible text, written for a wider audience than others in this chapter, and it has a pedagogic rather than a psychological perspective. Although it includes references to works of psychology, many more references are to books about children's art and creativity. It seems likely that teachers were the intended audience; Vygotsky was undertaking a good deal of writing for correspondence courses for teachers and this may have been part of such a project.

However, though not a specialist work, this study begins with a detailed account of how imagination is the product of retentive memory of past experiences on the one hand, and of combinatorial or creative activity on the other. To explain retentive memory Vygotsky draws an analogy with the way that soft earth retains the imprint of a wheel moving along a track. This he links to the 'plasticity of the neural substance' in the brain, which also readily retains impressions of experience. To explain the brain's creative activity Vygotsky suggests that we all constantly combine elements of our previous experience in new ways, imagining things that have never been:

It is precisely human creative activity that makes the human being a creature oriented towards the future, creating the future, and thus altering his own present.

(Vygotsky, 2004, p. 9)

So imagination is not just about fantasy, it is also a component of artistic, scientific and technical creation.

Vygotsky takes a scene from a work by Pushkin to show how fairy tales and fantasy are always drawn from reality. In this scene a green oak, girded by a golden chain, stands by a bow-shaped shore. A learned cat, leashed by the chain, goes walking round the oak in circles.

When he goes right he sings a folk song, when he goes left a tale he tells. What wonders there: the wood sprite wanders, a mermaid sits on a bough; strange creatures stalk forgotten trails; a hut stands there on chicken legs that has no windows and no door.

(Vygotsky, 2004, p. 14)

We all know, says Vygotsky, that despite the strange fantastic impression the scene makes, every single element in it is taken from reality; it is their combination that is fantastic. This is how the creative imagination combines memories and experiences to make new images.

Vygotsky is anxious not to present creativity as a possession of a few gifted individuals; he wants to make clear that 'an enormous percentage of what has been created by humanity is a product of the anonymous collective created work of unknown inventors' (ibid., p. 11). Creative processes are common to everyone and are manifest from earliest childhood.

Vygotsky regards creativity as one of the most important areas of child development. In his description of play, he brings in the example of the stick-horse again, but he also refers to other play situations with children imagining themselves as mothers, pirates or soldiers. Their play is often 'an echo' of adults' behaviour, but it is never just a reproduction, it is a creative reworking of impressions, for children's own purposes. In the examples Vygotsky gives, the combinatorial element in children's imaginative play is clear.

Vygotsky goes on to explore how imagination develops. It is always based on elements from reality and so its richness depends on the range and depth of experience:

the implication of this for education is that, if we want to build a relatively strong foundation for a child's creativity, what we must do is broaden the experiences we provide him with.

(Vygotsky, 2004, p. 15)

But imagination can also benefit from the products of *other* people's experience, as expressed through their writing and other artefacts. This is the main way in which we learn about things beyond our own limited experience and enlarge our worlds. Through books and stories (and now through film and television) we can travel through space and experience places, like the African desert, that we may never see in real life. And we can go back in time, reading accounts and seeing pictures of historical events like the French Revolution, which then become part of our store of virtual experiences. So imagination is based on experience, but in addition experience is enhanced by the imagination.

Imagination and emotion

Vygotsky now looks more deeply into the inner relationship between imagination and emotion. He suggests that the imagination draws on stored mental images that suggest particular moods, and these become 'an internal language for our emotion' (Vygotsky, 2004, p. 18). He quotes the psychologist Ribot saying that 'All forms of creative imagination include affective elements' (ibid., p. 19). He explains that this means 'every construct of the imagination has an effect on our feelings, and if this construct does not in itself correspond to reality, nonetheless the feelings it evokes are real feelings' (ibid.). He insists that 'the emotions that take hold of us from the artistic images on the pages of books or from the stage are completely real and we experience them truly, seriously, and deeply' (ibid., p. 20). This argument is strongly reminiscent of his discussion of literature and drama in *The psychology of art* (Vygotsky, 1971).

And finally in this exploration of the further development of the imagination, Vygotsky suggests that the imagination can actually *become* reality. This happens whenever the imagination is externally embodied and given material form; this 'crystallised imagination' then begins to actually exist in the world and affect people. Examples of this process include machines, tools, technical equipment, and innumerable products of human ingenuity and skill. But of course they also include products of the imagination: plays, music, works of art. Such works, once they are made to actually exist in the world, become part of reality, part of our experience and can also affect us 'truly, seriously and deeply'.

So there is a *cycle* whereby experience, imagination and emotion come together in the artist/writer during the making of a work of art – which then, when it has taken material form, becomes a real experience for those who see, hear or read. As we respond to artworks, they operate on our imaginations and affect us emotionally.

Vygotsky looks in more depth at the development of the imagination in children and at the 'conditions for creation'. He reflects on the skills and 'combinatorial abilities' that they need in order to create imaginative works. The development of these skills will depend of course on their experience – both their direct experience and their experience of any 'creative models' that they encounter. It will also depend on their technical abilities and how far they are helped to practise and develop them, and on the traditions in their communities. The influence of the environment, in the broadest sense, will be decisive.

Vygotsky emphasises the socio-historical aspect of the development of science, art and technology:

> Every inventor, even a genius, is also a product of his time and his environment ... No invention or scientific discovery can occur before the material and psychological conditions necessary for it to occur have appeared. Creation is a historical, cumulative process where every succeeding manifestation was determined by the preceding one.
>
> (Vygotsky, 2004, p. 30)

In later chapters Vygotsky considers how imagination changes and goes on changing through life, always according to changes in experience, in the environment, and in individual needs and drives. Although children's imagination is sometimes thought of as being richer and more diverse than that of adults, he observes that this has not been confirmed by objective study. Adults have wider experience and the possibility of achieving more complex imaginative transformations of experience than children have. The imagination, like other aspects of mind, *develops*, and only becomes fully mature in adults. In adolescence, however, the imagination is greatly stimulated and becomes a major means of expressing the growth and deepening of internal life at this age. Later in life, creative imagination may diminish as people 'get lost in the prose of everyday life'. But Vygotsky stresses that the creative imagination does not disappear completely in anyone; creativity is 'the province of everyone to one degree or another' (ibid., p. 35).

The three chapters that end the book deal with children's writing, dramatic art, and drawing. All give actual examples of children's work in these areas, with some references to work in classrooms. These are probably now mainly of historical interest, but they show Vygotsky's strong belief that the job of teaching includes developing in the child the creative urge that all children have.

In ch. 6, on 'Literary creativity in school-age children', which begins with a discussion of the beginnings of writing in young children's drawing, Vygotsky says that the key element in teaching writing is 'the proper development of the powers of the young author himself ... The best stimulus of creativity in children is to organize their life and environment so that it leads to the need and ability to create' (ibid., pp. 65–66). As an example, he refers to a class magazine written and organised entirely by children, the value of which is 'that it brings children's creative writing closer to children's life. The children begin to understand why a person would want to write. Writing becomes a meaningful and necessary task for them' (ibid., p. 66).

Vygotsky stresses the value of such writing experiences:

> The sense and significance of these creative endeavours lies only in the fact
> that they allow the child to make the sharp turn in the development of the
> creative imagination … one that persists throughout the rest of his life. Its
> significance lies in the fact that it deepens, expands, and purifies the child's
> emotional life, which for the first time is awakened and tuned to a serious
> key. Finally, it is important because it permits the child, by exercising his
> creative tendencies and skills, to master human language, this extremely
> subtle and complex tool for forming and expressing human thoughts,
> human feelings, and the human inner world.
>
> (Vygotsky, 2004, p. 69)

This long chapter contains some of Vygotsky's most deeply felt views on the
teaching of writing.

The next chapter, about theatrical creativity in school-age children, has some
authentic examples of what Vygotsky calls 'the drive for action for embodiment,
for realization' that is fulfilled by imitation and acting out. Vygotsky is convinced
that:

> Drama, more than any other form of creation, is closely and directly linked
> to play, which is the root of all creativity in children. Thus drama is the
> most syncretic mode of creation, that is, it contains elements of the most
> diverse forms of creativity.
>
> (Vygotsky, 2004, p. 71)

Again, in his descriptions of school practice, Vygotsky sees plays written by the
children themselves, or created and improvised by them, as much more
important than starting with a literary text, or trying to reproduce the forms of
adult theatre. One of the values of this kind of drama is that it gives different
roles and responsibilities to all children, involving them all in its creation. The
power of both play and dramatisation is 'this active way of portraying events
with one's own body' (ibid., p. 74) in a way linked to the child's imagination.

Finally, Vygotsky considers children's drawing, from its beginnings to adolescence. Vygotsky is known to have had a personal collection of children's
drawings and some of them are reproduced in an appendix at the end of the
book. In this final chapter he writes more as a psychologist and less as a teacher;
although his observations about the stages of development in children's drawing are of interest, they tell us less about teaching and learning. The problem
that he sees for art education is that 'on the one hand we need to cultivate
creative imagination; on the other hand, a special culture is needed for the
process of embodying the images created by the imagination' (ibid., p. 84).
Young people need to master the materials. 'Only by cultivating this mastery of
the material can we ensure that children's drawing is on the right

developmental path for their age' (ibid.). He is less concerned with the education of the class as a whole here, and more focused on the development of individuals and their mastery of techniques and conventions.

However, Vygotsky ends the book with a strong statement of principle:

> In conclusion we should emphasise the particular importance of cultivating creativity in school-age children. The entire future of humanity will be attained through the creative imagination: orientation to the future, behaviour based on the future and derived from this future, is the most important function of the imagination. To the extent that the main educational objective of teaching is guidance of school children's behaviour so as to prepare them for the future, development and exercise of the imagination should be one of the main forces enlisted for the attainment of this goal.
>
> (Vygotsky, 2004, pp. 87–88)

In these four texts Vygotsky makes an argument for an education which is concerned with children's affective development as well as their cognitive development, and one in which their creativity is recognised and fostered. Yet neither *Imagination and creativity in childhood* nor 'Play and its role in the mental development of the child' was included in Vygotsky's *Collected works*. This was presumably for the same reason that *The psychology of art* was omitted; they were not thought to be psychological texts. Unfortunately Vygotsky's thought has been consistently misrepresented by the omission from mainstream publications and commentaries of some of his major themes and preoccupations.

Note

1 See the discussion of the terms 'proximal' and 'proximate' in the Introduction.

References

Bruner, J., Jolly, A. and Sylva, K. (eds) (1976). *Play: its role in development and evolution.* New York: Basic Books.
El'konin, D.B. (1998). 'Epilogue', in Vygotsky, L.S., *The collected works of L.S. Vygotsky. Volume 5, Child psychology*, pp. 297–317. Rieber, R.W. (ed.). New York: Plenum Press.
Van der Veer, R. and Valsiner, J. (1991). *Understanding Vygotsky: a quest for synthesis.* Oxford: Blackwell.
Vygotsky, L.S. (1971). *The psychology of art.* Intro. A.N. Leontiev; commentary V.V. Ivanov. Cambridge, MA: MIT Press.
Vygotsky, L.S. (1978). *Mind in society.* Cole, M., John-Steiner, V., Scribner, S. and Souberman, E. (eds). Cambridge, MA: Harvard University Press.
Vygotsky, L.S. (1987). 'Lecture 5. Imagination and its development in childhood' [1932], in Vygotsky, L.S., *The collected works of L.S. Vygotsky. Volume 1, Problems of general psychology*, pp. 339–349. Trans. and intro. N. Minick; Rieber, R.W. and Carton, A.S. (eds). New York: Plenum Press.

Vygotsky, L.S. (1998a). 'Early childhood' [1932–1934], in Vygotsky, L.S., *The collected works of L.S. Vygotsky. Volume 5, Child psychology*, pp. 261–281. Rieber, R.W. (ed.). New York: Plenum Press.

Vygotsky, L.S. (1998b). 'Imagination and creativity in the adolescent' [1931], in 'Pedology of the adolescent', in Vygotsky, L.S., *The collected works of L.S. Vygotsky. Volume 5, Child psychology*, pp. 151–166. Rieber, R.W. (ed.). New York: Plenum Press.

Vygotsky, L.S. (2004). *Imagination and creativity in childhood* [1930]. *Journal of Russian and East European Psychology*, 42(1), pp. 7–97. Also available online in the Marxist Archive: www.marxists.org/archive/vygotsky/works/1927/imagination.pdf

Vygotsky, L.S. (2016). 'Play and its role in the mental development of the child' [1933]. Trans. N. Veresov and M. Barrs. *International Research in Early Childhood Education*, 7(2), pp. 3–25.

Vygotsky, L.S. and Luria, A.R. (1993). *Studies on the history of behaviour: ape, primitive, child* [1930]. Hillsdale, NJ: Lawrence Erlbaum Associates.

Vygotsky, L.S. and Luria, A.R. (1994). *Tool and symbol in child development* [1930], in Van der Veer, R. and Valsiner, J. (eds), *The Vygotsky reader*, pp. 99–174. Oxford: Blackwell.

Zavershneva, E. (2010). '"The way to freedom" (On the publication of documents from the family archive of Lev Vygotsky)'. *Journal of Russian and East European Psychology*, 48(1), pp. 61–90.

Zavershneva, E. and Van der Veer, R. (eds) (2018). *Vygotsky's notebooks: a selection.* Singapore: Springer.

Chapter 9

The zone of proximal/proximate development

A personal prologue

Vygotsky's article on 'The problem of teaching and mental development at school age' ('*Problema obučenija i umstvennogo razvitija v škol'nom vozraste*') was the first chapter in a posthumously published book of his writings entitled *Umstvennoe razvitie detej v processe obučenija* (*Children's mental development in the process of learning/teaching*; Vygotsky, 1935). It is probably the best known and most cited of all his works translated into English, but is generally known by a different title: 'Interaction between learning and development'. It appeared under this title (in a substantially edited form) as ch. 6 of *Mind in society*, a collection of Vygotsky's works published in 1978.

This chapter has been the main point of reference in English for all discussions of Vygotsky's concept of the zone of proximal/proximate development, frequently referred to as the ZPD. But over the past forty years it has become apparent that *Mind in society* contains many examples of highly interventive editing that affect the sense or obscure the point of the text. Some of the 'chapters' in *Mind in society* are truncated extracts from Vygotsky's work – such as the first three chapters, which are all taken from *Tool and symbol* (Vygotsky and Luria, 1994). In these cases the overall argument that the extracts were part of is lost.

In other cases the editors imported extracts from other sources. For instance, ch. 4 of *Mind in society*, said by the editors to be taken from *Tool and symbol*, was in fact made up of extracts from two different chapters in *The history of the development of higher mental functions* (Vygotsky, 1997a), which is the main text in volume 4 of the *Collected works* (Vygotsky, 1997). Joseph Glick pointed out in his introduction to this volume that the interventive editing of *Mind in society* had the effect of rewriting the original as a contemporary text:

> The processes of editing, clarifying, reducing seeming redundancies, eliminating polemical arguments of no contemporary interest and constructing volumes out of other volumes cannot but help to mold an author into a contemporary voice. *The judgments of what is dated, what is redundant, what is unclear, and in what terms, are contemporary judgments, and, as is inevitable,*

DOI: 10.4324/9780429203046-9

*contemporary construction addresses contemporary needs and understandings of what
the core problems are.*

(Glick, 1997, p. xii)

In 2010 I had been working on an article about *Tool and symbol* and was in
correspondence with Nikolai Veresov, whose *Undiscovered Vygotsky* (Veresov,
1999) I had read and admired. As a consequence of my work on *Tool and symbol*
I had become acutely aware of the failings of *Mind in society* to represent
Vygotsky's work fully. As far as I could ascertain, there was no recent translation
of the article about the ZPD, which appeared in *Mind in society* as ch. 6, and this
seemed to me to be a matter of concern. I was doubtful about how faithful the
Mind in society translation was to Vygotsky's original text. Might a new translation
throw more light on the ZPD, which had come to be seen as Vygotsky's signature concept? I asked Nikolai Veresov if he would be able to find a copy of
the 1935 text. Soon afterwards, Nikolai kindly sent me a scan of it.

At that point I had to obtain a very good translation. Fortunately I was able
to make contact with Stanley Mitchell, a Russian scholar and academic who
had recently translated Pushkin's *Eugene Onegin* into English for Penguin
Books. Mitchell agreed to take on the translation and completed it that
summer. I compared his new translation line by line with the chapter in *Mind
in society*, and discussed some points of difference with him. Chief among
these was the translation of '*obuchenie*', which in *Mind in society* was translated
as 'learning' but which Mitchell translated as 'teaching' or sometimes as
'education'. I had expected this; the word is an acknowledged crux in translating from Russian, as '*obuchenie*' can mean 'teaching' or 'learning' or
'teaching/learning' – it describes a two-sided process. However, Mitchell was
adamant that in this context the word should only be translated as 'learning' if
it meant 'learning with a teacher'.

My comparison of the two texts showed that *Mind in society* rarely used the
term 'teaching', generally preferring 'learning'. Moreover, when the use of
'teaching' was necessary in a sentence to keep to the sense of the argument,
Mind in society sometimes omitted the sentence altogether. This skewed the
meaning. The differences between the translations radically altered some of the
most familiar quotations from *Mind in society*.

For instance, the famous sentence 'Thus the notion of a zone of proximal
development allows us to propound a new formula, namely that the only
"good learning" is that which is in advance of development' (Vygotsky, 1978,
p. 89) now read, in the Mitchell translation, 'We have no hesitation after all
that has been said in stating the essential characteristic of teaching to be the
creation of the zone of proximate development' (Vygotsky, 2017, p. 368).

The other change of wording that stands out in the Mitchell translation is his
use of the word 'proximate' and not 'proximal'. As Luciano Mecacci (2017)
explains, there was no real point in the use of the word 'proximal' in *Mind in
society*. It was an obscure term from anatomy – the Russian original

('*blizhayshego*') simply means 'nearest', and the equivalent of 'proximate' was the translation used in other languages (e.g. '*zona di sviluppo prossimo*' in Italian). Mitchell (who had not seen the *Mind in society* version) had chosen 'proximate' as the most appropriate translation.

But these were not the only points of difference between the two texts. There were many omissions, insertions, and changes of emphasis in the *Mind in society* text. Some insertions came from other Vygotskyan texts, notably *The history of the development of higher mental functions* (Vygotsky, 1997a). One very long inserted passage – of over two pages – came from a different source, 'The dynamics of the schoolchild's mental development in relation to teaching and learning', which I could not identify as a source until Alex Kozulin's translation of it (Vygotsky, 2011) was published. Mitchell's new translation showed that this insertion completely interrupted the line of Vygotsky's thought in the article. Directly after introducing the concept of the ZPD, Vygotsky originally went on to say:

> Here we come straight to the central concept that is necessary for defining the zone of proximate development. This central concept is in turn linked with a reconsideration of the problem of imitation in contemporary psychology.
>
> (Vygotsky, 2017, p. 366)

And as well as these variants from the original text, there were also substantial other changes in the *Mind in society* version, principally the omission of several references to pedagogy and all references to pedology.

When the new translation and my commentary on it were published in 2017, I summed up the most important points highlighted by the new translation as follows:

> The Mitchell text, by its translation of the word '*obuchenie*' as 'teaching' and its inclusion of several previously omitted references to pedagogy, continually shifts the focus of the article from learning to teaching. It makes clear that part of Vygotsky's interest in the ZPD was to develop a more informed pedagogy – a science of teaching.
>
> By its greater emphasis on the central role of imitation in children's learning, which was underplayed or omitted in *Mind in society*, the new version links Vygotsky's ideas in this chapter to his writings about play and drama. It presents imitation as a natural and positive strategy for learning.
>
> Finally the new translation restores all of Vygotsky's original references to pedology as a science of children's development, and potentially a way of observing 'the processes of development as they occur in the head of each child'.
>
> (Barrs, 2017, p. 346)

Vygotsky ends the article with a statement of faith in the future of pedological research:

The task of pedological research in this sphere is the determination of the inner structure of school subjects from the point of view of the child's development and the change that takes place in this structure along with methods of school education.

We believe that together with this hypothesis we have introduced into pedology the potential for a boundless field of concrete research, which can alone solve our problem in all its plenitude.

(Vygotsky, 2017, p. 370)

It has become apparent from Mitchell's new translation, which restores the above passage as well as several others, that this article should be read as belonging to Vygotsky's considerable body of work in pedology. As Seth Chaiklin has indicated in his meticulous survey of the versions and inter-pretations of the ZPD, 'the zone of proximal development … must be related to development' (Chaiklin, 2003, p. 43).

The ZPD example in the Mitchell translation

At this point in the chapter it will probably be helpful to refer to Mitchell's translation of the most famous passage from this article, the (hypothetical) example that Vygotsky gives to explain the zone of proximal/proximate development:

> Imagine that we have examined two children and set their mental age at seven. This would mean that each child is capable of solving problems accessible to seven-year-olds. However when we try to move these children on with further tests we find a serious difference between them. One child, with the help of leading questions, examples, demonstrations, will easily answer the tests that are two years in advance of its developmental level. The second child will be able to answer tests that are only six months in advance of its level.
>
> (Vygotsky, 2017, pp. 365–366)

There follows the substantial passage about imitation, before a reiteration of the definition of the ZPD:

> Take the example just quoted. We have two children of an equal mental age, seven, but one of them with a minimum of help solves the problem of a nine-year-old, while the other reaches only seven and a half. Is the mental development of these two children the same? From the point of view of the independent activity it is the same, but from the point of view of proximate possibility it differs sharply. What the child is able to do with the help of an adult points to its zone of proximate development. This means that with the help of this method we can take into consideration

not only the process of development up to the present moment, not only the cycles completed, not only the processes of maturation, but also those processes which are taking place now and are beginning to grow and develop. What the child can do today with the help of adults, it will be able to carry out tomorrow on its own. In this way the zone of proximate development will help us to define tomorrow's achievements and the dynamics of the child's development, taking into account not only what it has already mastered, but also its process of growth.

(Vygotsky, 2017, p. 366)

A comparison of this translation with the better-known passage in ch. 6 of *Mind in society* reveals some significant differences. The most obvious of these is the ages of the children; whereas the Mitchell translation states that the children have a mental age of seven years, the corresponding passage in *Mind in society* speaks of 'two children ... both of whom are ten years old chronologically and eight years old in terms of mental development' (Vygotsky, 1978, p. 85). Vygotsky varies the ages of the children in some of his presentations of this concept, and we shall later explore where the *Mind in society* version may have come from.

A comparison with *Mind in society* will also show that in the Mitchell translation the role of assessment is more prominent. As Kellogg and Veresov note in their discussion of the ZPD: 'the purpose of the ZPD is not to facilitate teaching, but rather to diagnose development. In short, the ZPD is not pedagogical but pedological' (in Vygotsky, 2019, p. 154).

The ZPD and pedology

The zone of proximal/proximate development is Vygotsky's best-known concept (type it into Google and you get about seventeen million mentions) but it is also 'perhaps one of the most used and least understood constructs to appear in contemporary educational literature' (Palinscar, 1998, p. 370).

One reason for the many different interpretations that have been drawn from Vygotsky's explanation of this concept may be that he stated it in a variety of ways, emphasising different aspects of it in different publications. We shall consider some of these different statements in publications dated between 1932 and 1934.

Another reason for the disparity between later interpretations may simply be that Vygotsky left certain important aspects of the implementation of his theory unclear. Seth Chaiklin refers to the 'somewhat underspecified nature of the original formulation' (Chaiklin, 2003, p. 59).

It may be helpful at this point to consider how this important concept relates to pedology, and the situation for pedology at the time when it was formulated. This will involve us in revisiting some of the material discussed in Chapter 7.

We know that pedology had been promoted strongly from the late 1920s by the Commissariat for Education, as a way of supporting teachers in Soviet schools. Pedologists were expected to provide expertise particularly in relation to difficult pupils, pupils in need of special education, streaming and the use of testing. The trademark of pedology was widely seen as mental testing.

From 1930 the Commissariat for Education came under the aegis of the Communist Party. Initially the Commissariat maintained its supportive stance towards pedology; indeed in 1931 the Commissariat called for every district to have at least one person 'with pedological training' to work in schools. But from about 1932 onwards there was a growing backlash against pedologists. Their use of intelligence tests came in for particular criticism. There was an increasing tendency for pedologists to recommend that 'difficult children' be included with 'defective' children in special schools on the basis of their test scores; in Moscow pedologists identified 4000 children, about 1% of all those enrolled, for special schools. Pedologists were also blamed for consigning a disproportionate number of working-class children to special schools, and for not succeeding in the general social aim of 'rapid, massive and coercive social transformation' (Ewing, 2001, p. 479).

Schneuwly and Leopoldoff-Martin (2011, p. 14) suggest: 'For Vygotsky and for most of the scholars involved in the discipline the institutional refuge of pedology seems to find its limits in 1932.' Certainly by 1932–1934, the time when Vygotsky wrote his main papers on the ZPD, the growing hostility to pedology and to mental testing would have been unignorable.

In 1931 the Party's Central Committee called for struggle against deviations from Marxism-Leninism in science, and Stalin published an open letter calling for the fight for Party loyalty in science (Byford, 2020, pp. 211–212). This led to a general wave of criticism and self-criticism for perceived 'distortions'. The journal *Pedologija* invited pedologists to classify their 'grave mistakes' under labels such as 'mechano-Lamarckism', 'Freudian–Adlerian distortions' and others. In a journal editorial from 1931 Vygotsky was criticised as follows:

> Sharply expressed eclecticism can be seen in the work of Vygotsky, who has united in his theory of cultural development behaviourism and reactology with Gestalt-psychology that is idealistic in its roots.
> (Quoted in Van der Veer and Valsiner, 1991, p. 304)

Finally, in July 1936, two years after Vygotsky's death, the Central Committee issued a decree 'On pedological distortions in the system of Narkompros [the Commissariat for Education]' which banned the practice of pedology and all its institutions and publications, among which were included many works by Vygotsky. The Central Committee asserted that pedological theory was based on 'falsely scientific and anti-Marxist foundations' and was assigning an 'ever larger and larger number of children' to special schools, even though many of them 'were perfectly capable of attending normal schools' (Ewing, 2001, p. 480).

Vygotsky, of course, had always spoken out against the widespread use of mental testing in assessment, and had emphasised the need for more sophisticated and holistic ways of looking at children's progress in school. His theory of the ZPD was surely intended to introduce a much more dynamic and future-oriented dimension into the field of educational assessment, and also to create strong links between the study of development and the practice of teaching. But the fact that Vygotsky refers, in the *Mind in society*-edited example of the ZPD, to two ten-year-old boys, both with mental ages of eight years, and their ability to solve, with some support, tasks suitable for (in the one case) twelve-year-old students and (in the other case) nine-year-olds, has meant that he has tied his theory from the outset to existing standardised measures (Vygotsky, 1978, pp. 85–86).

Kellogg and Veresov point out (in Vygotsky, 2019, p. 152) that the 'tasks' referred to are most likely to be ones such as Binet and Simon produced in 1907 for 'abnormal' children. And the children's 'mental ages' were surely calculated in relation to a test such as the ubiquitous Binet/Simon IQ test. Thus, whatever new territory the ZPD theory marks out – and of course it does – the anchoring points of Vygotsky's statement of it still come from conventional mental testing.

Vygotsky had always derided Binet's traditional method of assessment, such as his developmental scale for establishing mental age. Such methods, he said, were 'basically limited to characterising a child in an exclusively negative fashion' (Vygotsky, 1993b, p. 253). He rejected the 'mechanical and arithmetic analysis of external symptoms' (ibid., p. 277) used by Binet. The translators of volume 2 of the *Collected works* indeed suggest in a footnote that his criticism of Soviet pedology, because of its concentration on measuring IQ, was actually in agreement with early Stalinist criticism (ibid., translators' footnote). It is therefore more than surprising to see the Binet/Simon tests and tasks used to underpin the ZPD assessment.

Vygotsky clearly intended the ZPD to become a new way of recognising the differences between children's potential capabilities and making those differences count in assessment. He may possibly have recognised a need for developing new tasks and tests to take the place of Binet/Simon tests in this assessment model. In his chapter on 'The problem of cultural age' (Vygotsky, 1997b) in *The history of the development of higher mental functions*, he imagines a kind of measurement of the transition from 'organic development' to 'cultural development', based on 'measuring relative indicators', which would enable a scale of cultural development to be developed, one which would yield 'equal, although abstract units' (ibid., p. 236).

The ZPD was very much a product of Vygotsky's work in pedology which – as we can see from his notebooks from the EDI clinic – used a battery of mental testing as well as teachers' observations and records, interviews with children and parents, sampling, reflective conversations between members of the EDI team, and other evidence to arrive at a diagnosis. Had pedology survived as a discipline, the ZPD would undoubtedly have been developed further and become an essential professional tool for diagnosis.

Different statements of the ZPD in Vygotsky's work

Chaiklin (2003), in his review of the different statements of the ZPD, identifies eight places where the ZPD is discussed, not all of which are available in English. I will consider five of these statements, in each of which there is a slightly different emphasis. Some of them have already been mentioned in the course of this book. In each case the context of the discussion influences the emphasis given to the concept.

'Play and its role in the mental development of the child' (2016)

The treatment of the ZPD in this lecture is quite different from any other because it refers to preschool children. In general the ZPD is always taken to refer to development and learning 'at school age' (i.e. from ages 7 to 12)[1] and to formal learning in school. Yet here, in an unexpected move, Vygotsky suggests that:

> play also creates the zone of proximal development of the child. In play a child is always above his average age, above his daily behaviour; in play it is as though he were a head taller than himself ... The play–development relationship can be compared with the instruction–development relationship, but play provides changes in needs and in consciousness of a much wider nature. Play is the source of development and creates the zone of proximal development.
>
> (Vygotsky, 2016, p. 18)

Other references to the zone of proximal/proximate development refer to its appearance only in situations where the child is working with a teacher, or with a more able/experienced peer. Yet in many of the play situations that Vygotsky describes in this lecture the child is involved in solo imaginative play. Vygotsky seems almost to be implying here that, in this kind of play, a child can become his own 'other' and create his own zone of proximal/proximate development. Play creates the possibility of becoming 'a head taller', of going beyond one's normal behaviour. This relates to Vygotsky's description of play as a 'leading activity' at this stage of development.

'The problem of age' (1998)

The next statement of the ZPD to be considered is from Vygotsky's text 'The problem of age'. Here the ZPD is part of an overall survey of his theory of child development, in which relatively stable periods are interrupted by periods of 'crisis', marked by 'neoformations' or new leading forms of behaviour. These critical periods act as transitions to new stable periods, where there has been a reconstruction of the child's personality as a consequence of the development of neoformations.

After Vygotsky's explanation of age periods, in a section on 'The problem of age and the dynamics of development' (Vygotsky, 1998, p. 199), we come to a statement of the ZPD, the aim of which is to explain how development can be assessed. Most of the statement is familiar; the ZPD is presented as a more positive and effective alternative to mental testing. Its relationship to imitation is explained, the hypothetical example used to illustrate it is identical to that used in some other ZPD texts, and it is quite closely related to teaching:

> the optimum time for teaching both the group and each individual child is established at each age by their zone of proximal development.
>
> (Vygotsky, 1998, p. 204)

In this pedological text there is more concern about the possible misuse of testing, and more emphasis on interpretation. Vygotsky quotes Gesell (a psychologist who developed a theory of maturation and development) as saying that we must not only measure the child, we must interpret him (ibid.). Data are not simply to be recorded, but critically and carefully interpreted.

'The problem of teaching and mental development at school age' (2017)

This is probably the most comprehensive stand-alone statement of the theory of the ZPD, and is the paper discussed earlier in this chapter. When we compare it with the other statements of the ZPD we see that its difference arises from the fact that its main focus is on pedagogy. Vygotsky criticises the existing relationship between developmental testing and teaching, which results in teaching orienting itself 'towards yesterday, towards stages that have already been gone through and completed'. But he is able to point to evidence from defectology and elsewhere to support his claim that teaching 'oriented towards yesterday' (Vygotsky, 2017, p. 367) is ineffectual and mistaken.

In the teaching of 'mentally backward children' he observes that there used to be a tendency to exclude anything to do with abstract thinking. There was widespread use of visual aids but no attempt to go beyond this kind of visual thinking. Children were not given the chance to develop any form of abstract thinking – yet the task of the school should be precisely 'to develop what by itself will remain inadequate' (ibid.). Similarly in the 'complex system' (the 'project method' of teaching based on the Dalton Plan which was briefly popular in Russia) there was no attempt to teach systematic forms of thinking.

These examples, Vygotsky maintains, provide exact parallels for what happens in mainstream schools when teaching is oriented only to completed cycles of development. The theory of the zone of proximal/proximate development supports the opposite view; it states that 'the only good method of teaching is that which runs ahead of development' (ibid.).

Vygotsky argues that just as 'higher psychic (mental) functions' develop in social relationships (as inter-psychic functions) and then as individual activities (as intra-psychic functions), in the same way a teaching approach directed towards developing processes can enable children to go much further than might be predicted on the basis of mental tests. He sees the 'essential characteristic of teaching to be the creation of the zone of proximate development' (ibid., p. 368).

Vygotsky maintains that 'the very lines of school education awaken inner processes of development'. He argues for further research in the internalisation of learning:

> To show how outward meaning and outward ability in the child become inward is a primary object for pedagogical research.
>
> (Vygotsky, 2017, p. 369)

So, while this is a pedological paper, the focus (in the Mitchell translation) is more clearly on pedagogy than in other statements of the ZPD. The omission of most references to teaching in the *Mind in society* version of this text was seriously misleading.

'The dynamics of the schoolchild's mental development in relation to teaching and learning' (2011)

This was the second chapter in the posthumously published 1935 book by Vygotsky. It is a detailed exposition of the ZPD, seen in the context of mental testing and school achievement. It covers issues such as the diagnostics of mental development, the relationship between actual and relative achievement, the concept of the ZPD, the relation between the ZPD and the optimal conditions for learning, and the use of the ZPD for grouping and the composition of classes.

Early in the paper Vygotsky begins his discussion of relative achievement by referring to special schools, where all the students are *absolute* underachievers but some have normal or high *relative* achievement, relating to how much their performance has improved over a period in school. Vygotsky suggests that only those children who display not only absolute but also relative underachievement should be referred to special education. The others are capable of benefiting from normal schooling.

Vygotsky then proceeds to explain the ZPD with the example of the two boys who have the same mental age of eight (two years lower than their chronological age) but who achieve differently on the same tests/tasks with the help of demonstrations, prompts, or leading questions. In these circumstances one is capable of solving tasks designed for twelve-year-olds, and the other can solve tasks designed for nine-year-olds. The gap between their level of actual development and their level of possible development defines their ZPD. The statement of the ZPD in this paper is extremely specific and the ages of the boys are identical to those in *Mind in society*. It seems likely that this example was excerpted and used by the *Mind in society* editors *instead of* the statement found in 'The problem of teaching and mental development at school age', when they 'constructed' the chapter 'Interaction between learning and development'.

Vygotsky goes on to cite a series of cases to illuminate various uses of the ZPD. In the first example he reminds us that children with the same IQ can have unequal ZPDs. So a child can have a high IQ and a large ZPD, a high IQ and a small ZPD, a low IQ and a large ZPD or a low IQ and a small ZPD. Vygotsky asks us to 'imagine that I select four students to follow their mental development during school study and their relative achievements' (Vygotsky, 2011, p. 205). Each student belongs to one of these four categories. He then reveals that these categories were used in an actual study:

> We took as an example just four students, but the study was carried out on a massive scale, so one could have taken 40, 400 or even 4000 students as long as they could be divided into these four groups.
>
> (Vygotsky, 2011, p. 206)

The results of the study showed that the ZPD was more important and influential than IQ for assessing students' relative achievement:

> In short for the dynamics of mental development and for school achievement, those functions that are in the process of maturation are more essential than those that are already well developed ...
>
> (Vygotsky, 2011, p. 206)

Vygotsky stresses the importance of the educational applications of this theory. It can help with:

> diagnosis, the selection of the mentally retarded, evaluation of achievement and underachievement – both global and partial – identification of latent achievement of failing students, problems of class composition.
>
> (Vygotsky, 2011, p. 210)

He suggests that homogeneous groupings are an essential feature of optimal learning, and that the most effective form of grouping is that which uses the ZPD as a grouping principle. There is little reference to pedagogy.

In the course of the paper Vygotsky is forceful about the importance of not referring children for special education if their relative achievement is normal or higher. He also debunks IQ tests which, he says, test family conditions rather than ability; children from cultured families do better because the tests are culturally biased. This shows his awareness of some of the contemporary criticisms of pedology.

This is a very sophisticated pedological paper in which the role of ZPD in educational assessment for diagnostic and administrative purposes is foregrounded. The issues raised in it are untypical of those we have met in most of Vygotsky's pedological texts; the focus is entirely on school achievement, viewed in relation to assessment which is underpinned by standardised measures. There is no discussion, as there generally is in Vygotsky's pedological texts, of interpretation of the assessment data in relation to other information.

Thinking and speech (1987), ch. 6

The discussion of the ZPD comes towards the end of ch. 6 in *Thinking and Speech*. This chapter is entitled 'Development of scientific concepts'. The chapter introduces Zhozefina Shif's work on concept development but also reviews the whole theory of spontaneous (or everyday) concepts, and scientific (or academic) concepts. This theory is related to, though distinct from, Piaget's theory of concept formation.

Vygotsky believes that the essential difference between spontaneous and scientific concepts comes from the fact that spontaneous concepts lack a system. Children who use them lack the 'conscious awareness and volitional control' which would enable the formation of systematic relationships. The scientific concept, on the other hand, 'presupposes a system. Scientific concepts are the gate through which conscious awareness enters the domain of the child's concepts' (Vygotsky, 1987, p. 193). The issue of scientific concepts then leads Vygotsky to his next main concern, the problem of instruction and development.

The ZPD is introduced and explained. In the predominantly educational context of this discussion Vygotsky focuses on the role of ZPD in guiding teaching. What the ZPD provides is a clear indication of the extent of the child's potential for instruction, because 'instruction is only useful when it moves ahead of development' (ibid., p. 212). Vygotsky terms instruction outside the ZPD – either above it or below it – as 'fruitless'.

Vygotsky compares the idea of the ZPD with that of the 'sensitive periods' identified by some other educators, such as Montessori. He suggests that the ZPD is the explanation for these 'sensitive periods'. They have nothing to do with biological development but are the product of social processes related to the development of higher mental functions. In general the 'school age period' (ages 7–12) is the 'sensitive period' for the development of all higher mental functions:

> The school age is the optimal period for instruction. It is a sensitive period for those subjects that depend on conscious awareness or volition in the mental functions. Consequently instruction in these subjects provides the ideal conditions for the development of the higher mental functions which are in the zone of proximal development during this period ... instruction organises their further development and partially determines their fate.
>
> (Vygotsky, 1987, p. 214)

Vygotsky goes on to say that as well as higher mental functions, scientific concepts *also* develop in the context of school instruction. So issues of the relationship between teaching and development are fundamental to the formation of higher mental functions, the ZPD and scientific concepts – which the chapter then goes on to discuss further.

Which ZPD?

The variations between these statements are striking. Obviously the treatment of the ZPD in 'Play and its role in the mental development of the child' needs to be seen in a different light from that in any of the other accounts, which all see the ZPD theory as referring to children's development and learning at school age. The differences between these other versions mainly derive from their contexts – the statement from 'The problem of age' is clearly pedological in character, whereas the statement in 'The problem of teaching and mental development at school age' is the most directly concerned with pedagogy. The statement that stands out from all the others is 'The dynamics of the schoolchild's mental development …' This narrowly assessment-focused account seems atypical of Vygotsky's usual approach to questions of development and education.

While Vygotsky's enthusiasm and conviction about the value of this theory of teaching, development and learning is evident in all these versions, the details of the methodology are sometimes blurred and there is a disappointing lack of documented evidence, especially in 'The dynamics…'. There is a sense in which the ZPD seems to be work in progress.

As I have already remarked, the ZPD is unquestionably Vygotsky's best-known concept, but is also the least well understood. It has given rise to very many diverse interpretations and most of these interpretations are based on only one version of the theory – ch. 6 of *Mind in society,* with its inaccurate translation and its interventive editing.

Joseph Glick, in his prologue to volume 4 of the *Collected works, The history of the development of higher mental functions,* remarks on the relatively small place the ZPD had in Vygotsky's theory:

> Some of the concepts with which he has been associated by modern understanding, e.g. the zone of proximal development, scarcely appear in these pages [i.e. of volume 4] … Instead the focus is on language, which was the main topic of *Thought and language* and only a subordinate topic in *Mind in society.*
>
> (Glick, 1997, p. xiii)

Glick sees Vygotsky as a 'thinker enmeshed in the core issues of developmental analysis', an aspect which is not reflected in *Mind in society.*

Margaret Gredler (2012) states that in the six volumes of Vygotsky's *Collected works* fewer than fifteen pages discuss the ZPD. Seth Chaiklin (2003) suggests that one could read the whole corpus of ZPD-related works in a few hours and become an 'expert' in Vygotsky's concept. As for the texts that I have presented in this chapter, which include some not found in the *Collected works*, they number in total about forty pages. The mismatch between the ZPD's 'relatively small place' in Vygotsky's work and the immensity of the interest that the theory has aroused is striking.

Major commentators on Vygotsky have outlined some of the problems that are presented by Vygotsky's presentation of the ZPD theory in its different statements, pointing to those aspects of the theory that are probably in need of further clarification. Other commentators have focused on the diversity of interpretations that the theory has given rise to, and the misapprehensions that have arisen around it.

Critiques of Vygotsky's presentation of the theory

The ZPD shows Vygotsky completely engaged in the field of developmental analysis. But very often Vygotsky's 'signature theory' is detached, as it was in *Mind in society*, from its context in pedology and child development, and this skews its meaning.

Several commentators, including Chaiklin and Kellogg and Veresov, have emphasised that the ZPD is *not* a ZPL – it is a concept that relates to development and not to learning. So the ZPD needs to be seen against the background of Vygotsky's theory of child development as expounded in his pedological writings. Fortunately these writings are now beginning to be published in their entirety, and not in the piecemeal fashion that was adopted in the *Collected works*, so in future it may be possible to appreciate the full complexity of Vygotsky's picture of development.

As noted earlier, Seth Chaiklin, who more than any other scholar has subjected Vygotsky's statements of the ZPD to close scrutiny, has remarked on the 'underspecification' of the original formulation of the theory. One of the aspects that he would have wished to be clarified further is the 'technical concept of imitation' on which the analysis depends. Vygotsky did not see imitation as a mechanical process, but believed that it was 'one of the basic paths of cultural development of the child' (Vygotsky, 1997a, p. 95). Unlike other species, children are capable of insightful intellectual imitation. Van der Veer and Valsiner regret Vygotsky's reliance, in his discussion of imitation, on comparisons between animal and human behaviour and the lack of a 'fully-fledged theory of imitation' such had been produced by other researchers (Van der Veer and Valsiner, 1991, p. 143).

Chaiklin also suggests that there is a serious lack of clear guidance about the nature or degree of the support that Vygotsky thought could be offered to children during the assessment of the ZPD. He takes a list of examples given by Vygotsky in 'The problem of age' as the most comprehensive:

we show the child how such a problem must be solved and watch to see if he can do the problem by imitating the demonstration. Or we begin to solve the problem and ask the child to finish it. Or we propose that the child solve the problem that is beyond his mental age by cooperating with another, more developed child or, finally, we explain to the child the principle of solving the problem, ask leading questions, analyse the problem for him, etc.

(Vygotsky, 1998, p. 202, quoted in Chaiklin, 2003, p. 55)

Chaiklin says that he cannot see any sequence to these suggested interventions or any discussion of children's responses to different interventions. Kellogg and Veresov similarly find Vygotsky's suggestions for interventions unsatisfactory in the context of an assessment:

we will have to work out a system of providing assistance to children doing the tasks that can be kept invariant in order to be able to compare children; otherwise, the variation in developmental age that we observe may simply be a function of variation in the forms of assistance.

(In Vygotsky, 2019, p. 154)

Again, in relation to measurement, some commentators find Vygotsky's reliance on standardised measures of mental age such as the Binet tests in establishing the ZPD unacceptable, and incompatible with other aspects of his work. Van der Veer and Valsiner say:

The specific application of this concept in the context of repeated IQ measurements, however, was rather unfortunate and seems at variance with several basic assumptions of his cultural-historical theory.

(Van der Veer and Valsiner, 1991, p. 347)

Misunderstandings and misinterpretations

The misunderstandings and misinterpretations of Vygotsky's theory of the ZPD have been widely commented on. Veresov sums up the situation:

So, the whole picture is that the concept of ZPD, being stripped from the theoretical framework, was gradually adapted to existing traditional educational practices and its strong methodological potential gradually disappears.

(Veresov, 2009, p. 257)

Veresov's whole article relates to the fragmentation of Vygotsky's theory.

What has happened is that certain words have been picked up and made the key to Vygotsky's whole theory. One of these is 'collaboration'. In *Mind in society* this word is used to suggest the way one child can be supported by another in working on a problem. In the passage from 'The dynamics ...' from which the *Mind in society* quotation is taken, the translation refers to cooperation. The Mitchell translation of the original article simply refers to the child working 'with the help of an adult'. But Gredler (2012) notes that the phrase 'in collaboration with more capable peers' in *Mind in society* (Vygotsky, 1978, p. 86) has become part of popular definitions of the ZPD, which have expanded the concept to include collaboration in general between peers, learning in adult/child dyads (for instance in planning a shopping list) and so on. As Gredler (2012, p. 117) suggests, this expanding concept of the ZPD has resulted in its being inappropriately transferred to learning situations with much younger children, even babies.

The ZPD has also been wrongly regarded as an example of 'scaffolding', a metaphor that originated with Bruner, and that Veresov (2009, p. 284) suggests owes its success to the fact that it resonates with teachers' own intuitive conceptions of effective intervention.

Veresov describes the 'stripping of the theoretical framework' from the ZPD as having simplified it and surrounded it with 'theoretical fuzziness'. As a consequence of working within the ZPD the child's 'learning process becomes developmental, learning goes ahead of development, which is the core principle of the ZPD' (ibid., p. 289). He emphasises that:

> The ZPD is not just a definition, it is a concept and concepts do not work alone. Their meaning could become clear only within the whole theory.
> (Veresov, 2009, p. 289)

To these different examples of misunderstanding and 'concept creep' can be added perhaps the most obviously harmful one of all, which is the reading of the 'zone of proximal development' as just another, more detailed, measure of attainment, or as a way of setting targets for children to reach or exceed. It is a fact that in some educational contexts children's ZPDs are now routinely measured and recorded alongside other indicators. Some commercial schemes make use of ZPDs and inform children of what ZPD they have reached. In our measurement-obsessed culture any form of assessment that results in a number is likely to be taken up and reified in this way.

And yet ...

It is important to appreciate just why the ZPD, in its *Mind in society* translation, captured the imagination of so many people in education when it first appeared and why it has entered the language, albeit in a corrupted form.

Perhaps at this point I could move back into reminiscence mode. *Mind in society* was published in 1978, two years before I began an MA in English in Education at the Institute of Education in London. It was one of the texts that we studied. The book, and especially some chapters, such as those on play, writing and the ZPD, had an extraordinary impact on us. The teachers on the course were excited by Vygotsky's many penetrating insights into learning and perhaps especially by his emphasis on the role of language in the development of thinking. The ZPD chapter showed how much more of their ability children could reveal in a dynamic assessment like the ZPD. It seemed to be a powerful critique of conventional assessment. The focus on collaboration and peer cooperation in problem-solving (which is what we took from the chapter) supported many of the practices that we were implementing in the classroom. This was the time of the language across the curriculum movement; the value of children's talk and writing in all curricular contexts was being explored and promoted in classrooms. Vygotsky's focus on language in this book and in *Thought and language* (Vygotsky, 1962) was enormously influential.

What the ZPD offers is the opportunity to assess children's performance in a supported situation. And it is a situation where the experimenter is providing positive help and encouragement. In this respect the procedures of the ZPD are exactly analogous with those used by Vygotsky's colleagues in the 'play experiments' described in detail in Chapter 5, on *Tool and symbol*. In those contexts Vygotsky also underlined the importance of language and interaction in the development of the child's understanding of higher mental functions. It seems doubtful, therefore, whether he would ever have thought it necessary to provide a standard formula for the experimenter's prompts, leading questions, or demonstrations. His approach to this kind of intervention was relaxed and it seems likely that he saw it as more like the interactive approach of a teacher than the detached input of an experimenter.

However poorly it has been interpreted or understood, the ZPD concept has made sense to teachers and many others. It appeals strongly to a practical sense of pedagogy; teachers see it as representing a teaching situation and providing a model of effective intervention. And they are not wrong in interpreting it as representative of Vygotsky's positive and empowering approach to education.

A future-oriented perspective

The powerfully optimistic and future-oriented character of Vygotsky's thought finds its full expression in the ZPD, a bold attempt to preview a child's future development rather than assess her or his past progress. The forward-looking nature of Vygotsky's work was apparent from his early publications in defectology onwards. One of the aspects of Adler's work that so attracted him was his 'new and profound future-oriented perspective' (Vygotsky, 1993a, p. 55).

Perhaps the most exciting account of the ZPD is that of Bernard Schneuwly (1994), who, quoting Vygotsky (1974) and passages of Vygotsky as cited in Mecacci (1976) and Fradkin (1990), sees the ZPD as an intrinsic part of Vygotsky's vision of development and of what powers development.

> Vygotsky defined development as 'an unceasing process of self-propulsion' and not a process induced from the exterior ... The question is, then, to

find out the driving force of this process. Vygotsky defines it particularly clearly in a curricular text on paedology in which he writes: 'The logic of the development process's self-propulsion must be shown ... To reveal [it] is to understand the internal logic, the mutual conditioning, the links, the mutual cohesion of various factors in the unity and struggle of opposites involved in the process of development.'

(Schneuwly, 1994, p. 283)

Schneuwly suggests that the dialectical 'struggle of opposites' here means, in Vygotsky's words from another text, 'the conflict between the evolved cultural forms of behaviour with which the child comes into contact and the primitive forms which characterise its own behaviour' (ibid.).

Relating this to Vygotsky's definition of the cultural and historical nature of the environment, Schneuwly concludes:

And therefore it is the confrontation with culture contemplated as a historical product of social life, as an ensemble of sign systems or semiotic systems, that is the driving force of development.

(Schneuwly, 1994, p. 284)

This confrontation happens in the process of education, through the kind of teaching that moves ahead of development while not losing sight of a child's actual level of development. This teaching works within the zone of proximal/proximate development, which Schneuwly defines as 'the creation of a tension between exterior and interior, the creation of a contradiction which is the basis of all movement' (ibid., p. 287). Development, as in all Vygotsky's pedological work, is not a smooth or conflict-free process, it is an 'abrupt restructuring':

They have to do what they do not (yet) know how to do, the requirements are beyond their present capabilities and therefore they can respond to them, at least partly, because of the didactic setting.

(Schneuwly, 1994, p. 287)

Schneuwly gives a very careful and responsive reading of Vygotsky's theoretical picture of development, rooted in the dialectic, future-oriented, and revealing a faith both in the ability of children to 'do what they do not yet know how to do' and of teachers to:

bring into existence, awaken and nourish a whole series of processes of internal development which at any given moment are only accessible to it in the context of communication with an adult and interaction with companions but which, once interiorised, will become the child's own conquest.

(Schneuwly, 1994, p. 287)

Coda

It is too late to put the ZPD back in the bottle. The innumerable versions, misunderstandings and interpretations will continue to proliferate. But now that Vygotsky's pedological works are being given their full value in his work and are appearing in good translations, now that reliable translations of other texts where the ZPD appears are becoming available, perhaps it is not too late to put together all the powerful evidence for what Vygotsky really meant by it. Now we are in a position to see it in its proper context and understand better how it can inform practice, both in teaching, in assessment, and in the many other fields where this idea is valued.

Note

1 In Russia, at the time when Vygotsky was working, compulsory schooling ended at age 12.

References

Barrs, M. (2017). 'Rediscovering Vygotsky's concept of the ZPD: Stanley Mitchell's new translation of "The problem of teaching and mental development at school age" [*Problema obučenija i umstvennogo razvitiya v škol'nom vozraste*]'. *Changing English*, 24(4), pp. 345–358.

Byford, A. (2020). *Science of the child in late imperial and early Soviet Russia*. Oxford: Oxford University Press.

Chaiklin, S. (2003). 'The zone of proximal development in Vygotsky's analysis of learning and instruction', in Kozulin, A., Gindis, B., Ageyev, V.S. and Miller, S.M. (eds), *Vygotsky's educational theory in cultural context*, pp. 39–64. Cambridge: Cambridge University Press.

Ewing, E.T. (2001). 'Restoring teachers to their rights: Soviet education and the 1936 denunciation of pedology'. *History of Education Quarterly*, 41(4), pp. 471–493.

Fradkin, F.A. (ed.) (1990). *Research in pedagogics: discussions of the 1920s and the early 1930s*. Moscow: Progress Publishers.

Glick, J. (1997). 'Prologue', in Vygotsky, L.S., *The collected works of L.S. Vygotsky. Volume 4, The history of the development of higher mental functions*, pp. v–xvi. Rieber, R.W. (ed.). New York: Plenum Press.

Gredler, M.C. (2012). 'Understanding Vygotsky for the classroom: is it too late?' *Educational Psychology Review*, 24, pp. 113–131.

Mecacci, L. (ed.) (1976). *La psicologia sovietica 1917–1936*. Rome: Riuniti.

Mecacci, L. (2017). *Lev Vygotskii: sviluppo, educazione e patologia della mente*. Florence: Giunti.

Palinscar, A.S. (1998). 'Keeping the metaphor of scaffolding fresh: a response to C. Addison Stone's "The metaphor of scaffolding: its utility for the field of learning disabilities"'. *Journal of Learning Disabilities*, 31(4), pp. 370–373.

Schneuwly, B. (1994). 'Contradiction and development: Vygotsky and paedology'. *European Journal of Psychology of Education*, 9(4), pp. 281–291.

Schneuwly, B. and Leopoldoff-Martin, I. (2011). 'Vygotsky's "Lectures and articles on pedology": an interpretative adventure'. *Tätigkeitstheorie*, 4, pp. 37–52.

Van der Veer, R. and Valsiner, J. (1991). *Understanding Vygotsky: a quest for synthesis*. Oxford: Blackwell.

Veresov, N. (1999). *Undiscovered Vygotsky: etudes on the pre-history of cultural-historical psychology*. Frankfurt-am-Main: Peter Lang.

Veresov, N. (2009) 'Forgotten methodology: Vygotsky's case', in Toomela, A. and Valsiner, J. (eds), *Methodological thinking in psychology: 60 years gone astray?*, pp. 267–295. Charlotte, NC: Information Age Publishing.

Vygotsky, L.S. (1935). '*Problema obučenija i umstvennogo razvitija v škol'nom vozraste*' ['The problem of teaching and mental development at school age']. In *Umstvennoe razvitie detej v processe obučenija* [*Children's mental development in the process of learning/teaching*], pp. 3–19. Moscow: Gosudarstvennoie Uchebno-pedagogicheskoie Izdatel'stvo.

Vygotsky, L.S. (1962). *Thought and language*. Trans. E. Hanfmann and G. Vakar. Cambridge, MA: MIT Press.

Vygotsky, L.S. (1974). 'Storia dello sviluppo delle funzioni psichiche superiori' [1931], in *Storia dello sviluppo delle funzioni psichiche superiori e altri scritti*. Veggetti, M.S. (ed.), pp. 41–223. Florence: Giunti-Barbèra.

Vygotsky, L.S. (1978). *Mind in society*. Cole, M., John-Steiner, V., Scribner, S. and Souberman, E. (eds). Cambridge, MA: Harvard University Press.

Vygotsky, L.S. (1987). *Thinking and speech* [1934], in Vygotsky, L.S., *The collected works of L.S. Vygotsky. Volume 1, Problems of general psychology*, pp. 37–285. Trans. and intro. N. Minick; Rieber, R.W. and Carton, A.S. (eds). New York: Plenum Press.

Vygotsky, L.S. (1993a). 'Defect and compensation' [1927], in Vygotsky, L.S., *The collected works of L.S. Vygotsky. Volume 2, The fundamentals of defectology*, pp. 52–64. Trans. and intro. J.E. Knox and C.B. Stevens; Rieber, R.W. and Carton, A.S. (eds). New York: Plenum Press.

Vygotsky, L.S. (1993b). 'The diagnostics of development and the pedological clinic for difficult children' [1936], in Vygotsky, L.S., *The collected works of L.S. Vygotsky. Volume 2, The fundamentals of defectology*, pp. 241–291. Trans. and intro. J.E. Knox and C.B. Stevens; Rieber, R.W. and Carton, A.S. (eds). New York: Plenum Press.

Vygotsky, L.S. (1997). *The collected works of L.S. Vygotsky. Volume 4, The history of the development of higher mental functions*. Rieber, R.W. (ed.). New York: Plenum Press.

Vygotsky, L.S. (1997a). *The history of the development of higher mental functions* [1931], in Vygotsky, L.S., *The collected works of L.S. Vygotsky. Volume 4, The history of the development of higher mental functions*, pp. 1–251. Rieber, R.W. (ed.). New York: Plenum Press.

Vygotsky, L.S. (1997b). 'The problem of cultural age' [n.d.], in Vygotsky, L.S., *The collected works of L.S. Vygotsky. Volume 4, The history of the development of higher mental functions*, pp. 231–239. Rieber, R.W. (ed.). New York: Plenum Press.

Vygotsky, L.S. (1998). 'The problem of age' [1932–4], in Vygotsky, L.S., *The collected works of L.S. Vygotsky. Volume 5, Child psychology*, pp. 187–205. Rieber, R.W. (ed.). New York: Plenum Press.

Vygotsky, L.S. (2011). 'The dynamics of the schoolchild's mental development in relation to teaching and learning' [1928]. Trans. A. Kozulin. *Journal of Cognitive Education and Psychology*, 10(2), pp. 198–211.

Vygotsky, L.S. (2016). 'Play and its role in the mental development of the child' [1933]. Trans. N. Veresov and M. Barrs. *International Research in Early Childhood Education*, 7(2), pp. 6–25.

Vygotsky, L.S. (2017). 'The problem of teaching and mental development at school age' ['*Problema obučenija i umstvennogo razvitiya v škol'nom vozraste*'] [1935]. Trans. S. Mitchell. *Changing English*, 24(4), pp. 359–371. Also available online in the Marxist Archive: www.marxists.org/archive/vygotsky/works/1931/school-age.htm

Vygotsky, L.S. (2019). *L.S. Vygotsky's pedological works. Volume 1, Foundations of pedology*. Trans. and notes D. Kellogg and N. Veresov. Singapore: Springer.

Vygotsky, L.S. and Luria, A.R. (1994). *Tool and symbol in child development* [1930], in Van der Veer, R. and Valsiner, J. (eds), *The Vygotsky reader*, pp. 99–174. Oxford: Blackwell.

Chapter 10

Thinking and speech I: Word meaning develops

1932

1932 was a turbulent year in education in the Soviet Union. Under the 'Five Year Plan', from the late 1920s schooling had been transformed by the requirement for school children to engage in 'socially useful work'. Schools were also encouraged to organise their teaching according to the 'project method' supported by Krupskaya, where subjects were integrated within topics that related to the Five Year Plan.

But in 1931 there was a resolution of the Central Committee that teaching in subjects must be reinstated and based on a centralised programme and a timetable. In January 1932 new subject programmes were sent out to schools. Teachers who had adapted to the 'activity methods' of a project-based curriculum had to learn how to teach traditional subjects with textbooks. However, the manner of teaching all subjects must still relate to political ideology: the grammar programme included a definition of a sentence as 'a unit of communication expressing objective reality through class consciousness' (Fitzpatrick, 1979, p. 223).

At the same time, the focus on self-criticism in all kinds of organisations including universities and schools was producing a culture of mutual suspicion and mistrust. In universities the Communist Party was organising public debates 'where carefully prepared opponents tried to demolish the scientific position of the researcher' (Van der Veer and Valsiner, 1991, p. 375). Vygotsky and Luria knew they were likely to be the target of such an attack, organised by the Party cell of the Psychological Institute, and had carefully prepared their defence (ibid., p. 376).

They were already a target for criticism. In 1931 a Party member of the Psychological Institute denounced them in a subsequently published talk for their insufficiently Marxist solution to the 'development of psychic processes' (ibid., p. 377). Vygotsky attended this talk. He later wrote to Luria saying that 'it had apparently been formally decided that they would be "beaten, but not killed"' (ibid., p. 378). Then in 1932 Vygotsky's work was systematically attacked in another article which denounced him for a 'biologistic approach', concluding, as we noted in Chapter 8, that his work gave 'an incorrect view of

DOI: 10.4324/9780429203046-10

the development of the Soviet child' and had a harmful educational influence (ibid., p. 380).

'Thinking and speech... a dim question'

By now it was necessary for books intended for publication to be submitted to a committee of members of the appropriate Party Cell. In the autumn of 1932, Vygotsky presented the content of his planned book *Thinking and speech* to a committee at the Psychological Institute. The book was severely criticised on ideological grounds (Zavershneva and Van der Veer, 2018, p. 311).

Vygotsky, in one of his small notebooks, kept detailed notes of the meeting. The notes begin with his plan for the book, the theoretical premises of which are given as 'consciousness and its functions' (ibid., p. 312). There follows an edited extract from Vygotsky's notes of the discussion, giving the names of the speakers and recording their contributions to the proceedings:

KOLBANOVSKY: The book does not yet exist. Is it consistent from the viewpoint of Marxist theory? ... It is not Marxist psychology in the proper sense of the word ...

VEDENOV: The experiments with concept formation do not show the process of concept formation. He [the child] does not form them himself but masters them. The experimental material does not confirm this: [The study was done] with artificial concepts, which obviously form no part of practice. The idea is correct, but it is not supported by the experimental method.

SHEMYAKIN: Thinking and speech ... a dim question. The classic answer will not do. Does it (the book) help to construct a Marxist-Leninist theory of thinking and speech, or does it muddle things. On the whole, idealism along the lines of Marxist-Leninism ...

The final speaker, Akimov, concludes his contribution with the remark: 'Methodologically careless' (ibid., pp. 313–314). At only one point in the notes does Vygotsky burst in with his own written response: 'I will not submit it to criticism' (ibid., p. 314).

In 1933 Vygotsky's work was subject to the judgement of the 'Purge Commission' of Party officials at the Institute who described it in their resolution as 'idealist and bourgeois theory' and as an 'anti-Marxist conception' (ibid., p. 316). Vygotsky declared in a draft response:

I have always considered my work to lie within the system of Soviet science and not outside it. I subjectively felt that with my work I consciously participated in the construction of a Marxist psychology ...

(Zavershneva and Van der Veer, 2018, p. 316)

Thinking and speech

Between 1931 and 1933 (according to the Russian editorial notes to volume 6 of the English *Collected works*), Vygotsky was working on a book about affect, *The teaching about emotions* (Vygotsky, 1999), which was unfinished when he died. He was also planning a book on consciousness, and actively defining in his notebooks both the contents and the shape of the book – but it was never written. However, *Thinking and speech*, which was written between 1929 and 1934 and was published in late 1934 after Vygotsky's death, contains key passages that reflect Vygotsky's deep interest in both affect and consciousness.

The main subject of *Thinking and speech* – the relationship between language and thought – had been a fundamental part of the development of his psychology from the outset. This book, a bringing together of different aspects of his work in this area, is the one for which he is best known. The Russian editorial notes, as they appear in volume 1 of the English *Collected works*, suggest that there were 'important external circumstances motivating this work' (Vygotsky, 1987, p. 375). Because his approach to psychology was, as we have seen, coming under sharp criticism at this time, 'Vygotsky felt the need of explaining his perspective' (ibid.). In his Afterword to this volume of the *Collected works*, Luria sees it as 'Vygotsky's most significant attempt to develop his general theory' (Luria, 1987, p. 359).

In the Preface to the book, Vygotsky writes that 'This book is the product of nearly ten years' work'[1] (Vygotsky, 1987a, p. 40). He explains that some chapters (2, 4 and 5) were taken from earlier works but that the remaining chapters and the book as a whole 'are published here for the first time' (ibid., p. 41). But he was never to see this publication; he completed the book while he was in hospital for tuberculosis in 1934, and died in June of that year.

Some recent commentators have suggested that this book is a collection of 'old work' and that it was put together in a hurry. This kind of suggestion seems absurd, however, when we look at the care that Vygotsky brought to the structuring of the argument of the book.

Chapter 1: The problem and the method of investigation

In this book, Vygotsky wants to investigate the relationship of thought to word. In traditional psychology, he explains, theories of thinking and speech have either seen thought and word as completely fused together, or else as quite distinct. The method of studying verbal thinking has been to break it down into its separate elements and study them separately. Vygotsky, on the contrary, wants to study the 'internal relationship of thought to word' (Vygotsky, 1987a, p. 45). In the first chapter he explains clearly why reductionist analysis, which attempts to break down a complex process or system into its constituent sub-skills or elements, must always fail – such analysis destroys the very phenomenon that it sets out to investigate. Only holistic analysis, which works with 'units of analysis' that contain the properties of the whole, is adequate to describe the kinds of complex processes that are the subject of psychological enquiry:

> A psychology concerned with the study of the complex whole must comprehend this. It must replace the method of decomposing the whole into its elements with that of partitioning the whole into its units.
>
> (Vygotsky, 1987a, p. 46)

Vygotsky therefore takes as his unit of analysis throughout the book 'word meaning', the semantic properties of words, which will allow him to observe, on a small scale, the interrelationship of thought and language:

> Clearly, then, the method to follow in our exploration of the nature of verbal thought is semantic analysis – the study of the development, the functioning, and the structure of this unit, which contains thought and speech interrelated.
>
> (Vygotsky, 1987a, p. 47)

The unit of analysis

We are already familiar with Vygotsky's use of a unit of analysis in his psychology. He first used one in his book *The psychology of art*, published in 1925 (Vygotsky, 1971; see Chapter 2). Here he was studying the psychological basis of literature and took as his 'unit of analysis' the complete work of art. The unit of analysis used in *Thinking and speech*, word meaning, could hardly be more different: these units are at opposite ends of the scale. Yet it is the same scale, and Vygotsky's concerns have not changed; he is still seeking ways of analysing complex systems without destroying the very features that make them function.

Initially, however, Vygotsky's choice of a unit of analysis does not look promising. A word cannot easily 'mean' by itself; and larger 'meanings' are not arrived at by combining individual units of meaning. In Luria's words:

> The listener or reader never is confronted with the problem of under-standing isolated words or sentences. Neither words nor sentences occur 'in vacuo' ... The basic process in comprehension consists of deciphering the meaning of the whole message.
>
> (Luria, 1982, p. 170)

Nevertheless, the study of language development in young children reveals that their interest in words, and in what things are called, is a critical aspect of their growth, and their growing awareness of word meanings reveals changes in their conceptual development. Vygotsky pointed out the difference between the syntactic and semantic aspects of language development:

In mastering external speech, the child starts from one word, then connects two or three words; a little later, he advances from simple sentences to more complicated ones, and finally to coherent speech made up of series of such sentences; in other words, he proceeds from a part to the whole. In regard to meaning, on the other hand, the first word of the child is a whole sentence. Semantically, the child starts from the whole, from a meaningful complex, and only later begins to master the separate semantic units, the meanings of words, and to divide his formerly undifferentiated thoughts into those units. The external and semantic aspects of speech develop in opposite directions – one from the particular to the whole, from word to sentence, and the other from the whole to the particular, from sentence to word.

(Vygotsky, 1987a, p. 250)

By selecting word meaning as his unit of analysis, Vygotsky enables himself to study these transitions, to look at the changes in the relationship between language and thought, and to study the development of both the external and the semantic aspects of speech.

The place of affect

At the end of ch. 1 Vygotsky foregrounds the issue of affect, and the connection between intellect and affect. He sees traditional psychology as having isolated 'the intellectual from the volitional and affective aspects of consciousness' (Vygotsky, 1987a, p. 50).

Thinking was divorced from the full vitality of life, from the motives, interests, and inclinations of the thinking individual ... By isolating thinking from affect at the outset, we effectively cut ourselves off from any potential for a causal explanation of thinking.

(Vygotsky, 1987a, p. 50)

Vygotsky suggests that if there were a research solution to this rupture it would lie, once more, in the analysis of the complex whole into its units. The affective and intellectual processes work together as part of a dynamic system; analysis into units would make it possible to see the relationship between affect (emotions, needs) and intellectual processes. Vygotsky sees this kind of investigation as an example of the future work that needs to be done in relationship to this problem.

The shape of the book

Vygotsky goes on to use word meaning as the unit of analysis in exploring the two aspects of consciousness that he has identified:

a   The cognitive external aspect, including both (i) the changing relation between children's thought and language through the development of word meaning, and (ii) the development of concepts, especially the relationship between children's everyday concepts and the 'scientific' concepts that are part of their school learning.

b   The affective interior aspect, including the development and internalisation of personal meanings, derived from social experience, which can be communicated in intimate talk or through literature – in such a way as to bring 'the most intimate and personal aspects of our being into the circle of social life' (Vygotsky, 1971, p. 249).

This would be one way of viewing the structure of this book. But another way would be to see it as divided (after the first chapter) into three studies of the development of word meaning, which correspond to three sections of the book:

Section 1 The study of the development of language and thought in young children

Chapter 2 Piaget
Chapter 3 Stern
Chapter 4 The genetic roots of thinking and speech

Section 2 The study of the development of concepts, especially scientific concepts, in older children

Chapter 5 Experimental study of concept development
Chapter 6 The development of scientific concepts

Section 3 The study of the development of inner speech

Chapter 7 Thought and word

These different ways of viewing the structure of the book and of the argument may help us in negotiating this long and complex text. Despite the fact that some parts of the book had been written earlier, the argument as a whole is coherent and the focus on word meaning as a unit of analysis is sustained throughout.

Chapters 2 and 3: Piaget and Stern

One of the ways in which Vygotsky defines his stance as a psychologist in this book is in opposition to other psychologists who had concerned themselves with the question of the development of language and thought. From the very first chapter, Vygotsky makes clear that one of his aims is to provide a thorough-going critique of the work of the one developmental psychologist, Jean Piaget, who had offered a theory of development which was in any way adequate to the facts (Vygotsky calls it 'the best available'). Two of Piaget's books had been published in Russian in 1930. In addition to the long ch. 2, which is entirely devoted to Piaget, Vygotsky returns to Piaget's work more than once in the book, particularly in the chapters on 'The development of scientific concepts in childhood' (ch. 6) and 'Thought and word' (ch. 7).

Ch. 2, 'The problem of speech and thinking in Piaget's theory', was originally Vygotsky's introductory essay to the Russian translation of Piaget's work, which included *The language and thought of the child* (Piaget, 1923). It is clear that Vygotsky followed Piaget's work closely, and that several of the experiments with children carried out in the 'instrumental period' of his work with his colleagues were based on Piaget's work. Van der Veer says that the team 'replicated virtually all of Piaget's investigations' (Van der Veer, 1996, p. 238). However, they sometimes made deliberate changes to the research model.

Vygotsky makes clear from the outset that he regards Piaget's work as having 'substantial historical significance'. He admired Piaget's emphasis on qualitative rather than quantitative approaches (Vygotsky, 1987a, p. 53) and his ability to gather and classify new empirical material (ibid., p. 55). But he regards Piaget as 'isolating himself in the narrow domain of empirical data'. Because of his focus on empirical facts, 'A veritable sea of facts gush from these pages' (ibid.).

Vygotsky's deep disagreement with Piaget stems from the fact that Piaget wants to dispense with theory in his studies. He has developed a superb clinical method for studying the 'complex, unified formations of the child's thought in transition and development' (ibid.) but he will not draw any theoretical conclusions from it. Yet, Vygotsky suggests, there *is* theory operating in Piaget's work: 'implicit and underdeveloped theory to be sure, but nonetheless ... theory of the kind that he had tried so hard to avoid' (ibid.). Vygotsky tracks through Piaget's work doggedly in his pursuit of its theoretical core and finds it in *The judgement and reasoning of the child* (Piaget, 1924), where Piaget suggests that the many diverse phenomena that characterise the child's thinking are linked by the idea of the 'egocentric nature of the child's thinking. That is the cornerstone of the entire structure' (Vygotsky, 1987a, p. 57).

Piaget's account of development sees the child's thought as originally and naturally autistic, egocentric, and egotistical. Only later, in his view, does a social instinct develop, and does speech become socialised. Vygotsky identified Piaget's theory in this respect very closely with the ideas of Freud, who had seen the pleasure principle as ruling all early behaviour, with the reality principle beginning to affect behaviour only much later in childhood. He draws constant parallels between Piaget's views and those of Freud. (Piaget had in fact taken a great interest in psychoanalysis and had been psychoanalysed for several months by Sabina Spielrein when she was a colleague of his at the Rousseau Institute in Geneva; see Santiago-Delefosse and Delefosse, 2002.)

Piaget's account of egocentric speech regards it as a transitional form between autistic (or 'subconscious') thought and rational, socialised thought. Egocentric speech and thought is described as egotistical, asocial and syncretic. Piaget writes:

Up till about 7½, therefore, all the child's thought ... will be tainted with the consequences of egocentrism and of syncretism in particular.

(Quoted in Vygotsky, 1987a, p. 60)

Egocentric speech is essentially monologue; the child is not interested in whether anyone is listening to him (ibid., p. 66). Piaget carried out a survey of egocentric speech which looked at the 'coefficient of egocentric speech' and found it was extremely high in children before the age of six or seven; more than half of their utterances were classified as egocentric. Piaget sees egocentric speech as being a reflection of egocentric thinking. Vygotsky comments:

The first postulate of Piaget's views on egocentric speech is that it has no necessary, objective, or useful function in the child's behaviour.

(Vygotsky, 1987a, p. 68)

So when the coefficient of egocentric speech decreases with age, 'Piaget maintains that it simply evaporates', withering away when speech becomes socialised (ibid., p. 69).

It is at this point that Vygotsky introduces a snapshot from his own empirical studies of egocentric speech, carried out with Luria, Leontiev and Levina, in which they organised the behaviour of the child 'in a manner nearly identical to that characteristic of Piaget's studies' (ibid.), but introduced factors that increased the difficulty of the child's activity. For instance, in a drawing task the child was not provided with the coloured pencil, paper, or paint that he needed. They found that when this difficulty was introduced, the coefficient of egocentric speech nearly doubled. The child attempted to assess the situation: 'Where is the pencil? I need a blue pencil now. Nothing. Instead of that I will colour it red and put water on it, that will make it darker and more like blue' (ibid., p. 70).

Vygotsky's theory of language development could not be more different from Piaget's. He dismisses Piaget's theory of autistic thinking:

Autistic thinking is not, however, the first stage in the mental development of either the human species or the child. It is not a primitive function, not the point of departure for the whole of development.

(Vygotsky, 1987a, p. 62)

He describes early development, particularly the development of speech, as being 'essentially social'; he sees babies as taking part in life from their earliest months. His is a far more optimistic and inclusive view of young children than the rather detached attitude taken by Piaget.

Vygotsky sees egocentric speech as being a key transitional stage in the development of language and thought. It can become a means of thinking, as when the child is faced with a difficult problem. He and his researchers observed how egocentric speech initially occurred in mid-activity and then began to occur towards the beginning, 'where it assumes a planning and directing function'. When it 'evaporates', Vygotsky's research suggests that it is becoming more fragmentary and being transformed into inner speech (ibid., p. 72).

Vygotsky's judgement of Piaget's whole stance as a scientist is extremely critical in this chapter. He considers that Piaget avoids the key responsibility of the scientist: to explain. Piaget's consistently empirical approach and unwillingness to generalise prematurely from the facts seems to Vygotsky to be a weakness. Piaget appears to think that he has avoided taking a philosophical position in his work but 'The absence of a philosophy is itself a very definite philosophy' (ibid., p. 80). Piaget wants to refrain from explaining psychological phenomena, and to substitute a factual account of genetic progression, in which one phenomenon is not seen to be the cause of another, but merely to precede it.

Vygotsky is scornful of this evasion:

> Piaget attempts to replace a causal understanding of development with a functional understanding of it. Though he does not notice it, he deprives the concept of development of any real content in the process. In this view of development everything is conditional. Phenomenon A can be viewed as a function of phenomenon B, but B can also be viewed as a function of A. The result is that the issue of cause ... disappears.
>
> (Vygotsky, 1987a, p. 81)

Piaget's scheme of development is the opposite of Vygotsky's. Piaget's begins with autistic thinking and ends with social speech/logical thinking:

autistic thinking $\rightarrow$ egocentric speech/thinking $\rightarrow$ socialised speech/logical thinking

Vygotsky and his colleagues begin their scheme with social speech, which moves inwards, becoming inner speech and thought:

social speech $\rightarrow$ egocentric speech $\rightarrow$ inner speech

Piaget's conception, Vygotsky says, 'does not correctly represent the basic dynamics of the developmental process nor does it properly represent the prospects for development' (Vygotsky, 1987a, p. 76).

Vygotsky is also very critical of Piaget's way of investigating children's thinking. The questions that he asks children are designed to be proof against any external influences, so as to capture empirically the child's own thinking. But this means that they are often completely outside the child's experience. To conclude, as Piaget does on the basis of these investigations, that children's thinking is irrational or alogical, is unreasonable. Children's answers to such questions as 'why doesn't the moon fall to earth' are bound to be syncretic (random). The question that Vygotsky's researchers ask in order to investigate thinking are designed to relate to children's experience, e.g. 'why did the child fall over?' (when he had tripped on a rock) – and in these cases the child can give a rational answer.

Chapter 3, on Stern's 'Theory of speech development', is very short. Vygotsky respects Stern's empirical observations of children's language development and thinks Stern made a 'real and substantial contribution' (ibid., p. 96) in this area, but deplores his treatment of the problem of thinking and speech. Stern declines to take a developmental approach to explaining how the meaningful character of speech arises, and Vygotsky attributes this to his 'personalistic' stance. All changes in speech derive from what Stern calls the 'integral, purposefully developing personality' (ibid., p. 99). Vygotsky criticises the lack of any social perspective in this account of development; he regards Stern's position as idealistic and 'purely intellectualistic' (ibid., p. 93).

Chapter 4: The genetic roots of thinking and speech

In this chapter Vygotsky sets out to make quite clear that inner speech is the result of the merging of speech and thinking, whose paths of development meet and intersect at around two years of age, at which point the child begins to actively expand his vocabulary by asking the name of each new thing. The argument of this chapter recapitulates several of Vygotsky's previous investigations.

First, Vygotsky looks at the question in terms of phylogeny (evolutionary development) – through a review of Köhler's and Yerkes's work with chimpanzees. This well-documented work shows that although these anthropoids are able to use tools and plan actions in a rudimentary way, and although they have a basic form of speech, mainly emotional in character, thinking and speech are not connected in chimpanzees in any way.

Second, he considers the question ontogenically (to do with individual development) in human infants. Here he finds that the development of thinking and speech are separate up to a certain point (about age two) when the two paths intersect and a new functional transformation begins: thinking becomes verbal and speech intellectual (ibid., p. 112).

Finally Vygotsky considers, as he had in the chapter on Piaget, the way in which social (external) speech, through a process of development – in which egocentric speech is a transitional form – becomes inner speech.

The key argument of the chapter, as of the whole book, is that 'thinking depends on speech ... the development of the child's thinking depends on his mastery of the social means of thinking.' (ibid., p. 120) Subsequently, after the major shift when thinking and language merge, 'the very type of development changes' and thinking and speech becomes 'the central problem of social psychology' (ibid.). Future development will depend on the social environment and on child-rearing – and of course on education.

The next two chapters of *Thinking and speech* deal with the later development of thinking and speech, through the development of concepts, and focus entirely on children of school age.

Interlude: a notebook from 1932

But perhaps before we leave the section of *Thinking and speech* that relates to young children's speech development we could take one last example from Vygotsky's observations of his daughter Asya, his living representation of language development. And Asya, at the time of Vygotsky's writing in this notebook from 1932, is operating with one-word sentences. One of her words is 'pu-fu' which can mean several things, since at this point (as Vygotsky suggests) 'there are more meanings than words' (Zavershneva and Van der Veer, 2018, p. 297).

'NB! 1. Asya: [written in green ink]

(a) pu-fu = an example of a complex = a bottle, iodine, a bruise, a cigarette, a match, to put out, to give;

(b) In her one-word sentence, the meaning of pu-fu changes both in the relation to the object (an empty bottle is not suited for a bruise, it can be used for whistling, i.e., sometimes: iodine; sometimes: vessels, a bubble) and in the general sense; this is the general law of the word and the one-word sentence in early childhood: Meaning is variable not just in the sense of transient meanings but also in the sense of its functioning. Sometimes: pu-fu = give the bottle and blow in it. Sometimes: pu-fu = the doll hurt herself; disinfect it with iodine;

(c) Her one-word sentence clearly shows the advantage of semantic differentiation of speech over phasic non-differentiation. Hence, the discrepancy: There are more meanings than words. The difficulty is in communicating: they do not understand her, she gladly welcomes the right question: yeees ... = right! Compare 'pu-fu.' Give pu-fu? Blow? No. Becomes angry. To disinfect the head of the doll with iodine (bobo, disinfect?). Yeees ... (= right!). Her two-word sentence develops from that (from the suggestive questions of the adults: Pu-fu! – Give?). The schema:

1   Pu-fu! – Give? – Yeees... (Here the two-word sentence is divided between her and me, but practically while thinking – psychologically it is already completely felt by her).
2   Give pu-fu. Hence her explanatory words: Asya, to me, write, etc.
(Zavershneva and Van der Veer, 2018, p. 297)

Chapter 5: Experimental study of concept development

The next step in Vygotsky's study of the development of word meaning is to consider what happens in the process of concept development. Among the psychological literature on concept development, Vygotsky particularly admires the work of a contemporary researcher, Narciss Ach. Ach had developed an experimental method which allowed him 'to study the process involved in concept formation in pure form' (Vygotsky, 1987a, p. 123) and also to enable different stages of concept formation to be identified. Vygotsky and his collea- gue Sakharov had carried out experiments with a variant of Ach's experimental model; these were written up in 1930 by Sakharov (1994). Vygotsky reports that more than 300 children and adults had taken part in these studies.

In the Sakharov version of the experiments with what are now generally known as 'Vygotsky blocks', children were presented with a motley, unorga- nised collection of wooden blocks of different shapes, sizes and colours, on a big board. They were told that these were toys belonging to children in a dif- ferent country. One of them was turned upside down and its name – in another language – was there. The children in the experiment were asked if they could put all the blocks with the same name as the first one onto a special area of the board – without turning them over or looking at the name under- neath. After each attempt the experimenter turned the blocks upside down one by one to reveal the names. Some blocks might have the same name, others were different and so, as the play-experiment continued, the children began to learn the names of different blocks.

Initially children's choices for grouping the blocks were random; there was no stable principle at work. The term used for this stage was 'syncretic'. The heaps that resulted were the result of pure trial and error. This early stage, which was typical of young children, was followed by a long stage with several different phases; Vygotsky termed this phase 'the formation of complexes'. In the first type of complex, the child grouped objects according to some per- ceived connection; it seemed that they belonged together. This was sometimes called an 'associative' complex.

Another type of complex was a 'collection': a group which was assembled on the basis of one feature which the child had decided would be the basis of the collection. This was a step further; the basis for choice was objective.

A further kind of complex was a 'chained' complex. In this kind of complex the blocks were chosen in relation to one feature, as in the 'collection'. But at a certain point the criteria might change – if a blue triangular block was chosen because it was a triangle, the next choice might be another blue block of any shape. Vygotsky said that because there was 'no structural centre' to the chained complex it was the 'purest form of complexive thinking' (Vygotsky, 1987a, p. 140). In no 'complex' does the child's thinking go beyond concrete, empirical connections.

The final stage of complexive thinking was the 'pseudo-concept', which appeared to have its basis in a general abstraction, but did not; the group of objects might be the same as that of the true concept, but the choice was based on no abstract principle. Vygotsky suggests that the true concept emerges at a comparatively late stage. The verbal interaction with adults about the principles of selection – the conceptual basis of the grouping – is a decisive factor in the move from pseudo-concepts to true concepts.

The Sakharov/Vygotsky experiment was thus a way of revealing the process of concept development by obtaining 'slices of the genetic process' (ibid., p. 147) – samples of behaviour at different developmental points that could be studied. But Vygotsky makes clear that the data from such experiments 'must be verified on the basis of data on the child's actual development' (ibid., p. 148). He ends the chapter with a caution: this elegant experiment is an experiment in the abstract, but in real life 'concepts are the product of the long and complex process that constitutes the development of the child's thinking' (ibid., p. 164). Concepts arise during intellectual operations, where the word has a function for the student and is a means of abstracting and isolating features and symbolising them. It is not until adolescence *'that he reaches the point where he is really thinking in concepts'* (ibid., p. 160).

Chapter 6: Development of scientific concepts

Vygotsky viewed the formation of concepts as being central to the development of thinking in every area. In *Pedology of the adolescent*, he had suggested that thinking in concepts could enable students to order the world and begin to perceive the systems that the concepts form part of:

> Recognising concrete reality with the help of words, which are signs for concepts, man uncovers in the world he sees connections and patterns that are confined within it.
>
> (Vygotsky, 1998, p. 48)

Vygotsky's next step in tracing the development of word meaning through concept development is the long chapter on the development of scientific concepts (ch. 6). He has investigated this subject through a formal laboratory experiment; now he wants to see how concept development comes about in more normal circumstances – in education. This long and sustained piece of thinking has substantial implications for teaching and learning.

Vygotsky refers to the research done by Zhozefina Shif (Vygotsky, 1987a, pp. 167–169) into the development of scientific and 'everyday' concepts in school-age children. The research was a study of understanding of cause-and-effect relationships in different situations, some encountered in social science lessons and some in everyday contexts. It showed that after instruction there was a higher conscious awareness of scientific concepts than of everyday concepts – but that rapid development in scientific thinking was soon followed by similar improvements in everyday concepts. This is the relationship that Vygotsky wants to consider throughout the chapter – how everyday concepts and scientific concepts are related, and how instruction can lead development.

Vygotsky recognises that the weakness of the everyday concept lies in its unsuitability for abstraction, while the weakness of the scientific concept lies in its 'insufficient saturation with the concrete' (ibid., p. 169). He also recognises that 'direct instruction in concepts is impossible. It is pedagogically fruitless ... the child learns not the concept but the word, and this word is taken over through memory rather than thought' (ibid., p. 170).

Vygotsky set out to study the development of *scientific* concepts, having realised that nearly all studies of concept formation had focused on everyday concepts. Once more the researcher whose work he chooses to engage with is Jean Piaget. He considers that Piaget, though a serious researcher, makes several mistakes in this field, one of which is his theory that only children's 'spontaneous' (everyday) concepts can illuminate the nature of the child's thought; 'non-spontaneous' (scientific) concepts always reflect adults' thought. This theory sets up a barrier between these two kinds of concepts, instead of seeing them as interacting in a single system.

Piaget's model of mental development, according to Vygotsky, is one in which the characteristics of the child's thought die out and are gradually replaced by the more powerful thought of the adult. Children's thought is seen as egocentric thought, and as having no function beyond childhood. Piaget does not see development as the emergence of new, more complex forms of thinking in the child, as scientific concepts begin to affect thinking. Instead he sees it as a process by which one form of thought is gradually pushed out and replaced by the more powerful thought of adults. So Piaget's view of conceptual development is exactly like his model of language development in young children; egocentric speech/thought dies away and is gradually replaced by adult speech/thought.

Vygotsky moves on to look at what happens in the course of education. Whereas Piaget sees the critical and objective approach taken by scientific thought as being foreign to the child's spontaneous intellectual state, Vygotsky considers that scientific concepts are '*not simply acquired or memorised by the child and assimilated by his memory but arise and are formed through an extraordinary effort of his own thought*' (ibid., p. 176). This effort will involve the child in making links with his existing knowledge; Vygotsky sees the development of everyday and scientific concepts as being related and these two forms of thought as continually influencing one another.

Vygotsky considers actual examples of learning, to highlight the difference between everyday and scientific concepts. For instance, learning a foreign language in school is an entirely different process from learning one's native language. The learning of a foreign language is based on the child's knowledge of the native language, yet the foreign language then influences the development of the native language – increasing the child's conscious awareness of linguistic forms and abstract knowledge of language. Vygotsky compares it with the learning of algebra which 'frees the child's thought from the grasp of concrete numerical relations and raises it to the level of more abstract thought' (ibid., p. 180). The main cause of the lack of conscious awareness in spontaneous concepts is the absence of this abstract level, and the child's unawareness of any *system* linking the concepts.

We already know from Vygotsky's writing on the development of higher psychological functions that he sees the relationships and connections between functions as changing in the process of mental development:

> Changes in these interfunctional connections – *change in the functional structure of consciousness* – is the main and central content of the entire process of mental development.
>
> (Vygotsky, 1987a, p. 188)

Conscious awareness is, for Vygotsky, the key to mental development and he sees it arising, in his example, through the growing awareness of the forms of language gained by acquaintance with a second language. The other essential quality that he sees as enabling intellectual development and the mastery of new learning is *voluntary control* of one's own mental processes – self-mastery.

Scientific concepts are central to intellectual development, and so is instruction. Understanding scientific concepts, as Vygotsky has suggested, requires 'an extraordinary effort' of thought, which involves voluntary control of thinking and leads to a different *way* of thinking – conscious awareness. The new generalisations and ways of thinking that the student is now able to use can be transferred to other domains of thought. Vygotsky concludes:

> Thus, *conscious awareness enters through the gate opened up by the scientific concept.*
>
> (Vygotsky, 1987a, p. 191)

This is what Vygotsky meant, in relation to the zone of proximal/proximate development, by saying that 'the only good method of teaching is that which runs ahead of development' (Vygotsky, 2017, p. 367). This statement is absolutely not an argument for fast-paced transmission teaching. Vygotsky is committed to the kind of teaching which will *develop* children's thinking, by expanding their understanding and systemisation of concepts, their conscious awareness and their self-mastery. He sees the teaching of scientific concepts as the way of 'opening the gate' to these developed forms of thinking.

From now on ch. 6 focuses on the relation between instruction and development. Piaget sees children's thinking passing through certain stages regardless of whether or not they receive instruction. Vygotsky, however, takes the view that instruction is key to the development of thinking. He discusses four studies which look at the relationship between instruction and development, one of which is about writing and grammar, and another about the ZPD.

The section on writing complements Vygotsky's earlier study of the development of writing abilities, which was discussed in Chapter 6 of this book. It is a consistently interesting study of the reasons why writing is often difficult for children – why there can be such a disparity between their spoken and their written language. Vygotsky's discussion of this is complex and fascinating; we will consider some of the main points that emerge from it.

Written speech

Written speech is not just the translation into writing of oral speech; it is a different speech form, with different structures.

Written speech requires a high degree of abstraction. Vygotsky calls it 'the algebra of speech' (Vygotsky, 1987a, p. 203). It lacks intonation and expression, it lacks an immediate interlocutor – it is speech-monologue. This means that there is no external 'speech-motive'. The writer is in a conversation with a blank sheet of paper.

The abstract nature of written speech differentiates it from conversational speech. It is a form of symbolism – a *second-order* symbolism, since the written word is a symbol of a symbol.

All this means that writing requires a different relationship to the communication situation; the writer must act with more *conscious awareness* of the process and purpose of the writing and exercise more *voluntary control*.

Written speech stands between two other forms of speech:

- oral speech, which is spontaneous, expansive, lacking in any set structure, dialogic, involuntary, sometimes repetitious or given to diversions; and
- inner speech, which is dense (maximally contracted), idiomatic (addressed to the self), abbreviated, elliptical and implicit in its meanings.

Written speech is the most expanded form of speech; it needs to be thoroughly clear and comprehensible to the reader.

And writing is difficult because, in the writing process, the writer is drawing on thought, or inner speech (maximally contracted speech) and expanding it into written speech (maximally expanded speech). The implication of this is that there is an obvious bridge between inner speech and written speech – oral speech. Talking it through is often the way to get past a writing problem.

So writing has all the features of a scientific concept, and Vygotsky makes clear that all scientific concepts develop more fully with use over a period of time and do not become mature functions until adolescence.

The ZPD, and concept development

We have already visited the statement of the ZPD that Vygotsky provides in this chapter, where it relates closely to education, instruction, and the relation between teaching and development. But it is important, before we leave the treatment of scientific concepts in *Thinking and speech*, to consider the overall conclusion he comes to about the relationship between scientific and everyday concepts. He makes a point of stressing the relationship between them, and towards the end of the chapter makes a long summative statement:

> The strength of the everyday concept lies in spontaneous, situationally meaningful, concrete applications, that is, in this sphere of experience and

the empirical. The development of scientific concepts begins in the domain of conscious awareness and volition. It grows downward into the domain of the concrete, into the domain of personal experience. In contrast, the development of spontaneous concepts begins in the domain of the concrete and empirical. It moves toward the higher characteristics of concepts, towards conscious awareness and volition. The link between these two lines of development reflects their true nature. This is *the link of the zone of proximal and actual development.*

(Vygotsky, 1987a, p. 220)

This image of one line of development growing up from deep roots, putting up shoots which will develop in a different but related domain – and the other line of development putting down roots in a way which will connect it with a related aspect of development, is easy to understand. Each needs the other and the job of education is to connect the two.

The key difference between the two kinds of concept is the presence or absence of a system. Within a system, the relationships between concepts begin to emerge. Without a system, children's concepts remain syncretic; they lack order or relationship.

But for Piaget, 'The child is not systematic' (ibid., p. 234). Piaget is not interested in school concepts, which he sees as having no significance for research into children's thought. 'Therefore, he pursues the study of thinking outside the context of instruction' (ibid., p. 237). For Vygotsky this is the major limitation of Piaget's theory.

At the end of this penultimate chapter of *Thinking and speech* Vygotsky reminds us of 'the central point – the main thought – of our entire work': the development of a concept is not completed when a new word is learned; it is only beginning.

The gradual, internal development of the word's meaning leads to the maturation of the word itself. Here, as everywhere, the development of the meaningful aspect of speech turns out to be the basic and decisive process in the development of the child's thinking and speech.

(Vygotsky, 1987a, p. 241)

The final chapter of *Thinking and speech* is the subject of the next chapter of this book.

A letter to Luria

In June 1932 Vygotsky wrote a letter to Alexander Luria:

Dear Alexander Romanovich, I am still in Moscow and still do not know whether an operation will be done this summer or in the fall. I have grasped from the doctors' comments and intonation that I will apparently be unable to avoid it. I am staying at the clinic for a few days to decide the matter … Please write me about your experiments, and conduct them with all confidence in their great objective importance and their special significance for us. I shake your hand. Sincerely yours, L. Vygotsky.

(Vygotsky, 2007, pp. 43–44)

Vygotsky's tuberculosis was worsening, the cavities in his lungs were not closing up and surgery was the obvious option. But he was resisting a stay in hospital; he had too much to do.

Note

1 Quotations from *Thinking and speech* are taken from the English edition of the *Complete works,* volume 1 (Vygotsky, 1987), but in my view this translation lacks the economy and grace of Kozulin's translation (Vygotsky, 1986).

References

Fitzpatrick, S. (1979). *Education and social mobility in the Soviet Union 1921–1934.* Cambridge: Cambridge University Press.

Luria, A.R. (1982). *Language and cognition.* Wertsch, J. (ed.). Washington, DC: V.H. Winston.

Luria, A.R. (1987) 'Afterword to the Russian edition', in Vygotsky, L.S., *The collected works of L.S. Vygotsky. Volume 1, Problems of general psychology*, pp. 359–373. Trans. and intro. N. Minick; Rieber, R.W. and Carton, A.S. (eds). New York: Plenum Press.

Piaget, J. (1923). *Le langage et la pensée chez l'enfant* [*The language and thought of the child*]. Neuchatel: Delachaux and Niestle.

Piaget, J. (1924). *Le jugement et le raisonnement chez l'enfant* [*The judgement and reasoning of the child*]. Neuchatel: Delachaux and Niestle.

Sakharov, L. (1994). 'Methods for investigating concepts' [1930]. Trans. M. Vale, in Van der Veer, R. and Valsiner, J. (eds), *The Vygotsky reader*, pp. 73–98. Oxford: Blackwell.

Santiago-Delefosse, M., and Delefosse, J.-M. (2002). 'Spielrein, Piaget and Vygotsky: three positions on child thought and language'. *Theory and Psychology*, 12(6), pp. 723–747.

Van der Veer, R. (1996). 'Vygotsky and Piaget: a collective monologue'. *Human Development*, 39, pp. 237–242.

Van der Veer, R. and Valsiner. J. (1991). *Understanding Vygotsky: a quest for synthesis.* Oxford: Blackwell.

Vygotsky, L.S. (1971). *The psychology of art.* Intro. A.N. Leontiev; commentary V.V. Ivanov. Cambridge, MA: MIT Press.

Vygotsky, L.S. (1986). *Thought and language* [1934]. Trans. A. Kozulin. Cambridge, MA: MIT Press.

Vygotsky, L.S. (1987). *The collected works of L.S. Vygotsky. Volume 1, Problems of general psychology.* Trans. and intro. N. Minick; Rieber, R.W. and Carton, A.S. (eds). New York: Plenum Press.

Vygotsky, L.S. (1987a). *Thinking and speech* [1934], in Vygotsky, L.S., *The collected works of L.S. Vygotsky. Volume 1, Problems of general psychology*, pp. 37–285. Trans. and intro. N. Minick; Rieber, R.W. and Carton, A.S. (eds). New York: Plenum Press.

Vygotsky, L.S. (1998). 'Pedology of the adolescent' [1931], in Vygotsky, L.S., *The collected works of L.S. Vygotsky. Volume 5, Child psychology*, pp. 3–184. Trans. M.J. Hall; Rieber, R.W. (ed.). New York: Plenum Press.

Vygotsky, L.S. (1999). *The teaching about emotions: historical-psychological studies* [1931–1933], in Vygotsky, L.S., *The collected works of L.S. Vygotsky. Volume 6, Scientific legacy*, pp. 71–235. Trans. M.J. Hall; prologue D. Robbins; Rieber, R.W. (ed.). New York: Plenum Press.

Vygotsky, L.S. (2007). 'In Memory of L.S. Vygotsky (1896–1934): L.S. Vygotsky: Letters to Students and Colleagues'. Trans. M.E. Sharpe; Puzyrei, A.A. (ed.). *Journal of Russian and East European Psychology*, 45(2), pp. 11–60.

Vygotsky, L.S. (2017). 'The problem of teaching and mental development at school age' ['*Problema obučenija i umstvennogo razvitiya v škol'nom vozraste*'] [1935]. Trans. S. Mitchell. *Changing English*, 24(4), pp. 359–371. Also available online in the Marxist Archive: www.marxists.org/archive/vygotsky/works/1931/school-age.htm

Zavershneva, E. and Van der Veer, R. (eds) (2018). *Vygotsky's notebooks: a selection.* Singapore: Springer.

Chapter 11

Thinking and speech 2: The final 'why'

> Without philosophy (one's own personal philosophy of life) there can be nihilism, cynicism, suicide, but not life ... Crises are not a temporary state, but the path to one's inner life ... In particular, all of us, peering into our past, see that we are drying up. And indeed we are. This is so. To develop is to die.
>
> (From Vygotsky's letter to Roza Levina, 16 June 1931; Vygotsky, 2007, p. 38)

'The possibility of implementing all of our plans'

In 1934 Vygotsky was working harder than ever, travelling between Moscow and Leningrad to give lectures, planning for a new research institute, and of course writing. In the period from 1931 to 1934 he delivered a series of six lectures in psychology at Leningrad, which are published in volume 1 of the *Collected works* (Vygotsky, 1987b, pp. 289–358). He also gave many lectures on pedology in Leningrad, only some of which were included in volume 5 of the *Collected works* (Vygotsky, 1998). (A translation of the complete pedological works into English is currently being carried out by David Kellogg and Nikolai Veresov; the first volume is Vygotsky, 2019.)

During this period Vygotsky was exploring further the relation between psychology and neuroscience, and continuing to practise as a clinical psychologist at the EDI (Experimental Defectological Institute) and at the Donskaya Clinic, both in Moscow. But he was also looking forward to a new development: he had been offered the post of head of the psychology department at a new research institute, VIEM, the All-Union Institute of Experimental Medicine, in Moscow. Vygotsky's elder daughter, Gita, in her memoir 'Through a daughter's eyes', tells how Vygotsky was preparing for this post:

> It not only took a lot of time, it also occupied the mind and imagination. It gave inspiration in that it outlined new, unprecedented possibilities for work and new scientific research. It was this time Luria had in mind when he said: 'For the first time, we found ourselves faced with the possibility of implementing all of our plans and creating the organized team of

DOI: 10.4324/9780429203046-11

researchers about which he dreamed all his life and which could undertake to carry out everything that was hidden in his brilliant brain.'

True, at times Father's health was poor, and he even sometimes allowed himself to be cared for, which had never been the case before. I remember one conversation between my parents that I witnessed. Mama said that he had to rest and recuperate, that the doctors also insisted on this. It was even better, as his permanent physician advised, to go to a hospital for this. My father's firm answer was: 'I can't do this now. I have no right to interrupt the school year for the students. Once the school year is over, then I'll go to be treated.' This was said in such a way that it was senseless even to discuss the matter. But he was not fated to complete the school year.

Yet, even feeling bad at the time did not dampen his spirits. He was preparing for some new work, and this created a very good mood: it gave him strength.

(Vygodskaya and Lifanova, 1999, p. 11)

At this time Vygotsky was also planning two major books, one on consciousness and the other on emotion.

Consciousness

'No one can doubt that Vygotsky was, first of all, the psychologist of consciousness', writes Nikolai Veresov in *Undiscovered Vygotsky* (Veresov, 1999, p. 43). But he also adds that there was a 'dramatic evolution' in Vygotsky's views on consciousness and its nature. Consciousness had been a central theme in Vygotsky's psychology since (at least) 1925, when he gave a celebrated talk on the topic, and he continued to develop his theory of the construction of consciousness. Several notebooks from 1932 contain outlines for his planned book, which was intended to provide a systematic semantic analysis of consciousness, in which *meaning* would be a key concept. Although Vygotsky was very preoccupied with defining the thesis and the contents of the book, it was never written.

Throughout the development of Vygotsky's theory, however, he argued that consciousness was built and developed, from the earliest years, through language. In a late work, a lecture from 1933/34 on 'Early childhood' (ch. 9 in volume 5 of the *Collected works*), he observed that:

in early childhood, together with the development of speech, what seems to me the most essential positive trait of human consciousness at later stages of development appears, specifically, [to be] the interpreted and systemic structure of consciousness ...

As systemic construction of consciousness, it seems to me, we should understand the unique relation of separate functions to each other, that is, that at each age level, certain functions are in a certain relation to each other and form a certain system of consciousness ...

> In the form of a general thesis I will say that the change in the system of relations of functions to each other consists of a direct and very close connection with the meaning of words and, specifically, with the result that the meaning of words begins to mediate mental processes.
>
> (Vygotsky, 1998a, p. 278)

Consciousness as an overall system, within which other psychological functions and systems interrelate, with these interrelationships and the nature of the system always changing; consciousness developing as part of the development of speech and thinking: this is a broad description of the picture of consciousness that Vygotsky was working with while he was writing *Thinking and speech*.

Affect and emotion

Between 1931 and 1933 Vygotsky was also working on a book about the emotions. In *The teaching about emotions* (Vygotsky, 1999b), only one part of which was completed, he began to articulate his own theory, as he often did, through engaging with the work of other theorists, in this case William James, Lange, Descartes and Spinoza. In Spinoza's work he was focusing particularly on affects and emotions as the forces that power and drive human thoughts and actions. He was considering how to further investigate the role of affect and emotion in thought and action.

Vygotsky had been emphasising affect in his writing and his talks, particularly in the context of pedology and child development, for several years. The importance of '*perezhivanie*' (lived experience), with its focus on the personal and affective aspect of experience, and of the social context of experience, was already established in his psychology. Although it is sometimes seen as a theme of Vygotsky's later work, Pascale Severac suggests that *perezhivanie* had in fact been associated with consciousness from the mid-1920s when Vygotsky wrote that 'consciousness is the experiencing of experiences' – '*soznanie est' perezhivanie perezhivanii*' (Severac, 2017, p. 94).

Despite his conviction of the centrality of emotion and affect in consciousness, Vygotsky never expanded his ideas on affect into a complete theory. Yet, if he had, it is clear that it would have followed the paths of his other models of mental development, since emotions were not different from other mental functions. In his paper 'On the problem of the psychology of the actor's creative work', he concluded:

> Like other mental functions, emotions do not remain in the connection in which they are given initially by virtue of the biological organization of the mind. In the process of social life, feelings develop and former connections disintegrate; emotions appear in new relations with other elements of mental life, new systems develop, new alloys of mental functions and unities of a

higher order appear within which special patterns, interdependencies, special forms of connection and movement are dominant.

(Vygotsky, 1999a, p. 244)

In his lecture 'Imagination and its development in childhood' (Vygotsky, 1987a) Vygotsky had suggested that the imagination could unite several other functions, including emotion, in a psychological system, and participate in advanced thinking. In his article 'The problem of mental retardation' he had also stressed 'the unity between the affective and intellectual processes' (Vygotsky, 1993, p. 232) and insisted that:

> The whole point is that thought and affect are part of the same, single whole and that whole is human consciousness ... we might say that any stage in the development of thought has a corresponding stage in the development of the affect.
>
> (Vygotsky, 1993, p. 236)

The symposium on consciousness

On 4 December 1932 Vygotsky had held a staff conference for his colleagues and ex-colleagues. He had prepared very thoroughly for this symposium and his notes can be found in ch. 17 of his *Notebooks* (Vygotsky, 2017, pp. 271–290). Just as when he had presented his talk on 'psychological systems' to his colleagues in 1930, Vygotsky was suggesting another change of direction for their work. He was proposing they study the most important psychological system of all, the semantic system and structure of consciousness.

The editors' introduction to the notes on the symposium observes: 'Vygotsky sharply criticises his previous views and underlines the need for a new research direction.' (ibid., p. 274) (This self-criticism was typical of the way in which Vygotsky moved on in his theory – he was always looking for the next step on the ladder.) The notebook begins with a plan of his introduction:

> The need for a new stage in the research does not follow from the fact that a new idea came up, because a new idea became interesting, but because the development of the research itself required it. The new facts impel us to the search for new, more complex explanations. The limited, conventional, narrow nature of the older viewpoint led to an incorrect assessment of the central aspects, which we have taken for secondary ones: the interfunctional connections ... Thus, we have lots of poorly explained facts and wish to look deeper into the facts, i.e., we wish to re-interpret them theoretically.
>
> (Vygotsky, 2017, p. 274)

He explains his proposal in this way:

> The most important thing, which has no equal in the organic world, is: (a) the change of the interfunctional connections … (b) one and the same function is performed by different processes, *ergo* functions are not tied to activities, they are *polyvalent, polyfunctional*, pure, free, and auxiliary unbound activities of consciousness.
>
> (Vygotsky, 2017, p. 274)

Following Vygotsky's presentation there was a very long discussion; the conference went on for two days. Vygotsky's own notes make clear that there was some dissension and disagreement, including the questioning of whether this change of direction was necessary. Leontiev, particularly, was unhappy about Vygotsky's statement that the new stage of research should go beyond the study of sign uses; he was reluctant to give up this fruitful research route. But Luria supported Vygotsky, stating that speech was a phenomenon of consciousness and that there was no reflection of reality without speech.

Andrey Maidansky suggests that:

> The contradictory unity of concept and affect, of reason and passion, of thought and speech, is the main theme of Vygotsky's latest works.
>
> (Maidansky, 2018, p. 357)

Human beings' ability to unite these conflicting attributes is part of the 'progressive freeing' that Vygotsky, like Spinoza, sees as enabling the development of mind.

Maidansky observes that in Vygotsky's *Notebooks* (Russian edition), freedom is defined, in the spirit of Spinoza's *Ethics*, as '*conceptualised affect*' (ibid.). He quotes Vygotsky:

> The concept of affect is an active state, freedom as is.
>   Freedom: affect within the concept.
>   The central problem of all psychology is freedom …
>   The grandiose picture of the development of personality: the path to freedom.
>
> (Vygotsky, 2017, pp. 255–256)

Leontiev rejected Vygotsky's 'neo-Spinozist' proposal for the research. Maidansky refers to an account by Leontiev of his disagreement with Vygotsky, going back to 1931, over the theoretical move towards consciousness and affect. He could not at all comprehend Vygotsky's proposal to investigate the relationships between *concept* and *affect*; he described this as 'a step backward' (Maidansky, 2018, p. 357). He was unable to see affect as a driving force. He himself was developing a psychology based on 'objective activity'. In his autobiography he described a dramatic confrontation between two groups of members of Vygotsky's school as a 'confrontation of two lines for the future':

> My line: the return to initial theses and developing them in a new direction. Study of the practical intellect (= objective action). ...
>   Vygotsky's line: affective tendencies, emotions, feelings. They are behind consciousness. The life of affects: hence the turn to Spinoza.
>   (Leontiev, 2005, quoted in Maidansky, 2018, p. 358)

After this the relationship between Leontiev and Vygotsky deteriorated. Leontiev continued to develop his theory of activity with his colleagues in Kharkov.

Thinking and speech: Vygotsky's last chapter[2]

Concept and *affect*, the two ideas between which Leontiev could see no relationship, are both fundamental to Vygotsky's overall argument in *Thinking and speech*. In ch. 1–6 of the book Vygotsky had investigated the changing relationship between thought and word: first through a study of how word meaning develops in young children's language, and then through a long investigation of conceptual development in secondary-school students. In both these cases, the emphasis was on the denotative function of words and on the developing of increasingly precise meanings. Now in ch. 7 he comes to a third kind of development, the developing relationship between thought, word and affect, which counterposes to the stable and precise nature of 'meaning' (*znac'enie*) the changing, connotative and affective nature of 'sense' (*smysl*).

In the last chapter of *Thinking and speech*, Vygotsky returns to the subject of his earliest book, and to the personal manifesto represented by that book. In *The psychology of art* (Vygotsky, 1971), he had striven to show how literature works, both in terms of the internal organisation of works of art and of the function of art in human society. He had made a strong case for art as a major means by which human consciousness is developed, a 'tool of society'. In revisiting this subject, his argument is immeasurably strengthened by his experiences of the intervening years: his experimental work in psychology, his experience of theory-building and planning a major research programme, and his work on the place of higher mental functions and systems and of psychological tools in human development.

This chapter, 'Thought and word', is an extraordinary document and one cannot really imagine what its effect might have been on its readers, particularly its readers in the world of psychology, at the time of publication. In it, Vygotsky seems to turn with pleasure, perhaps some relief, to the world of literature. His study of word meaning and of the deep semantics of inner speech is here mainly carried on in relation to literary discourse, which is admitted as completely legitimate evidence of the workings of mind. Vygotsky seems not to acknowledge that he is making any kind of statement through this approach, and yet it must have been a very challenging demonstration of his belief that psychology should not confine itself to the study of behaviour in experimental contexts, but should study mind in all its manifestations, including works of art. It was this refusal to limit psychology to its traditional empirical sphere that led to Vygotsky being rejected by the psychological community both in his own country and in the West for many years, and makes him still, in some respects, a marginal figure today.

As Vygotsky was writing this chapter, Party control of scientific and intellectual activity was tightening. The need to demonstrate orthodoxy as a psychologist, both politically (in deriving one's work from Marxist–Leninist and materialist principles) and scientifically, was becoming more acute. Yet Vygotsky focuses the chapter on the problem of consciousness, a subject that was bound to expose him to rigorous scrutiny, and chooses as its epigraph a verse from Mandelstam, a poet who had been under increasing political suspicion and whose work was finally banned in 1934, the year when *Thinking and speech* was published and when Vygotsky died.

The Mandelstam quotation is about the difficulty of voicing thought, or more specifically, for the poet, of writing thought down:

> But I have forgotten what I wanted to say
> And a thought without flesh flies back to its palace of shadows.
>   (From 'I have forgotten the word ...', in
>   Mandelstam, 1989, p. 58)

Vygotsky had been reading Mandelstam, especially his essay 'On the nature of the word' (Mandelstam, 1991). It is clear that some of Mandelstam's themes and preoccupations were continuous with his own. In fact the last quotation in this chapter, the quotation from Gumilev describing the death of the word, was part of the epigraph of Mandelstam's essay.

Vygotsky's argument

Vygotsky's argument in the last chapter concerns (a) the development of word meaning, (b) the formation and nature of inner speech, and (c) the nature of non-verbal thought and the path it must take to be realised in language. He is concerned to stress the role of affect in this process; emotions, desires and needs are what give birth to both thought and language. Vygotsky's argument in this chapter has running through it many examples that underline the role of affect and emotion in the genesis of thought.

The development of word meaning

The first two parts of the chapter define the shifting nature of the relationship between thought and word. Vygotsky is impatient with most theorists who have written about word meaning (Kulpe, Selz, Ach and the Gestalt psychologists are discussed). All of this work errs in his view because it is tinged with 'associationism', the theory that words acquire meanings simply by being constantly associated with them. This view leads into a blind alley, for it ignores the dynamic nature of word meanings and the fact that they both change and develop. In an outstanding passage, Vygotsky describes how 'the development of the semantic and external aspects of speech move in opposite directions' (Vygotsky, 1987c, p. 251) – words come to mean both *less* and *more*: as children's vocabulary grows, words become more denotative, more precise and explicit, but they also lose some of the layers of connotative meaning that they have held. This focus on the way that language travels between the outer and the inner worlds, the nature of both the voyage out and the voyage in, will preoccupy Vygotsky for the rest of the chapter.

The formation and nature of inner speech

Vygotsky turns to inner speech and resumes his ongoing quarrel with Piaget about the function and development of egocentric speech. The experiments of Vygotsky and his team had revealed important information about the changing nature of egocentric speech, demonstrating its increasingly idiosyncratic syntax, fragmentation and abbreviation, and an increasingly predicative style, like the speech of intimates. Further investigations and other data, including Piaget's own, 'provide consistent support for a single idea, the idea that *egocentric speech develops in the direction of inner speech*' (ibid., p. 262).

In order, apparently, to clarify still further the nature of inner speech, Vygotsky refers back to the contrastive analysis he made (in ch. 6 of the book) of the characteristics of inner, outer and written speech. In this passage, he is also concerned with the antipodal relationship between these forms – the way oral speech is abbreviated and internalised as inner speech, and the way that inner speech must be expanded and elaborated in the act of writing. Though Vygotsky does not entirely acknowledge what he is doing, from now on his focus in the rest of the chapter will largely be on the 'voluntary construction of the fabric of meaning' (ibid., p. 204) which takes place in writing. (Kozulin's memorable translation of this phrase is the 'deliberate structuring of the web of meaning'; Vygotsky, 1986, p. 182.) This focus will enable him to look at the longest journey that thoughts have to travel:

thought → meaning → inner speech → (oral drafts) → writing

Moreover, out of all the many kinds of written language, Vygotsky refers more and more from now on to literature and particularly to poetry. Of the 45 references in this chapter, over half are to literature, and of these about half are to poetry. These poetic references are particularly predominant in the last part of the chapter.

The reason for this becomes clear as Vygotsky unfolds his description of the characteristics of inner speech. He begins to explore the essence of this speech form, which is that it works with semantics, not phonetics.

> In inner speech the syntactic and phonetic aspects of speech are reduced to a minimum ... Word meaning advances to the forefront.
>
> (Vygotsky, 1987c, p. 275)

Words in inner speech become concentrates of sense, which need considerable expansion in order to be expressed in oral speech. 'Inner speech is speech carried on almost without words' (ibid.).

Vygotsky identifies three basic characteristics of inner speech:

i   the predominance of a word's 'sense' (*smysl*) over its meaning (*znac'enie*);

ii   the *agglutination* of words in inner speech – the way words are combined and unified into complex new forms; and

iii the way words acquire layers of meaning and become 'saturated with sense'. (Vygotsky, 1987c, p. 278)

Implicitly, as Vygotsky explores these characteristics of inner speech, he is showing what it is that writers and poets have to work with in their creation of symbols for others. The connotative character of inner speech, the predominance of moods, sounds, shades of meaning, allusions, the texture and feel of words, the dynamic, fluid and personal nature of inner language, are the resources that poetry exploits.

There is a paradox in this, for what Vygotsky goes on to show is that all these characteristics of inner speech make it likely to be incomprehensible or opaque to others, even if there were any way of recording it fully or sharing it with others. Yet it is this very density that poetry taps into. The condensed semantics of inner speech find their closest outer parallel in poetic language. This goes some way to describing what it is that poets, in particular, do when they turn private language and private symbols into language and symbols for others. Vygotsky suggests that in inner speech a single word can become a 'concentrated clot of sense', needing 'a whole panorama of words' (ibid.) to translate it into the language of external speech. Part of the power of poetry, however, lies in *not* completely unpacking these 'concentrated clots of sense', but allowing them to enter the inner speech of others and unfold in the mind of the reader.

Yet at the same time, of all the ways of 'structuring the web of meaning', poetry is the most deliberate. It is this paradox in poetry, the fact that it is both the most conscious and artful way of using language, yet that which is most responsive to the subterranean and condensed meanings of inner speech, that makes it a uniquely powerful medium. In this chapter, Vygotsky quotes frequently from poets – from Mandelstam, Pushkin, Tiutchev, Fet, Klebnikov, Gumilev and Goethe – while his own writing, particularly in the last pages, takes on more and more the character of poetry.

The nature of non-verbal thought

Vygotsky has not yet completed his voyage into the interior. He now looks at what lies beyond inner speech, on a still more inward plane: 'That plane is thought itself' (ibid., p. 280).

Vygotsky's analysis leaves unexplained whether 'thought itself' is intended to be understood as a yet deeper internalisation of language – what James Britton has illuminatingly termed 'post-verbal symbols' (Britton, n.d.) – which would be the logical and seemingly necessary conclusion from the general argument of the book. Vygotsky has, on the other hand, always maintained that there are areas of thought which lie outside language, and at this point in the chapter he stresses that there is no necessary or exact correspondence between thought and speech, as can be seen when 'thought does not move into word' (Vygotsky, 1987c, p. 280). Thought has its own structure, and is not made up of separate units, as language is. In further expounding this idea, Vygotsky refers to mental or eidetic imagery, and to the way in which a complex thought can be contained in a single graphic image, which will have to be translated into linear form as it is put into words. He seems to be suggesting that other semiotic systems and ways of symbolising meaning may, in an internalised form, help to make up thought, but this part of his argument is weaker for the lack of any indication of what he really intends by 'thought itself', and what he sees as its genetic roots.

The rest of the chapter deals with two major questions:

i   the role that affect and emotion play in the engendering of thought; and

ii   the path that thought must follow in its 'voyage out', particularly in order to find its fullest and most elaborated expression in written language.

Vygotsky has stressed from the first chapter of the book that thought is not an abstract, purely cognitive process; it is powered by desires, needs, interests and feelings. Intellect and affect are often separated by psychology, but this is a serious defect since it cuts off the intellectual aspects of consciousness from the affective aspects:

> The inevitable consequence of the isolation of these functions has been the transformation of thinking into an autonomous stream. Thinking itself became the thinker of thoughts.
>
> (Vygotsky, 1987c, p. 50)

And thinking was thus 'divorced from the full vitality of life, from the motives, interests, and inclinations of the thinking individual' (ibid.).

Stanislavski's analysis of the sub-text behind a text provides Vygotsky with a neat illustration of what is involved in understanding spoken language:

> Understanding of the words of others also requires understanding their thoughts. And even this is incomplete without understanding their motives or why they repressed their thoughts. In precisely this sense we complete the psychological analysis of any expression only when we reveal the most secret plane of verbal thinking – its motivation.
>
> (Vygotsky, 1987c, p. 283)

The work of the actor consists of uncovering the true meaning of the utterance, which may be different from the overt meaning of the words.

Essentially, both of these points have to do with tracing the path of the 'voyage out'. In thinking about what is involved in expanding thought into written language, Vygotsky focuses on the shifts that occur during the successive 'drafting' that takes place during this structuring of a text. His model of the drafting can be represented like this:

thought → meaning → inner speech → (oral drafts) → written speech

(In this representation written speech may, or may not, be rehearsed in talk.)

In considering the affective basis of thought, however, Vygotsky draws the map of the journey slightly differently:

affective volitional basis → thought → emergence of meaning → meaning realised in language

Here the stress is on what lies behind even thought itself – the feeling or impulse (the affective-volitional basis) that leads to the original thought and its successive stages of expression.

Inner speech

The linguist Volosinov, like Vygotsky, considered that:

> the semiotic material of the psyche is preeminently the word – inner speech ... Were it to be deprived of the word, the psyche would shrink to an extreme degree.
>
> (Volosinov, 1986, p. 29)

Inner speech, its development, status, and particular characteristics, lie at the heart of the last chapter of *Thinking and speech*. The nature of this speech function, which Vygotsky recognises as being the most difficult to investigate, is demonstrated through his experiments on egocentric speech. But these experiments, referred to in section 3 of the chapter, allow Vygotsky to study only the ontogenesis of inner speech, its very beginnings, and not its later developments, which have to be glimpsed through the (mainly literary) examples that begin to be widely used in the latter part of the chapter. Moreover, the early experiments lead Vygotsky to view inner speech mainly as interiorised monologue.

Yet although Vygotsky unhesitatingly classes written speech and inner speech together as monologic, and in one place in the chapter expresses the view that monologue is a 'higher, more complicated speech form' and 'developed later than dialogue' (Vygotsky, 1987c, p. 272), this classification of inner speech presents him with a difficulty. When he comes to look at the characteristics of inner speech he finds that in many ways this speech form has more in common with dialogue than with monologue, for instance in its tendency to predication. 'This same tendency for predicativity is a constant characteristic of inner speech' (ibid., p. 273), though in outer speech it is only found in particular contexts, such as between intimates who share perceptions. This leads Vygotsky to suggest that in inner speech we are in fact in dialogue – an inner dialogue with ourselves:

> This shared apperception is complete and absolute in the social interaction with oneself that takes place in inner speech.
>
> (Vygotsky, 1987c, p. 274)

Vygotsky knew the work of the linguist Lev Jakubinskij, and had read Jakubinkij's article 'On verbal dialogue' (Jakubinskij, 1979), which was originally published in 1923. There are overlaps between the examples from literature that he uses in this chapter and Jakubinskij's examples. These include the long quotation from Dostoevsky's *A writer's notebook*, which Vygotsky quotes to illustrate a point about the abbreviation of speech in dialogue, and is used by Jakubinskij to make the same point. It seems likely that Vygotsky absorbed a good deal from the article, whether or not he referred to it directly during the writing of the chapter.

In his article Jakubinskij sets out to examine dialogue, or direct verbal interaction. In the course of a brief but illuminating paper he touches on the place of mime, gesture, facial expression and intonation in direct face-to-face dialogue, on the abbreviation of speech between intimates ('speaking by hints'), and on the tendency of all speech, even monologic speech, towards dialogue. The whole of Jakubinskij's argument in the article very interestingly prefigures – as Jane Knox points out in her introduction to her translation of the article in *Dispositio* (Knox, 1979) – the later work of Bakhtin on the 'dialogic imagination'.

Ladislaw Matejka points out that both Volosinov and Vygotsky borrowed Jakubinskij's Dostoevsky quotation, and wrestled with the question of the relationship between inner speech and outer or oral speech (Matejka, 1986, p. 171).

Matejka finds them coming to very similar conclusions, with inner speech being defined by both of them as a completely different speech function from oral speech. Volosinov's views on this matter –

> It is clear from the outset that without exception all categories worked out by linguistics for the analysis of the forms of external language-speech (the lexicological, the grammatical, the phonetic) are inapplicable to the analysis of inner speech ...
>
> (Volosinov, 1986, p. 38)

– are very like Vygotsky's argument.

Luciano Mecacci believes that Vygotsky had read Volosinov's *Marxism and the philosophy of language*, from whose English translation I have quoted, and probably also knew (at the least) Bakhtin's *Problems of Dostoevsky's poetics* (1984) (Mecacci 1992, p. 417, n. 399). If so, it is perhaps surprising that Vygotsky did not explore more fully the dialogic aspect of inner speech. For the words of others, as Volosinov points out, are in fact taken into inner speech; it is there that 'Word comes into contact with word' (Volosinov, 1986, p. 138). The background to all spoken dialogue is the inner dialogue taking place in the inner speech of both parties. 'After all, it is not a mute wordless creature that receives such an utterance but a human being full of inner words' (ibid, p. 118).

Inner planes

For both Volosinov and Vygotsky, inner speech is key territory because it is the area where the inner and outer worlds of experience meet. It is where the formation and development of mind takes place, and is thus of importance both in psychology and philosophy. It is interesting to observe the metaphors used by these and other thinkers to picture this territory. Volosinov describes the relations between inner speech and outer speech as those between a sea, and an island rising from the sea:

> The outwardly actualised utterance is an island rising from the boundless sea of inner speech; the dimensions and forms of this island are determined by the particular situation of the utterance and its audience.
>
> (Volosinov, 1986, p. 96)

The form of the island is decided by the context of the utterance, but the sea from which it rises is formless, boundless, infinitely potential.

In this chapter Vygotsky habitually refers to the 'planes' of verbal and non-verbal thought. He conceives of a series of inwardly receding planes, which range from the outermost plane of external speech to the inmost plane of feeling, motivation, intention – the 'affective-volitional' basis of all cognition.

Between these are the planes of inner speech and that of 'thought itself'. *Affect is thus imagined as lying at the core of all verbal and intellectual activity.*

I have already suggested that although the plane of inner speech is explored thoroughly by Vygotsky, the plane of 'thought itself' is unexplored, while that of affect and emotion is only sketched on this inner map. Volosinov's work might have helped him to fill out the picture. Volosinov's brilliant contribution to this area of psychology lies in his argument about the fundamental role of signs in experience. He maintains that 'experience exists even for the person undergoing it only in the material of signs. Outside that material there is no experience as such' (ibid., p. 28). All experience is potential expression – through gesture or intonation or movement or facial expression, even if not through language. And Volosinov proceeds to demonstrate the wide vocabulary of sign material available to the psyche by his astonishing list of examples of what can count as sign:

> What then is the sign material of the psyche? Any organic activity or process: breathing, blood circulation, movements of the body, articulation, inner speech, mimetic motions, reaction to external stimuli (e.g. light stimuli) and so forth. In short, anything and everything occurring within the organism can become the material of experience, since everything can acquire semiotic significance, can become expressive.
>
> (Volosinov, 1986, pp. 28–29)

At the same time Volosinov acknowledges that the most important sign material of the psyche is language: 'The semiotic material of the psyche is preeminently the word ...' (ibid., p. 29).

D.W. Harding, in his essay on 'The hinterland of thought', describes these kinds of inner signs as: 'much finer postural sets and movements: shrinking, local tensions, twistings, asymmetries of muscle tone, and also contractions of smooth muscle in the viscera and changes in the circulatory system' (Harding, 1974, p. 178). He calls this kind of physical behaviour 'an intimate gesturing of the whole body, which may accompany or precede or entirely replace the outcropping of a belief or attitude in cognitive terms' (ibid.). He stresses that behaviour of this kind, which is sometimes difficult or impossible to detect, may be the only way in which some ideas, beliefs or attitudes exist – though psychoanalysis or psychotherapy may bring them 'to verbal formulation or other ideational recognition' (ibid.).

These powerful contributions enable us to conceptualise more clearly what might be found on Vygotsky's inner planes. There is the *plane of inner speech*, that most fully described by Vygotsky, where speech becomes abbreviated and is marked by predication, compression and agglutination. This plane is clearly a continuum – Vygotsky's experiments on the development of this speech form suggest that there must be a zone close to the border with external speech where inner speech is almost as elaborated as oral speech, and another, close to the border of the more inward plane of thought, where inner speech is maximally compressed and at the point of being transmuted into 'post-verbal symbols'.

Next comes the *plane of thought*. Here we would find post-verbal symbols but also other thought material from other symbol systems – including 'presentational symbols', in Suzanne Langer's term (Langer, 1980, p. 97). Her distinction between presentational and discursive symbolism provides a helpful means of describing ways of thinking that lie beyond language: 'the abstractions made by the ear and the eye – the forms of direct perception' (ibid., p. 92). These non-discursive symbols constitute a different kind of semiotic material.

Finally there is the *'affective-volitional' plane* of feelings, needs, desires and intentions. Because this plane is still less available to scrutiny, it becomes even harder to envisage what is to be found there. But Volosinov's and Harding's lists give us a suggestive start. The sign material of affect will be expressions of the feelings that lie behind thought. Vygotsky's use of Stanislavski's directions to actors emphasises how, behind every line of the text in a play, stand the 'parallel desires' that the character is feeling. And this is also true in life:

> The affective and volitional tendency stands behind thought. Only here do we find the answer to the final 'why' in the analysis of thinking.
>
> (Vygotsky, 1987c, p. 282)

In travelling outward, thought moves further away from its affective roots and further towards the cognitive. Language becomes progressively less connotative and more denotative as it moves from the more condensed and private imagery of the plane of thought, and towards the elaborated discursive nature of public language. And words which in the furthest recesses of inner speech are 'clots of sense' (ibid., p. 278), saturated with profound feelings, begin to be used in less idiosyncratic ways as they move outwards into external speech and take on more clearly differentiated public meanings.

Mandelstam's poem

The poem that Vygotsky quotes from as his epigraph in the last chapter of *Thinking and speech* is resonant with his preoccupations in the chapter. The imagined setting for the poem seems to have a strange affinity with one of Vygotsky's inner planes, the plane of inner speech. The voyage out into the world of external speech, and the difficulty of making that voyage, of expressing private meanings in public language, is the topic of Mandelstam's poem.

Vygotsky's choice of the quotation from Mandelstam's poem as an epigraph at such a time is obviously meaningful – it is a political act. It must be seen as a manifesto, a statement of his determination to define psychology and its legitimate concerns in his own terms, despite the likely reaction of the regime. For several years before 1934, the year when *Thinking and speech* was published and Mandelstam was exiled, the poet had been suspect in the eyes of the regime and had been the subject of investigation and criticism; his privately circulated epigrammatic poem on Stalin was the event that led to his arrest.

But Vygotsky's choice of Mandelstam was also a personal choice. Mandelstam and Vygotsky had evidently known each other for years; Vygotsky's copy of Mandelstam's *Tristia*, from which the poem he quotes is taken, was dedicated to him personally by Mandelstam in a printed dedication at the time of publication in 1922.

The setting of the poem is the classical underworld, the shores of the Styx. Dead souls rustle like leaves. The scene is a barren one:

> No birds are heard. No blossom on the immortelle.
> The manes of the night horses are transparent.
> An empty boat floats on an arid estuary
> And, lost among grasshoppers, the word swoons.
> (Mandelstam, 1989, p. 58)

This underworld is both a place of exile, and yet a refuge full of 'Stygian affection', tender and nurturing. Mandelstam's attitude towards this silent world set apart is full of ambiguity.

It may have been as much as anything the setting and atmosphere of this poem that drew Vygotsky towards it. It pictures a shadowy world before speech – on the other side of speech. This underworld, or underside of things, like D.W Harding's 'hinterland of thought', is largely unmapped and unmappable. The poem, moreover, takes place on the brink of the river that marks the boundary between the worlds of the living and the dead. It is a powerful symbol for the moment that Vygotsky returns to again and again in this chapter, the moment when a thought enters words, when the boundary between two 'inner planes' is crossed. And of course it is also a reminder of how near Vygotsky himself was to this same brink; he was dictating the chapter in the Serebryany Bor Sanatorium shortly before his death. It is the *liminality* of the world that Mandelstam pictures, and where the swallow hovers, that creates the strongest link between the thought and feeling of the poem and those of Vygotsky's last chapter.

In the poem, Mandelstam reveals his private images and allows them to enter the consciousness of others. Perhaps no other poet celebrates and explores the world of the inner and private senses of words so unceasingly as Mandelstam. His poem is an embodiment of what Vygotsky saw as creative activity, in which 'inner context-dependent senses gradually unfold their meanings as symbols-for-others' (Kozulin, 1986, p. xxxviii). It may stand both for poetry, the most developed use of written speech, and as a 'tool of society', the cultural tool that Vygotsky knew literature to be, and strove to prove it to be through his psychology.

The construction of consciousness

Vygotsky's focus on literature in this chapter implicitly proposes it as a major site for exploring issues to do with word meaning, inner speech, thought and affect. In this respect his argument is like that of Bakhtin, who considered that literature was a means of understanding human consciousness. Because literature, in Bakhtin's view, is continuous with, and the furthest development of, ordinary speech, and because human consciousness is formed through language, literature 'reveals such capacities of human consciousness and communication which remain undeveloped or invisible in other media of communication' (quoted in Kozulin, 1990, p. 183).

Although he was not able, in the time left to him, to write either his book on consciousness, or his book on affect and emotion, Vygotsky managed to include in *Thinking and speech*, especially in this last chapter, the essence of what he wanted to say in relation to both subjects. Through his use of quotations from literature, particularly poetry and drama, he shows how art finds symbols to express the deepest feelings and the richest moments of emotional life. His treatment of this theme is strongly reminiscent of his statement in *The psychology of art*:

> Art is the social technique of emotion, a tool of society which brings the most personal and intimate aspects of our being into the circle of social life.
> (Vygotsky, 1971, p. 249)

Vygotsky has shown throughout *Thinking and speech* how consciousness – the meta-system of all psychological systems and functions – is constructed through the interaction and development of language and thought. His preoccupation with the problem of consciousness had been the subject of his early forays into psychology; one of his first conference papers had taken as its subject the problem of conscious behaviour. He persisted to the end in labouring to establish objectively the role of thought and language in the development of the mind. But he now also stressed the place of affect in this development:

> Only here do we find the answer to the final 'why' in the analysis of thinking.
> (Vygotsky, 1987c, p. 282)

Consciousness and affect had been termed 'idealistic' in psychology. By enlarging the boundaries of psychology to take in more than *external* behaviour and activity, Vygotsky laid the basis of a new cultural, historical and humanistic psychology.

At the end of the chapter, Vygotsky's summary of what his argument has shown is confident and unequivocal. Thought is born through words, and words are seen as the culmination of development. Briefly, in a paragraph, he sketches what would have been his response to Leontiev and Leontiev's research group, who had criticised and revised his work in their 'theory of activity'. He perfectly accepts that activity has a fundamental part to play in human development, but places language at the *peak* of development:

The word did not exist in the beginning. In the beginning was the deed. The formation of the word occurs nearer the end than the beginning of the development. The word is the end that crowns the deed.

(Vygotsky, 1987c, p. 285)

This statement, beginning with a quotation from Goethe, was also used at the end of *Tool and symbol* (Vygotsky and Luria, 1994), an earlier argument for the central place of language, rather than activity, in the development of mind and of consciousness.

Vygotsky's closing paragraphs are condensed, almost notes. In the 1962 English translation this passage was even more condensed, as it was cut by the translators to about a third of its length, with most of the philosophical content omitted. As Mecacci notes, in the Russian *Sobranie Sočinenij* of 1982 most of the text was restored, but of three quotations from Marx and Engels's *A critique of the German ideology* (1968), which Vygotsky originally used on this final page, only two were included, without quotation marks or any citation; the third[1] was omitted (Vygotsky, 1992, p. 419, n. 411). The English translation of 1987 simply follows the flawed Russian text.

Vygotsky's tone in these last sentences is triumphant; in 'word meaning' he has found his 'cell', the unit of analysis that has allowed him to investigate the furthest recesses of the psyche. Using this one building block he has constructed an immense piece of architecture, his *Capital*.

Consciousness is reflected in the word like the sun is reflected in a droplet of water. The word is a microcosm of consciousness, like a living cell is related to an organism, like an atom is related to the cosmos. The meaningful word is a microcosm of human consciousness.

(Vygotsky, 1987c, p. 285)

How much more Vygotsky could have gone on to do with a longer lease of life, and in different times, can only be guessed at. Luria said of him:

Through more than five decades in science I never again met a person who even approached his clearness of mind, his ability to lay bare the essential structure of complex problems, his breadth of knowledge in many fields, and his ability to foresee the future development of his science.

(Luria, 1979, p. 38)

The text of *Thinking and speech*

The text of *Thinking and speech* is still a matter of some controversy. It was a compilation from different sources, and Vygotsky in his Preface detailed clearly which chapters had been previously published. Some commentators now think that the text was assembled not by Vygotsky himself, but by his friends and collaborators. However, it is very difficult to believe that Vygotsky had no hand in the decisions involved. The argument of the book is coherent and clearly developed, even though some chapters are somewhat repetitive – not an unusual feature of Vygotsky's writing, which often had its origin in stenographic records.

Vygotsky died on 11 June 1934, in the sanatorium, working till the end. Luciano Mecacci reports that on the day after he died the secret police were in his house requisitioning his papers, 'among which there could have been, had they not been secreted, the pages of the last chapter of this book, dictated by Vygotsky' (Mecacci, 1992, p. vi).

Note

1 'From the start the "spirit" is afflicted with the curse of being "burdened" with matter, which here makes its appearance in the form of agitated layers of air, sounds, in short, of language. Language is as old as consciousness, language is practical consciousness that exists also for other men, and for that reason alone it really exists for me personally as well; language, like consciousness, only arises from the need, the necessity, of intercourse with other men' (Marx and Engels, 1968).
2 Parts of this chapter originally appeared in my article 'Vygotsky's "Thought and Word"' (see reference list).

References

Bakhtin, M. (1984). *Problems of Dostoevsky's poetics* [1929]. Emerson, C. (ed. and trans.). Minneapolis, MN: University of Minnesota Press.
Barrs, M. (2016). 'Vygotsky's "Thought and Word"'. *Changing English*, 23(3), pp. 241–256.
Britton, J. (n.d.). 'Post-verbal symbols': a description of Vygotsky's 'thought itself'. Personal communication.
Harding, D.W. (1974). 'The hinterland of thought', in *Experience into words*. London: Penguin, pp. 176–198.
Harris, O. (ed.) (1991). *Osip Mandelstam: The collected critical prose and letters*. London: Harvill Press.
Jakubinskij, L.P. (1979). 'On verbal dialogue' [1923]. Trans. J.E. Knox. *Dispositio: Revista Hispanica de Semiotica Literaria*, IV(11–12), pp. 321–336.
Knox, J. E. (1979). 'Lev Jakubinskij as a precursor to modern Soviet semiotics'. *Dispositio: Revista Hispanica de Semiotica Literaria*, IV(11–12), pp. 317–320 [introduction to Jakubinskij, 1979 above].
Kozulin, A. (1986). 'Vygotsky in context', in Vygotsky, L.S., *Thought and language*, pp. xi–lxi. Trans. A. Kozulin. Cambridge, MA: MIT Press.
Kozulin, A. (1990). *Vygotsky's psychology: a biography of ideas*. Hemel Hempstead: Harvester Wheatsheaf.
Langer, S. (1980). *Philosophy in a new key*. Cambridge, MA: Harvard University Press.
Leontiev, A.N. (2005). 'Study of the environment in the pedological works of L.S. Vygotsky: a critical study' [1937]. Trans. M.E. Sharpe. *Journal of Russian and East European Psychology*, 43(4), pp. 8–28.
Luria, A.R. (1979). *The making of mind: a personal account of Soviet psychology*. Cole, M. and Cole, S. (eds). Cambridge, MA: Harvard University Press.

Maidansky, A. (2018). 'Spinoza in cultural-historical psychology'. *Mind, Culture and Activity*, 25(4), pp. 355–364.

Mandelstam, O. (1989). *The eyesight of wasps*. Trans. J. Greene. London: Angel Books.

Mandelstam, O. (1991). 'On the nature of the word', in Harris, O. (ed.), *Osip Mandelstam: The collected critical prose and letters*, pp. 117–132. London: Harvill Press.

Marx, K. and Engels, F. (1968). *A critique of the German ideology* [1846]. Moscow: Progress Publishers. Also available online in the Marxist Archive: www.marxists.org/archive/marx/works/download/Marx_The_German_Ideology.pdf.

Matejka, L. (1986). 'On the first Russian prolegomena to semiotics'. Appendix to Volosinov, V.N., *Marxism and the philosophy of language*, pp. 161–174. Trans. L. Matejka and I.R. Titunik. Cambridge, MA: Harvard University Press.

Mecacci, L. (1992). 'Introduzione', in Vygotsky, L.S., *Pensiero e linguaggio*, pp. v–x. Trans. L. Mecacci. Bari: Editori Laterza.

Severac, P. (2017). 'Consciousness and affectivity: Spinoza and Vygotsky'. *Stasis*, 5 (2), pp. 80–109.

Van der Veer, R. and Valsiner, J. (eds) (1994). *The Vygotsky reader*. Oxford: Blackwell.

Veresov, N. (1999). *Undiscovered Vygotsky: etudes on the pre-history of cultural-historical psychology*. Frankfurt-am-Main: Peter Lang.

Volosinov, V.N. (1986). *Marxism and the philosophy of language* [1929]. Trans. L. Matejka and I.R. Titunik. Cambridge, MA: Harvard University Press.

Vygodskaya, G.L. and Lifanova, T.M. (1999). 'Through a daughter's eyes'. *Journal of Russian and Eastern European Psychology*, 37(5), pp. 3–27. doi:10.2753/RPO1061-040537053.

Vygotsky, L.S. (1962). *Thought and language* [1934]. Trans. E. Hanfmann and G. Vakar. Cambridge, MA: MIT Press.

Vygotsky, L.S. (1971). *The psychology of art* [1925]. Cambridge, MA: MIT Press.

Vygotsky, L.S. (1986). *Thought and language* [1934]. Trans. A. Kozulin. Cambridge, MA: MIT Press.

Vygotsky, L.S. (1987). *The collected works of L.S. Vygotsky. Volume 1, Problems of general psychology*. Trans. and intro. N. Minick; Rieber, R.W. and Carton, A.S. (eds). New York: Plenum Press.

Vygotsky, L.S. (1987a). 'Imagination and its development in childhood' [1932], in Vygotsky, L.S., *The collected works of L.S. Vygotsky. Volume 1, Problems of general psychology*, pp. 339–349. Trans. and intro. N. Minick; Rieber, R.W. and Carton, A.S. (eds). New York: Plenum Press.

Vygotsky, L.S. (1987b). 'Lectures on psychology' [1931–1934], in Vygotsky, L.S., *The collected works of L.S. Vygotsky. Volume 1, Problems of general psychology*, pp. 289–358. Trans. and intro. N. Minick; Rieber, R.W. and Carton, A.S. (eds). New York: Plenum Press.

Vygotsky, L.S. (1987c). *Thinking and speech* [1934], in Vygotsky, L.S., *The collected works of L.S. Vygotsky. Volume 1, Problems of general psychology*, pp. 37–285. Trans. and intro. N. Minick; Rieber, R.W. and Carton, A.S. (eds). New York: Plenum Press.

Vygotsky, L.S. (1992). *Pensiero e linguaggio* [1934]. Trans. L. Mecacci. Bari: Editori Laterza.

Vygotsky, L.S. (1993). 'The problem of mental retardation' [1935], in Vygotsky, L.S., *The collected works of L.S. Vygotsky. Volume 2, The fundamentals of defectology*, pp. 220–240. Trans. and intro. J.E. Knox and C.B. Stevens; Rieber, R.W. and Carton, A.S. (eds). New York: Plenum Press.

Vygotsky, L.S. (1998). *The collected works of L.S. Vygotsky. Volume 5, Child psychology*. Trans. M.J. Hall; Rieber, R.W. (ed.). New York: Plenum Press.

Vygotsky, L.S. (1998a). 'Early childhood' [1932–1934] in Vygotsky, L.S., *The collected works of L.S. Vygotsky. Volume 5, Child psychology*, pp. 261–281. Trans. M.J. Hall; Rieber, R.W. (ed.). New York: Plenum Press.

Vygotsky, L.S. (1999a). 'On the problem of the psychology of the actor's creative work' [1932], in Vygotsky, L.S., *The collected works of L.S. Vygotsky. Volume 6, Scientific legacy*, pp. 237–244. Trans. M.J. Hall; prologue D. Robbins; Rieber, R.W. (ed.). New York: Plenum Press.

Vygotsky, L.S. (1999b). *The teaching about emotions: historical-psychological studies* [1931–1933], in Vygotsky, L.S., *The collected works of L.S. Vygotsky. Volume 6, Scientific legacy*, pp. 71–235. Trans. M.J. Hall; prologue D. Robbins; Rieber, R.W. (ed.). New York: Plenum Press.

Vygotsky, L.S. (2007). 'In Memory of L.S. Vygotsky (1896–1934): L.S. Vygotsky: Letters to Students and Colleagues'. Trans. M.E. Sharpe; Puzyrei, A.A. (ed.). *Journal of Russian and East European Psychology*, 45(2), pp. 11–60.

Vygotsky, L.S. (2017). *Notebooks. Selected writings*. Zavershneva, E. and Van der Veer, R. (eds). Moscow: Kanon+.

Vygotsky, L.S. (2019). *L.S. Vygotsky's pedological works. Volume 1, Foundations of pedology*. Trans. and notes D. Kellogg and N. Veresov. Singapore: Springer.

Vygotsky, L.S. and Luria, A.R. (1994). *Tool and symbol in child development* [1930], in Van der Veer, R. and Valsiner, J. (eds), *The Vygotsky reader*, pp. 99–174. Oxford: Blackwell.

Chapter 12

After Vygotsky

Vygotsky's books

After Vygotsky's death in June 1934, he would become his books. But when he died much of his writing was still unpublished, so one of the most urgent concerns of his friends and colleagues was to make sure that as much as possible of his work was in print.

This applied particularly to the book that Vygotsky had been finishing at the very end of his life, *Thinking and speech* (Vygotsky, 1987a). Kolbanovsky, who had been appointed director of the Moscow Institute of Psychology in 1931, was determined to see it in print. David Joravsky sees Kolbanovsky as an orthodox Party member who had been appointed to the Director's role in order to 'set the place in order', but suggests that 'Once there, under the spell of Vygotsky's theorising, he became a defender of psychological science' (Joravsky, 1989, p. 359). Initially Kolbanovsky had been one of the Party cell committee that reviewed and criticised Vygotsky's plan for *Thinking and speech* in 1932. Now, however, he did everything he could to make sure that the book was published. With the help of Zankov and Shif he edited it, making only the most necessary corrections (ibid., p. 360). It was prefaced by an introduction and a short essay by Kolbanovsky, expressing some reservations about Vygotsky's theory (Mecacci, 1992, p. xiii). This was presumably to ward off possible ideological criticism.

The book that was published, however, did not include – as Kolbanovsky had hoped – Vygotsky's *The historical meaning of the crisis in psychology* (Vygotsky, 1997b). Kolbanovsky greatly admired this still unpublished work and in his oration at Vygotsky's funeral said that he hoped it would be published soon. But presumably the authorities would not allow that, and *The crisis in psychology* did not appear until 1982 when it became the main item in volume 1 of the Russian *Collected works* (*Sobranie Sočinenij*). *Thinking and speech* was thus, as Joravsky concludes, 'the public's chief access to Vygotsky's thought ... until the post-Stalin thaw' (Joravsky, 1989, p. 360). It appeared in late 1934.

Meanwhile Mina Levina, a close colleague of Vygotsky at the Leningrad Herzen Pedagogical Institute, put together the writings on the *Foundations of*

DOI: 10.4324/9780429203046-12

pedology, a stenographic record of a course of lectures that Vygotsky had delivered at the Institute. The lectures were originally published in Moscow and in Leningrad in 1934/1935 (Van der Veer and Valsiner, 1991, p. 384), in Iževsk in 2001 (edited by G.S. Korotaeva), and later by Kellogg and Veresov (Vygotsky, 2019).

1935 saw the publication of a book of Vygotsky's lectures and articles, which was edited by a group of Vygotsky's co-researchers, El'konin, Shif and Zankov. It contained talks about the zone of proximal/proximate development, and other articles relating to pedology and pedagogy. The overall title was *Umstvennoe razvitie detej v processe obučenija* (*Children's mental development in the process of learning/teaching*; Vygotsky, 1935).

Vygotsky's old friend from Gomel, Israel Daniushevsky, who was the Director of the Moscow Defectological Institute, and who had co-written 'The problem of mental retardation' with him, ensured that this long article was published in 1935. The article was later included in volume 2 of the *Collected works* (Vygotsky and Daniushevsky, 1993).

Daniushevsky also arranged that Vygotsky's long pedological article from 1931, 'The diagnostics of development', should be published as a pamphlet (edited by R.E. Levina). It appeared in 1936. The article is now the final item in volume 2 of the *Collected works* (Vygotsky, 1993).

But in June 1936 the mounting ideological criticism of pedology, apparent since 1930, culminated in the Decree on Pedology, which declared it to be a reactionary bourgeois science. It outlawed the discipline, closed all pedological institutes, and dismissed the staff. Many pedological publications were destroyed (Minkova, 2012, p. 93).

Van der Veer and Valsiner comment:

> It was because of his contributions to pedology that Vygotsky was damned by the authorities, and any study of his ideas banned in the Soviet Union, between 1936 and 1956; which explains the curious modifications of terminology in later republications of selected parts of his work.
>
> (Van der Veer and Valsiner, 1991, p. 327)

After the Pedology Decree there were attacks on Vygotsky's work. The timing and language of these suggested that they were written to order.

> The authors clearly followed the procedure that now had become distressingly widespread in the Soviet Union: on the premise of a Party directive, the work of an author would be scrutinised for (dis)agreement with that directive's content.
>
> (Van der Veer and Valsiner, 1991, p. 386)

In 1936 Kozyrev and Turko, who worked at the Herzen Institute, wrote an article criticising Vygotsky's work in pedology. They dismissed the concept of the zone of proximal/proximate development as 'fatalistic' and accepting of 'biological determinism'. They also claimed that Vygotsky's theory of the different roots of thought and speech, in *Thinking and speech*, was 'scientifically worthless' (ibid., p. 385).

Rudneva's critique of 1937, in a 32-page brochure, was simply a disorganised rant:

> Eclecticism is very distinctly reflected in Vygotsky's concepts: it is difficult to find any current in bourgeois psychology that has appeared in the last two decades that has not found a place in his writings ... Hence, the work of Vygotsky and his pupils on children has essentially been a mockery of our Soviet children and amounted to stupid, absurd tests and questionnaires associated with Piaget, Claparede, and others.
>
> (Rudneva, 2000, p. 76)

And at some time in the late 1930s (González Rey, 2014, puts it as 1937) Leontiev wrote an article with the title 'Study of the environment in the pedological works of L.S. Vygotsky', which presented the view of the social environment in Vygotsky's pedology as mistaken. First Leontiev considers Vygotsky's account of the development of word meaning and finds it to be a 'spiritual' and 'idealistic' theory. Then he describes Vygotsky's view of the environment as lacking an essential dimension: an understanding that all human relationships are based on the process of labour, of activity. Finally, Vygotsky's view of the child's *perezhivanie* (experience of the social environment) is dismissed as 'a secondary and derivative fact'; what is primary, in Leontiev's view, is the child's *action* 'as a completely practical and material being'. He concludes:

> Only the unity of activity and experience, and not experience as such, contains the internal driving force of the psychological development of man.
>
> (Leontiev, 2005, pp. 26–27)

With this article Leontiev made his declaration of independence. And thereafter, while on the one hand trying to monopolise Vygotsky's legacy, on the other he continued to develop his Activity Theory as a true 'Marxist psychology', becoming the leading figure in Soviet psychology (González Rey, 2014).

The role of Alexander Luria

After the Pedology Decree, Vygotsky's books were available in some libraries but with restricted access: special permission to read them was required. Even after Stalin's death in 1953 this atmosphere persisted; Vygotsky was under a cloud. In this atmosphere it would have been difficult to take forward Vygotsky's work in any public way, but several of his ex-colleagues and students continued to do research, and some of their researches related to projects that they had begun with Vygotsky, or that drew on parts of his theory. This was particularly true of Alexander Luria, who had moved into the field of neurology.

Vygotsky and Luria had carried out research together on what happens when, in a condition like aphasia, language begins to break down. They believed that a study of aphasia would enable them to look at the *obverse* of the process by which children, while retaining elementary mental functions, develop, through the mediation of language, 'higher mental functions' such as *voluntary* attention or *logical* memory. This would help to confirm their theory of mental development. They continued this work with patients with Parkinson's disease, and were able to show that with the help of signals patients could sometimes regulate their own behaviour.

Luria continued to work in the field of neurology and neuropsychology for the rest of his career and carried out analyses of thousands of cases over more than 25 years. But he maintained that:

> In each case the progress of diagnosis and the methods of treatment bear an obvious and close relation to the principles put forward by Vygotsky, who first suggested that the dissolution of higher psychological functions could serve as the path for their analysis ... The methods of therapy that have proved useful are exactly those methods that would have been predicted by Vygotsky on the basis of the general theory of the socio-historical origins of higher psychological functions.
>
> (Luria, 1979, p. 156)

Luria always acknowledged Vygotsky's role in his life's work. Tatiana Akhutina, who was a student of Luria's, recalls that when she showed her dissertation to Luria he made a single correction: 'in one place, concerning the detailed development of neuropsychological principles, he crossed out his own name and wrote "L.S. Vygotsky"' (Akhutina, 2003, p. 159).

Akhutina regards Vygotsky as having identified the fundamental problem of the localisation of mental functions. On these beginnings, Luria, 'in agreement with Vygotsky's theory, built a new psychological discipline − neuropsychology' (ibid., p. 183).

After the death of Stalin, things began moving more rapidly. In 1956 Luria and Leontiev edited a new edition of *Thinking and speech* in Russian. Oddly they did not simply republish the 1934 book but went through it omitting all references to pedology and making other minor cuts and changes. Then in 1960 *The history of the development of higher mental functions* was also published − but only the first five chapters (Mecacci, 2017, p. 153). Soon after this Vygotsky's books began to travel beyond the Soviet Union, and Luria played an active part in this process.

In 1962 there was the first edition in English of *Thinking and speech* (then entitled *Thought and language*), translated by Eugenia Hanfmann and Gertrude Vakar and with an introduction by Jerome Bruner. Hanfmann had been born in Russia and educated in Lithuania and Germany. In 1930 she went to the USA where she worked as a researcher and a lecturer in psychology. In 1957 Alexander Luria invited her to take part in translating *Thought and language* into English. She suggested that the translation should not include 'excessive repetition and certain polemical discussions that would be of little interest to the contemporary reader' (Vygotsky, 1962, p. xii). Consequently this version is very much shorter than later translations and omits many passages ('certain polemical discussions') from Vygotsky's critiques of Piaget's work.

Over the years Luria had maintained his international correspondence; he wrote to psychologists all over Europe and the USA. At every opportunity Luria tried to get his international contacts and visitors to take an interest in Vygotsky's work, and to get it published in the West. Both Michael Cole and Luciano Mecacci went to study with him (Cole in 1962 and Mecacci in 1972) and both eventually devoted a great deal of time to making Vygotsky's work better known outside the USSR.

Michael Cole and *Mind in society*

Michael Cole went to Moscow to work with Alexander Luria for a year in 1962. According to his own account (Cole, 2004), his aim was to study work on conditioned reflexes, and other Soviet work using Pavlovian conditioning techniques. He did not know that Luria had been a colleague of Vygotsky's, and did not choose to work with him because of that. Cole's whole background, and the focus of his work, were in the American behaviourist tradition.

Luria tried to encourage Cole to read Vygotsky's work, but Cole was resistant. He recalls his reactions on first reading *Thought and language*:

> Both Vygotsky's prose and the style of his thought defeated my attempts to understand Luria's admiration of him. I had read Vygotsky's *Thought and language* as a graduate student, but except for some observations on concept learning in children, which at the time I knew nothing about, I could see little in his work to generate enthusiasm.
>
> (Cole, 1979, p. 194)

It was not until Cole began to edit Luria's autobiography, and to understand how his career and thought had been influenced by Vygotsky, that he gradually saw the point of Luria's insistence.

At around this time, Cole promised Luria that he would ensure that two long essays by Vygotsky would appear in English. Luria had been urging him to publish Vygotsky in English for some time, but Cole confesses that 'as I did not understand Vygotsky well, I could see no point in it' (ibid., p. 196). Once he had actually undertaken the project and was engaged in the editorial work, he began to read the manuscripts in question more closely and came to a realisation of the significance of Vygotsky's work:

In struggling to understand Vygotsky well enough to resolve our editorial group's different interpretation of his ideas, I slowly began to discern the enormous scope of his thinking. His goal had been no less than the total restructuring of psychological research and theory. This undertaking would never have occurred to me or, I suspect, to very many other psychologists of my generation as anything but a crackpot scheme. Yet Vygotsky was no crackpot, and his scheme was extremely interesting.

(Cole, 1979, pp. 196–197)

Mind in society (Vygotsky, 1978) is a product of the struggle of Cole and his colleagues to understand Vygotsky's work, and to present him to a sceptical psychological community as a psychologist that it would be worth taking seriously. The book has no sense of being conceived as a whole, or of having a coherent and developing argument; its shape is simply a construction of Vygotsky's editors in the USA.

In the resultant text, one of Vygotsky's central theories, the role of language in mental development, is seriously under-represented. Joseph Glick, in his Prologue to *The history of the development of higher mental functions*, volume 4 of the *Collected works*, from which a chapter in *Mind and society* was taken, observes that in that volume 'the focus is on language which was the main topic of *Thought and language* and only a subordinate topic of *Mind in society*' (Glick, 1997, p. xiii).

Distorting history

The book which resulted from this editorial process is a very unsatisfactory production. Instead of printing the two complete manuscripts that had been made available to them as a whole (one of which was the manuscript of *Tool and symbol*), the editorial team chose to edit the texts in a highly interventive fashion. This is freely acknowledged in the editors' preface:

The reader will encounter here not a literal translation of Vygotsky, but rather our edited translation of Vygotsky, from which we have omitted material that seemed redundant and to which we have added material that seemed to make his points clearer.

(Cole, John-Steiner, Scribner and Souberman, 1978, p. x)

The editors confess that they have, in several places, inserted material from additional sources in order to make the meaning of the text clearer, and elucidate passages that seemed 'dense and elliptical'. They explain that they have used extracts from *The history of the development of higher mental functions* for this purpose, but have also included extracts from writings *not* by Vygotsky, but by his collaborators. Summing up what they have done, they end:

We realise that in tampering with the original we may have distorted history; however, we hope that by stating our procedures and by adhering as closely as possible to the principles and content of the work, we have not distorted Vygotsky's meaning.

(Cole, John-Steiner, Scribner and Souberman, 1978, p. x)

However, although these general procedures are stated, there is no detailed information in the notes to the volume about *where* particular changes have been made, or about the nature of the omissions and insertions. There are no summaries or translations of omitted passages, nor any indications of the extent of these editorial changes. All that readers of this volume know is that this is a text that has been substantially altered from the original. Sections that did not originally appear together are juxtaposed and made to appear as part of one work. Although a second edition could have provided more information about these missing details, in more than forty years since the publication of *Mind in society* none has been produced.

The distortions in the presentation of Vygotsky's psychology evident in *Mind in society* have continued in subsequent publications by Michael Cole, James Wertsch and others. The nature of these distortions, and the changes to and omissions from Vygotsky's writings, are described in detail by Ronald Miller in his book *Vygotsky in perspective* (Miller, 2011). Chief among these changes is the misrepresentation of Vygotsky's theory of 'mediating activity'. Vygotsky makes quite clear the different purposes of tools (directed outward to change things in the world) and signs, including language (directed inward as a means of psychological action, to change one's own behaviour). Miller argues that both Cole and Wertsch ignore this clear distinction and thus provide a misleading view of Vygotsky's work, in which language has virtually no place.

Luciano Mecacci

Mecacci went to Moscow in 1972 to work with Alexander Luria, and stayed there for several months. He worked at the Institute of Psychology, in the laboratory of psychophysiology, which used a modified version of Pavlov as its theoretical framework. However, all the researchers he met – the older and younger alike – were 'anti-Pavlovians'. They were most interested in the work of Vygotsky, Luria and Leontiev. At that time, Mecacci recalls:

the dissemination of Vygotsky's works was limited, implicitly, by the official decree of the Soviet Communist Party of 1936 … Nevertheless, Vygotsky was the main topic of our discussions triggered by the release of his unpublished papers in *samizdat*.

(Mecacci, 2012, p. 83)

Mecacci explains the neglect of Vygotsky in the USSR, four decades after his death, in terms of the deliberate ostracism of the man and his work that had become the norm among the psychological community during the Stalin era, and that lasted well after the death of Stalin. There was a general unwillingness, for ideological reasons, to initiate a revival of the work. This situation makes it possible to understand why the first international conference dedicated to Vygotsky was held in Rome in 1979. Only in 1981 was a conference organised in Moscow, specifically on the work of Vygotsky, 'the most celebrated Russian psychologist in the West' (Mecacci, 2017, p. 8).

One of the biggest obstacles to the study of Vygotsky in Russia between 1950 and 1980 was the unavailability of authentic versions of his writings. Mecacci drew attention to this in a speech that he made at an international Vygotsky conference in Budapest in 1988. At that time he was working on his translation of *Thinking and speech* into Italian (*Pensiero e linguaggio* – Vygotsky, 1992), based on the original Russian edition published in 1934. That Italian translation is still, at the time of writing, *the only one to be based on the 1934 publication*. All of the translations into English, and many other languages, have been based on the edition edited by Leontiev and Luria, and published in 1956. This includes the edition of *Thinking and speech* in volume 2 of the Russian *Collected works* of Vygotsky, published in 1982, and also – since they were a translation of the Russian original – in volume 1 of the *Collected works* in English (Vygotsky, 1987).

Mecacci began reconstructing and investigating the history of Russian psychology. He wrote three histories of Soviet psychology and translated into Italian numerous texts by Vygotsky, Luria and other Russian psychologists. This was a period when Western researchers sometimes seemed to be better informed about Vygotskyan topics than their Russian peers. At a Budapest conference in 1988, the Russian delegates presented Vygotsky 'as a harmless, highbrow and abstract theoretician, but they failed to ever mention that he was occupying a few governmental positions and for his practical applications of psychology was censored and avoided' (Mecacci, 2012, p. 84).

Mecacci's meticulous scholarship has provided for Italian speakers a group of reliable texts and a short but thorough guide to Vygotsky in Italian (Mecacci, 2017). The bibliography included in that book is one of the fullest and most carefully annotated Vygotskyan bibliographies that exists.

Manolis Dafermos: international studies of Vygotsky

> Multiple interpretations about the theoretical background and possible applications of Vygotsky's theory have developed. Many educators and psychologists extol the benefits of Vygotsky's theory, but actually they know little about his works. Many researchers accept only a few fragmented ideas, taken out of the specific context within which these ideas have developed.
>
> (Dafermos, 2016, p. 27)

Manolis Dafermos has provided one of the most comprehensive reviews of what happened in Vygotsky studies after the publication of *Mind in society* in

1978 (Dafermos, 2016, 2018). He makes the point that the majority of researchers still use only two of Vygotsky's books, *Thinking and speech* (or *Thought and language*) and *Mind in society*. But he emphasises: '*Mind in society* is not written by Vygotsky' (Dafermos, 2016, p. 27).

Dafermos suggests that the lack of respect shown to Vygotsky's original texts in *Mind in society*, and the way in which his theories were reinterpreted and made to fit other paradigms, have influenced the reception of Vygotsky's work ever since. For instance, in the *Cambridge companion to Vygotsky*, the editors write:

> There is a growing interest in what has become known as 'socio-historical or cultural historical theory' and its subsequent close relative 'activity theory'.
> (Daniels, Cole and Wertsch, 2007, p. 2)

But Vygotsky never used the term 'socio-historical', and he most certainly did not regard activity theory as a close relative of his own theory.

Dafermos also deplores the use of the term 'sociocultural' as applied to Vygotsky's theory. This is not a term used in Vygotsky's work; it is 'the theoretical framework of its reception and incorporation in North American settings' (Dafermos, 2016, p. 31). He also considers that 'cultural-historical activity theory', a conflation of Vygotsky's theory with that of Leontiev, 'offers a decontextualized account and obscures the gaps, tensions, and inconsistencies in the history of cultural-historical psychology and activity theory' (ibid.). Leontiev's activity theory was in fact originally part of his move to *distance* his work from that of Vygotsky.

In surveying the international reception of Vygotsky's work, Dafermos quotes Edward Said's argument that when a theory is moving into a new environment it will be transformed as a result of changes in place and time.

Dafermos's own view is that:

> Vygotsky's theory has been essentially transformed under the influence of multiple contexts in its reception and implementation. The main problem is that frequently researchers and practitioners are not aware of the difference between Vygotsky's theory and its own frames, and filters in its reception.
> (Dafermos, 2016, p. 29)

Vygotskyan pedagogy

Although it took a long time for more than a few of Vygotsky's theoretical works to be produced in reliable editions in Soviet Russia, his practical ideas about pedagogy continued to influence research and practice. A remarkable testimony to this is the book edited by Brian and Joan Simon, *Educational psychology in the USSR*, published in 1963.

In 1955 Professor Brian Simon, a professor in education, and Joan Simon, his wife, a writer on the history of education and a Russian translator, had visited the USSR, with a small party of teachers and educationalists, to study developments in Soviet psychology. The visit resulted in a book edited by Brian Simon, *Psychology in the Soviet Union* (Simon, 1957), which contains twenty papers by Soviet psychologists. It makes surprising reading: nearly every paper begins with an acknowledgement of the work of Pavlov and there are numerous references to his work and to reflexology. Only in the contributions by Alexander Luria, especially his Appendix, are there references to the work of Vygotsky.

Soon after this, Luria asked the Simons if it might be possible to get his own short book (co-authored with Yudovich) *Speech and the development of mental processes in the child* (published in the USSR in 1956), translated into English. The English translation by Joan Simon was published in 1959. Luria's first chapter contains an extended passage on the work of Vygotsky.

The Simons, now knowing more about Vygotsky's work, planned a second book, *Educational psychology in the USSR* (Simon and Simon, 1963). Out of 20 articles there were six by ex-associates of Vygotsky, including Leontiev, Luria, El'konin and Zankov. In the Preface Brian Simon notes that in the five years since their previous book 'the position has considerably changed' (ibid., p. vi). This time hardly any of the articles have ritual references to Pavlov. And the first article in the book, in a translation by Joan Simon, is by Vygotsky; it is his article on the relationship between children's mental development and their education (later translated in 2017 by Stanley Mitchell: Vygotsky, 2017) and it introduces the idea of the 'zone of potential development' (Simon and Simon, 1963, p. 28). Several other articles contain references to Vygotsky.

It is as if a starting pistol has been fired. What had happened between the two books was the publication, in 1956, of Luria and Leontiev's editions of Vygotsky's *Thinking and speech* and of a volume of his *Selected psychological works*, followed in 1960 by *The history of the development of higher mental functions*.

Brian Simon's introduction to *Educational psychology in the USSR* gives a comprehensive picture of the structure of the Institute of Psychology of the Academy of Educational Sciences of the USSR (known as APN), which had a network of specialised research institutes, each with a staff of 40–80 full-time workers, in different locations (12 are listed). In some of these institutes we find ex-associates of Vygotsky: at the head of the pre-school Institute is Professor Zaporozhets, at the head of the Institute of the theory and history of education is Professor Zankov, and Professors Luria and Leontiev are fully involved. Two institutes are concerned with child and educational psychology. In the secondary-school section of the child psychology department Lydia Bozhovich, one of Vygotsky's five original research students, is working on the formation of personality (i.e. the pedology of adolescence). In the primary-school section of APN, three years of research have been directed to discovering the capacities of children aged 7–11. Simon comments that the research has found that 'certain concepts, usually held to be beyond the capacity of primary children, can be formed at this age by the use of special methods'. For example:

> The teaching programme should be so organized that it is always a little way ahead of the children's development ... oriented towards what is to come, since learning prepares the way for development. (This is the essence of the approach advocated by Vygotski.)
>
> (Simon and Simon, 1963, p. 12)

Simon expresses great interest in the experimental schools that work with the institutes, each with six attached research workers. This enabled lessons to be planned, observed and evaluated jointly by teachers and researchers:

> there was no sense of formality or strain; on the contrary there was considerable exchange between teacher and pupil ... and the pupils themselves were lively in both question and answer.
>
> (Simon and Simon, 1963, p. 13)

The research into learning being undertaken by the institutes is concerned with 'the formation of mental actions, concept formation ... individual differences in learning' (ibid., p. 14). Simon notes: 'the approach to this question by way of mental testing has been abandoned since 1936' and that testing is regarded as misleading; it cannot offer practical guidance in relation to teaching methods. Instead there has been a 'concentration on learning as a process which in turn involved research into the development, the *formation* of mental processes' (ibid., p. 16).

Brian and Joan Simon, going to Soviet Russia as educationalists rather than psychologists, were able to observe what was happening after Vygotsky in educational research and in schools. Despite the atmosphere of caution around his books and theories, his influence on practice in both research and education was alive.

As an aside, we could note that James Britton, a lecturer in the English Department of the London University Institute of Education, read Joan Simon's 1959 translation of Luria and Yudovitch's *Speech and the development of mental processes in the child*, with its references to Vygotsky's work, when it came out. But before that he may have attended three special university lectures that Luria gave at University College London in 1958, and he certainly read Luria's book based on these lectures, *The role of speech in the regulation of normal and abnormal behaviour* (Luria, 1961). He also read *Thought and language* when it appeared in 1962 and developed a lifelong interest in Vygotsky, whose ideas became part of the English Department courses at the London Institute of Education. Britton's own book, *Language and learning* (Britton, 1970), contained extensive references to Vygotsky. When Penguin Books published *Speech and the development of mental processes in the child* (Luria and Yudovich, 1971), Britton wrote the introduction (Britton, 1971). It was at the London Institute of Education, in classes and discussions with James Britton and his colleagues, that I first came to know Vygotsky's work.

Zankov's schools

Leonid Zankov worked as a research student and a defectologist with Vygotsky in the late 1920s. He continued to research in the field of defectology and from 1944 to 1947 was the director of the Institute of Defectology. He was a full member of the Academy of Pedagogical Sciences (APN) and from 1951 to 1955 was director of the Scientific Institute of the Theory and History of Pedagogy.

From 1955 to his death in 1977, Zankov's work was closely connected with his 'Experimental Didactics Laboratory'. By now he was an expert in experimental methods and he launched a project involving the in-depth study of children's learning processes. With a team of three researchers, he set out to identify the most efficient approaches to furthering children's development. The team looked at the whole teaching process, drawing on the disciplines of child studies, psychology, physiology and defectology. On the basis of this they planned a new system of school curricula, with textbooks and methods to support its implementation (Guseva and Sosnowski, 1997).

The first experiment took place in a real school, School 172 in the middle of Moscow. Children were not given grades; they were encouraged to be cooperative, not competitive and to share their opinions and feelings. School life was varied and active. There were regular field trips in Moscow and beyond, and a range of optional after-school clubs: crafts, drawing, rhythm and dancing, choir, engineering, some taught by Zankov. There were also frequent celebrations, contributing to a feeling of fellowship. There was evidence that children were mastering the material in the programme rapidly. By 1962 teachers from 18 schools were involved.

The pedagogy at the heart of the schools was based on the following principles:

- teaching at an optimal level of difficulty (zone of proximal development);
- emphasising theoretical knowledge;
- proceeding at a rapid pace;
- developing students' awareness of the learning process; and
- the purposeful and systematic development of every student.

(Guseva and Solomonovich, 2017)

The system encouraged teachers to emphasise the development of thinking, observing and doing. The development of the imagination was foregrounded. There were class discussions based on what students had read or seen, pedagogical games, intensive independent learning, and team 'quests' based on observation, comparison, identifying patterns, and reasoning.

The experiment grew, but there was no room for alternative schools within the Soviet system. The Ministry of Education seriously considered implementing Zankov's programme across the whole of Soviet Russia, but Zankov did not think it was ready for this; the majority of elementary-school teachers had not completed his professional-development courses. So the Ministry introduced some elements from the system into mainstream schools without any training for teachers. As Zankov had predicted, this did not work and the Ministry dropped the experiment.

Zankov and his team concentrated on a publishing project to make his system known to a wider audience, but the book describing the project was not given official backing; after Zankov's death in 1977 his Instruction and Development Laboratory was closed (Boguslavsky, 2015).

However, in 1991 there was a conference devoted to Zankov's work and in 1993 the Russian Ministry of Education launched a research centre named after him. His teaching materials were brought back into print. In 1996 the system was given nationwide status and officially recognised as one of three variants of Russian elementary-school education. His mathematics teaching programme has been implemented in Norway and in Edmonton in Canada.

There have been other well-known schools in Russia aiming to follow Vygotsky's theories of teaching and learning, such as that of Davydov, but the example of Zankov shows a continuous line of development from Vygotsky, at the level of educational practice, throughout the years when his books were frowned on. Zankov's system strove to implement Vygotsky's views on pedagogy on a large scale and to provide a broad education, which took into account affect, imagination and the development of the personality as well as cognitive growth.

Meshcheryakov: Awakening to life

To fully understand the meaning of Vygotsky's famous phrase 'teaching is the source of development' (Vygotsky, 2017, p. 368), it is enough to read about the extraordinary living experiment that was the school for deaf-blind children in Zagorsk, near Moscow, which opened in 1963. This is described in *Awakening to life* by Alexander Meshcheryakov (2007), the psychologist who worked at the school. Meshcheryakov was a student of Alexander Luria and became totally involved with the education of deaf-blind children. He worked in this field for the rest of his life.

Meshcheryakov makes clear that in the initial period of deaf-blind children's rearing they need to master practical day-to-day skills and learn how to dress themselves, to use 'a fork, a table, a chamber pot, a plate, a chair, a shirt, a bed' (ibid.). The first focus is self-care; then gradually children can begin to take some part in a community they cannot hear or see. This is achieved through touch, first with physical help that is very gradually withdrawn, and next with signs:

The main objective for the teacher at this stage is the fostering of communication activity, which makes the child a part of human society and
allows him to assimilate social experience on the basis of sign systems.

(Meshcheryakov, 2007)

The progress of each child is recorded daily.

The deaf-blind child, says Meshcheryakov, is: 'as yet bereft of a human mind,
while possessing the capacity of full mental development. Thus the unique task
arises of a deliberate moulding of a child's human behaviour and mind, keeping in
view all factors influencing a child' (ibid.).

Deaf-blind children have to be taught every detail of the skills they need to
become to some degree self-sufficient. They must also be taught to play – to
build a sorting pyramid, to take apart a *matryoshka* doll, and to take part in
children's action games.

Meshcheryakov cites Vygotsky as paving the way for this work. He sees him
as providing 'theoretical justification for regarding the moulding of a child's
mind as his assimilation (appropriation, in Karl Marx's words) of social experience' (ibid.). In many countries deaf-blind children are regarded as ineducable.
But at Zagorsk, through developing active sign language, the possibility of
communication opens up innumerable opportunities and gives shape to the
world. Every means possible is used to teach language. Children learn finger
spelling, and eventually to read and communicate using Braille. They learn to
count and use an abacus, to recognise model shapes, to look after plants and
work in the garden. They make relief maps of the countryside around the
school. Later some can follow a higher programme of academic work.

Four of the students who were educated at Zagorsk went on to study psychology and philosophy at Moscow University. In 1990 the BBC made a film
about the children of Zagorsk, the title of which is *The butterflies of Zagorsk*
(British Broadcasting Corporation, 1990). In the film we see the routine of the
school, the children communicating by fluttering hand movements (which
gives rise to the film's title), by sign language, finger spelling and oral speech,
which some can learn to 'hear' by feeling the vibrations in a teacher's voice
box. Even the profoundly deaf have music lessons and we meet a girl whose
greatest pleasure is playing the piano.

We also meet Natalya K, one of the four students who went on to Moscow
University, who at the time of the film was a psychologist. Natalya started at
Zagorsk when she was 13. She was taught finger spelling:

at first it seemed like a childish game to me … This was the first stage of
my education when I discovered I could see and hear not only with my
eyes and ears but also with my hands. In this way order came to my world.

Natalya quotes Vygotsky as saying that the most serious of disabilities can be
overcome with constant stimulation in other areas:

Vygotsky said that handicapped children should not be approached through their handicap ... I remember when I was completely crushed ... When you overcome difficulties it gives you the knowledge of your own strength ... I feel myself to be a woman and a very strong one.

(Quotations transcribed from film)

The deaf-blind school of Zagorsk is another example of a continuous line in the development of Vygotskyan pedagogy – this time in the field of defectology – that ran, through Luria, to the ground-breaking work of Meshcheryakov and his teacher colleagues.

Vygotsky in the UK

Language and learning: Barnes, Britton and Rosen and the LATE

Vygotsky was one of the first psychologists to acknowledge the role of language in organising our understanding of the world. His work was therefore of intense interest to teachers whose business was language. In the 1960s and 1970s, teachers in the English department at the University of London Institute of Education engaged in in-depth exploration of Vygotsky's work. They were interested in his theories about the internalisation of talk, how it is initially dialogic, but then internalised, becoming inner speech and thought. Both in the Institute courses and in study groups run by the London Association for the Teaching of English (LATE), teachers studied tape recordings of children's small-group discussions to trace how learning developed through interactive talk, and through writing.

Some of the working groups operating at this time focused on the language of secondary-school subject teaching and learning. This resulted in the publication in 1969 (with a revised edition in 1971) of *Language, the learner and the school*, by Douglas Barnes, James Britton and Harold Rosen and the LATE, a seminal book that focused attention on the role of language in learning across the curriculum. In part one (Barnes, 1971), Barnes's fine-grained analyses of the language of secondary classrooms showed that to be effective teachers needed 'far more sophisticated insights into the implications of the language they use' which they could gain from examining examples of classroom interaction. He remarked that 'the purposes of such study would be frankly pedagogical' and would 'contribute dramatically to the effectiveness of teaching in secondary schools' (ibid., p. 75).

Robin Alexander

More recently, Robin Alexander's study of the relationship between classroom talk, pedagogy and learning in five countries (England, France, India, Russia and the United States), which foregrounded the idea of 'dialogic teaching', sought to compare different national approaches to pedagogy and learn from the comparison:

The English tradition emphasises the importance of equal distribution of teacher time and attention among all the pupils, and participation by all of them in oral work, in every lesson. So with only one teacher and 20–30 pupils in a class it is inevitable that competitive bidding and the gamesmanship of 'guess what teacher is thinking', and above all searching for the 'right' answer, become critical to the pupil's getting by. But in many of the Russian lessons we observed, only a proportion of children were expected to contribute orally in a given lesson. Here, instead of eliciting a succession of brief 'now or never' answers from many children, the teacher constructs a sequence of much more sustained exchanges with a smaller number. Because the ambience is collective rather than individualised or collaborative, the child talks to the class as much as to the teacher and is in a sense a representative of that class as much as an individual … And because there is time to do more than parrot the expected answer, the talk is more likely to probe children's thinking.

(Alexander, 2005, p. 9)

Alexander's work has focused attention on dialogic teaching, over many projects and publications. He advocates a Vygotskyan view of development that requires children to engage, through the medium of spoken language, with adults, other children and the wider culture. This kind of social interaction is critical for children's understanding of school knowledge. Dialogic teaching is open, reciprocal, cumulative (with learners building on each other's answers to make a coherent line of thinking) and purposeful. It requires pupils to think. It advocates a range of different groupings for learning, not just class teaching.

Neil Mercer

Neil Mercer is the director of Oracy Cambridge: the Centre for Effective Spoken Communication. His work has always aimed to raise awareness of the importance of effective group talk and how it can be taught and learned, in the interests of improving effective thinking. For him 'the relationship between "intermental" (collective) activity and "intramental" (individual) intellectual activity' is the key to learning and teaching in education (Mercer, 2013).

What teachers say

While writing this book I talked to a number of teachers about the influence that Vygotsky had had on their thinking and practice.

A head of a nursery school said:

My underlying theory is that unless adults themselves have an intellectual life, and curiosity, and reflectiveness, it'll be difficult to create the right conditions for learning with children. I've asked practitioners to do regular structured observations of children, to see whether it changed their ideas. They became much more observant about small things. They had thought that if they provided the conditions for play the children would play independently. But having observed the first inklings of pretend play in a child with English as a second language, they realised that they could take a more active role in supporting and extending this essential form of play. This realisation of the importance of social interaction is a Vygotskyan insight. They are becoming enormously more thoughtful and capable of theorisation.

A drama teacher said:

> 'Play and the development of mental processes' has always been the underlying text for my ideas about drama education. It's the most extra-ordinary, complex, rich argument about play and learning, with great subtlety of observation. Drama's all about generating an imaginative experience together, with the pupils becoming a 'head taller'. Being a teacher in role has always been very important for me, I can often communicate better with the children, even ones with minimal English, within the drama, and I do see them become 'a head taller' when working in role. I have been very influenced by the work of Dorothy Heathcote who worked in role with a class, but would regularly ask them to come out of role to discuss the drama, where it was going and what should happen next. This kind of switch, from language in the context of dramatic action to language for reflection and thinking, moves children on.

A writing consultant said:

> Vygotsky was completely attuned to the foundations of writing, its prehistory in gesture, in picturing and in storying. He regards all those activities as the precursors of writing, and his observations of them are acute. The impulse to write often comes from a desire to make things – like a birthday card for your mother – or to tell things, to make stories – true or imagined. He describes learning to write as 'learning to draw speech' and this is a wonderful way of putting it because it makes quite clear that children's own spoken language is where you have to start.

A deputy head of a primary school said:

> The national curriculum we have now has content but not concepts. I am interested in Vygotsky's emphasis on concept development. Earlier this year I worked with a class of Y5 children. I based the project on some-thing Einstein said: 'If all the bees died the human race would last four years.' Everything we did followed from that. We made a scrapbook of

their research questions and hypotheses and planned the project; first of all we went to see some beehives in Kennington, met a beekeeper and were shown the hives. I expected this project to have a mainly ecological character, looking at bees' place in the ecosystem, but one of the first questions was 'Does the queen bee own the worker bees?'. The bees were a whole society, with its roles and social strata, and that question led to a discussion of social structures; so now we had two big questions to explore. It was all cut short by lockdown, but the class had already generated a great deal of discussion, art and writing. I am in favour of taking the scaffold away; I think children can often do more than we expect of them.

A teacher educator said:

What I am most excited about in Vygotsky is the idea that 'word meaning develops'. That idea comes from a tradition that goes right back to John Locke, but what Vygotsky does is turn it from a philosophical question to one about the development of mind and learning. The idea that language and mental development – language and concept development – go hand in hand is transformative. It's an essential idea to have in your head in a classroom, it can underpin all your observations of the things children say and how they can be built on. The other idea that struck me forcibly the second time I came to *Thinking and speech*, when I was doing my PhD, was his extraordinary focus on very delicate approaches to methodology – he magnificently rejected reductive methods and always aimed to respond to the complexity of children.

An Italian coordinator of Early Years services said:

Play reveals so many things and is expressive of creativity and mental health – that's why psychologists are interested in it. It's not just recreation, it's the child's voice expressing the child's self and view of the world. Our nurseries are resourced and set up to encourage dramatic play, but although the potential is there it doesn't mean it's going to happen. I have always been interested in Vygotsky's description of the ZPD in play. It gives particular importance to make-believe play as a source of development, and it has huge pedagogic implications. In play, the adult can become involved in the child's world and understand what sea they're fishing in! This kind of participation requires observation and empathy; it enables the teacher to see what matters to children and to shape what they offer them.

One of the main lessons that I draw from Vygotsky relates to his work in assessment. In recent years his name, and the concept of the ZPD, have sometimes been used to justify school reforms that have led to more didactic approaches to teaching and intensified approaches to assessment. But this is a misrepresentation of Vygotsky's psychology. In his writings on defectology, Vygotsky often made clear that he was interested in 'experimentation, observation, analysis, generalisation, description and qualitative diagnosis' (Vygotsky, 1993b, p. 29) rather than counting and measuring. A qualitative approach to the observation, teaching and evaluation of children (similar to the approach which I and my colleagues at the Centre for Language in Primary Education, Sue Ellis, Hilary Hester and Anne Thomas, took in the writing of the Primary Language Record; Barrs, Ellis, Hester and Thomas, 1988) is a hallmark of all Vygotsky's work. Despite the frequent tendency to see the ZPD as a better way of measuring achievement, this is a misreading of that concept (and of Vygotsky's position as a psychologist).

Conclusion

Texts

Luciano Mecacci (1992), in his introduction to his translation of *Thinking and speech, Pensiero e linguaggio* (Vygotsky, 1992), laments the fate of Vygotsky's books at the hands of those whom Mandelstam termed 'the enemies of the word' (ibid., p. vi). For many years the very scholars and colleagues who would have been able to preserve Vygotsky's words for others to read were involved in censoring them. He describes Leontiev and Luria, in their 1956 version of *Thinking and speech*, 'eliminating references to Freud and Sapir, to pedologists like Blonsky, changing the word pedology into pedagogy, substituting the word "task" for "test" (used in pedological research), introducing italics where Vygotsky hadn't used them and eliminating them where he had, and so on' (ibid., p. ix). He ends with a description of the cemetery of Novodevic, where Vygotsky and 'other poets and intellectuals of the Revolution, cut down by Stalinism, rest in tombs covered with dead leaves'. In his view the translation of *Thinking and speech* in volume 1 of the *Collected works* (Vygotsky, 1987a), based on Leontiev and Luria's 1956 version, had buried him again, 'under piles of invented words that he never said' (ibid.).

But by 2017, when his own book on Vygotsky was published, Mecacci was more optimistic about Vygotsky's texts; more and better editions were appearing, the *Collected works*, revised and expanded, were being published in Russian, and other texts that had been suppressed (such as some pedology texts) were being published. He felt that for the first time it was possible to read Vygotsky in reliable texts (Mecacci, 2017).

Nikolai Veresov (2020) is also positive about the recent publication in Russia of many previously unavailable texts 'creating a new reality in Vygotsky's legacy'. Although some foundational works are still unavailable in English they are gradually being translated. This means that 'theoretical links which were hidden now become clear'. There are new examples of concrete research conducted by Vygotsky and his collaborators.

Due to the contemporary publication of Vygotsky's archival materials and notebooks and deep investigation of key periods of Vygotsky's theoretical evolution *there are no more blank spaces left.*

(Veresov, 2020, p. 111)

This is a good time to be reading and studying Vygotsky. The time really is past when the only texts most people knew or used were *Thought and language* and *Mind in society*. Future students of Vygotsky will be able to explore the whole range of his work in psychology and pedology, and I have tried to represent that range in this book. I am aware that there are areas of Vygotsky's work that I have not touched on or only touched on lightly, such as his relations and professional arguments with the Gestaltist psychologists. I have tended to keep to texts that are included in the *Collected works*, and to certain key texts, like *Educational psychology* (Vygotsky, 1997a), *The psychology of art* (Vygotsky, 1971), *Studies on the history of behaviour* (Vygotsky and Luria, 1993), *Imagination and creativity in childhood* (Vygotsky, 2014), 'Play and its role in the mental development of the child' (Vygotsky, 2016) and 'The problem of teaching and mental development at school age' (Vygotsky, 2017), which are not included in the *Collected works*.

Commentators

There is an enormous secondary literature on Vygotsky, and I have included references to only a fraction of the books and papers that are published. I have tended to prioritise more recent contributions and have relied heavily on certain commentators: Manolis Dafermos, Fernando González Rey, Ludmilla Hyman, David Kellogg, Bella Kotik-Freidgut, Luciano Mecacci, Ronald Miller, Bernard Schneuwly and Irina Leopoldoff-Martin, René Van der Veer and Jan Valsiner, Nikolai Veresov, Ekaterina Zavershneva and, of course, Gita Vygodskaya. I have consulted many others.

In recent years there have been signs of moves to 'deconstruct Vygotsky', to focus on the flaws and deficiencies in his work, his own occasional disappointments with its progress, his 'failures'. I hope this book has shown that this is a distortion of Vygotsky's achievements. What is needed now is construction rather than deconstruction: the task, as Veresov has said, is to follow the theoretical links that are now clearer, to put Vygotsky together.

Several Vygotskyan commentators have focused on the 'periodisation' of Vygotsky's theoretical development: on defining the 'periods' that his work went through in his short working life, and pinning down the exact years that mark the shifts and transitions, the discontinuities and the beginnings of new phases. Obviously the uncertainty that there has been about the dating of Vygotsky's texts, and of the *writing* of those texts has, as Dafermos has pointed out, complicated that task.

For myself, when I look at the whole sweep of Vygotsky's work, most of which was written in his last ten years, from 1924–1934, I am much more aware of the continuities than of the discontinuities – of what we could call, in Vygotsky's words from *The psychology of art* (Vygotsky, 1971) the 'interpretational curve' of his work. I am aware of the large themes that recur, in different guises, throughout his life as a psychologist and a pedologist: child development, consciousness, language and the development of thinking, concept development and abstraction; play and the imagination; affect, emotion and *perezhivanie*; teaching and learning. Although Vygotsky shifted his focus at different points in his development, and although he often became dissatisfied with what he had done and criticised his own work, this was always a prelude to a new approach, a new proposal for exploring these constant themes.

'A very difficult path'

It's a long time since we heard Vygotsky's voice, and I thought that to hear it again would be the best way to end this book. When lecturing he had a 'soft baritone, rich and flexible in intonation', and 'it was difficult to refrain the involuntary feeling of disappointment when he stopped' (Kolbanovsky, quoted in Van der Veer and Valsiner, 1991, p. 14).

We can hear his voice most clearly in his letters, as in the following one written to his five new research students in April 1929, talking about psychology:

> The road is a long one ... A sense of the enormity and massive scope of modern-day psychology (we are living in an era of geologic cataclysms in psychology) – this is my main feeling. But this makes the situation of those few who are pursuing the new avenue in science (especially in the science of man) an *extremely* responsible one that is serious in the highest degree and almost tragic (in the best and current, not pathetic, sense of that word). One has to check oneself a thousand times, to endure and withstand the test before making one's decision, because this is a very difficult path that demands a person's all.
>
> (Vygotsky, 2007, p. 21)

References

Akhutina, T. (2003). 'L.S. Vygotsky and A.R. Luria: foundations of neuropsychology'. *Journal of Russian and East European Psychology*, 41(3/4), pp. 159–190.

Alexander, R. (2005). '*Culture, dialogue and learning: notes on an emerging pedagogy*', address to International Association for Cognitive Education and Psychology (IACEP) 10th International Conference, University of Durham, 10–14 July. Available online: http://lpuae.pbworks.com/w/file/fetch/47478116/Dialogic%20teaching.pdf.

Barnes, D. (1971). 'Part one: language in the secondary classroom', in Barnes, D., Britton, J.N., Rosen, H. and the LATE, *Language, the learner and the school*, pp. 9–77. Harmondsworth: Penguin Education.

Barnes, D., Britton, J.N., Rosen, H. and the LATE (1971). *Language, the learner and the school* (revised edition). Harmondsworth: Penguin Education.

Barrs, M., Ellis, S., Hester, H. and Thomas, A. (1988). *The primary language record: handbook for teachers*. London: Inner London Education Authority/Centre for Language in Primary Education.

Boguslavsky, M.V. (2015). 'Vital pedagogy of Leonid Zankov'. *Russian–American Education Forum*, 7(3). Available online: www.rus-ameeduforum.com/content/en/?task=art&article=1001153&iid=23.

British Broadcasting Corporation (1990). *The butterflies of Zagorsk*. Documentary film written, produced and presented by M. Dean; directed by A. Paul.

Britton, J.N. (1970). *Language and learning*. Harmondsworth: Penguin Books.

Britton, J.N. (1971). 'Introduction', in Luria, A.R. and Yudovich, F.I., *Speech and the development of mental processes in the child*, pp. 7–13. Harmondsworth: Penguin Books.

Cole, M. (1979). 'Epilogue' in Luria, A.R., *The making of mind: a personal account of Soviet psychology*, pp. 189–225. Cambridge, MA: Harvard University Press.

Cole, M. (2004). 'Prologue: reading Vygotsky', in Rieber, R.W. and Robinson, D.K. (eds), *The essential Vygotsky*, pp. vii–xii. New York: Springer.

Cole, M., John-Steiner, V., Scribner, S. and Souberman, E. (1978). 'Editors' preface', in Vygotsky, L.S., *Mind in society*, pp. ix–xi. Cole, M., John-Steiner, V., Scribner, S. and Souberman, E. (eds). Cambridge, MA: Harvard University Press.

Dafermos, M. (2016). 'Critical reflection on the reception of Vygotsky's theory in the international academic community'. *Cultural-Historical Psychology*, 12(3), pp. 27–46.

Dafermos, M. (2018). *Rethinking cultural-historical theory: a dialectical perspective to Vygotsky*. Singapore: Springer.

Daniels, H., Cole, M. and Wertsch, J.V. (eds) (2007). *The Cambridge companion to Vygotsky*. Cambridge: Cambridge University Press.

Glick, J. (1997). 'Prologue', in Vygotsky, L.S., *The collected works of L.S. Vygotsky. Volume 4, The history of the development of higher mental functions*, pp. v–xvi. Rieber, R. W. (ed.). New York: Plenum Press.

González Rey, F.L. (2014). 'Advancing further the history of Soviet psychology'. *History of Psychology*, 17(1), pp. 60–78.

Guseva, L. and Solomonovich, M. (2017). 'Implementing the zone of proximal development: from the pedagogical experiment to the developmental education system of Leonid Zankov'. *International Electronic Journal of Elementary Education*, 9(4), pp. 775–786.

Guseva, L. and Sosnowski, A. (1997). 'Russian education in transition: trends at the primary level'. *Education Canadienne et Internationale*, 26(1), pp. 14–31.

Joravsky, D. (1989). *Russian psychology: a critical history*. Oxford: Blackwell.

Leontiev, A.N. (2005). 'Study of the environment in the pedological works of L.S. Vygotsky: a critical study' [1937]. Trans. M.E. Sharpe. *Journal of Russian and East European Psychology*, 43(4), pp. 8–28.

Luria, A.R. (1961). *The role of speech in the regulation of normal and abnormal behaviour*. Tizard, J. (ed.). Oxford: Pergamon Press.

Luria, A.R. (1979). *The making of mind: a personal account of Soviet psychology*. Cole, M. and Cole, S. (eds). Cambridge, MA: Harvard University Press.

Luria, A.R. and Yudovich, F. I. (1959). *Speech and the development of mental processes in the child*. Simon, J. (ed. and trans.). London: Staples Press.

Luria, A.R. and Yudovich, F.I. (1971). *Speech and the development of mental processes in the child*. Simon, J. (ed. and trans.). Harmondsworth: Penguin Books.

Mecacci, L. (1992). 'Introduzione', in Vygotsky, L.S., *Pensiero e linguaggio*, pp. v–x. Trans. L. Mecacci. Bari: Editori Laterza.

Mecacci, L. (2012). 'Russian psychology and Italian psychology and psychiatry in the second half of the 20th century'. *PsyAnima, Dubna Psychological Journal*, 3, pp. 81–87.

Mecacci, L. (2017). *Lev Vygotskii: sviluppo, educazione e patologia della mente*. Florence: Giunti.

Mercer, N. (2013). 'The social brain, language, and goal-directed collective thinking'. *Educational Psychologist*, 48(3), pp. 148–168.

Meshcheryakov, A. (2007). 'Awakening to life: forming behaviour and the mind in deaf-blind children' [1979]. Available online in the Marxist Archive: www.marxists. org/archive/meshcheryakov/awakening/index.htm.

Miller, R. (2011). *Vygotsky in perspective*. Cambridge: Cambridge University Press.

Minkova, E. (2012). 'Pedology as a complex science devoted to the study of children in Russia: the history of its origin and elimination'. *Psychological Thought*, 5(2), pp. 83–98.

Rieber, R.W. and Robinson, D.K. (eds) (2004). *The essential Vygotsky*. New York: Springer.

Rudneva, E.I. (2000). 'Vygotsky's pedological distortions'. *Journal of Russian and East European Psychology*, 38(6), pp. 75–94.

Simon, B. (ed.) (1957). *Psychology in the Soviet Union*. London: Routledge and Kegan Paul.

Simon, B. and Simon, J. (eds) (1963). *Educational psychology in the USSR*. London: Routledge and Kegan Paul.

Van der Veer, R. and Valsiner, J. (1991). *Understanding Vygotsky: A quest for synthesis*. Oxford: Blackwell.

Veresov, N. (2020). 'Discovering the Great Royal Seal: new reality of Vygotsky's legacy'. *Cultural-Historical Psychology*, 16 (2), pp. 107–117.

Vygotsky, L.S. (1935). *Umstvennoe razvitie detej v processe obučenija* [Children's mental development in the process of learning/teaching]. Moscow: Gosudarstvennoie Uchebno-pedagocheskoie Izdatel'stvo.

Vygotsky, L.S. (1962). *Thought and language* [1934]. Trans. E. Hanfmann and G. Vakar. Cambridge, MA: MIT Press.

Vygotsky, L.S. (1971). *The psychology of art* [1925]. Intro. A.N. Leontiev; commentary V. V. Ivanov. Cambridge, MA: MIT Press.

Vygotsky, L.S. (1978). *Mind in society*. Cole, M., John-Steiner, V., Scribner, S. and Souberman, E. (eds). Cambridge, MA: Harvard University Press.

Vygotsky, L.S. (1987). *The collected works of L.S. Vygotsky. Volume 1, Problems of general psychology*. Trans. and intro. N. Minick; Rieber, R.W. and Carton, A.S. (eds). New York: Plenum Press.

Vygotsky, L.S. (1987a). *Thinking and speech* [1934], in Vygotsky, L.S., *The collected works of L.S. Vygotsky. Volume 1, Problems of general psychology*, pp. 37–285. Trans. and intro. N. Minick; Rieber, R.W. and Carton, A.S. (eds). New York: Plenum Press.

Vygotsky, L.S. (1992). *Pensiero e linguaggio* [1934]. Trans. L. Mecacci. Bari: Editori Laterza.

Vygotsky, L.S. (1993). 'The diagnostics of development' [1936], in Vygotsky, L.S., *The collected works of L.S. Vygotsky. Volume 2, The fundamentals of defectology*, pp. 241–291. Trans. and intro. J. Knox and C.B. Stevens; Rieber, R.W. and Carton, A.S. (eds). New York: Plenum Press.

Vygotsky, L.S. (1993b). 'Introduction: The fundamental problems of defectology' [1929], in Vygotsky, L.S., *The collected works of L.S. Vygotsky. Volume 2, The fundamentals of defectology*, pp. 29–51. Trans. and intro. J. Knox and C.B. Stevens; Rieber, R.W. and Carton, A.S. (eds). New York: Plenum Press.

Vygotsky, L.S. (1997a). *Educational psychology* [1926]. Trans. R. Silverman. Davydov, V. V. (ed. and intro.). Boca Raton, FL: CRC Press.

Vygotsky, L.S. (1997b). *The historical meaning of the crisis in psychology: a methodological investigation* [1926–1927], in Vygotsky, L.S., *The collected works of L.S. Vygotsky. Volume 3, Problems of the theory and history of psychology*, pp. 233–343. Trans. and intro. R. Van der Veer; Rieber, R.W. and Wollock, J. (eds). New York: Plenum Press.

Vygotsky, L.S. (2007). 'In Memory of L.S. Vygotsky (1896–1934): L.S. Vygotsky: Letters to Students and Colleagues'. Trans. M.E. Sharpe; Puzyrei, A.A. (ed.). *Journal of Russian and East European Psychology*, 45(2), pp. 11–60.

Vygotsky, L.S. (2014). 'Imagination and creativity in childhood' [1930]. *Journal of Russian and East European Psychology*, 4(1), pp. 7–97. Also available online in the Marxist Archive: www.marxists.org/archive/vygotsky/works/1927/imagination.pdf.

Vygotsky, L.S. (2016). 'Play and its role in the mental development of the child' [1933]. Trans. N. Veresov and M. Barrs. *International Research in Early Childhood Education*, 7(2), pp. 3–25.

Vygotsky, L.S. (2017). 'The problem of teaching and mental development at school age' ['*Problema obučenija i umstvennogo razvitiya v škol'nom vozraste*'] [1935]. Trans. S. Mitchell. *Changing English*, 24(4), pp. 359–371.

Vygotsky, L.S. (2019). *L.S. Vygotsky's pedological works. Volume 1, Foundations of pedology*. Kellogg, D. and Veresov, N. (eds). Singapore: Springer.

Vygotsky, L.S. and Daniushevsky, S.M. (1993). 'The problem of mental retardation' [1935], in *The collected works of L.S. Vygotsky. Volume 2, The fundamentals of defectology*, pp. 220–240. Trans. and intro. J. Knox and C.B. Stevens; Rieber, R.W. and Carton, A.S. (eds). New York: Plenum Press.

Vygotsky, L.S. and Luria, A.R. (1993). *Studies on the history of behaviour: ape, primitive, child* [1930]. Hillsdale, NJ: Lawrence Erlbaum Associates.

Afterword

I have dedicated this book to Gordon Pradl, who was its 'midwife'. This is how he described himself, and it's a good description. From the mid-1990s on, when I had completed my PhD (about a third of which was devoted to Vygotsky), Gordon urged me, persistently, to write 'the Vygotsky book'. He was working at New York University and we used to meet sporadically, when he came with NYU students to England, or when I was working in New York or at an English teaching conference in the UK or USA. Every time we met it was 'How's the Vygotsky book going?'

More recently we met frequently online and he helped me through a very difficult time. Late in 2018, I had put in a proposal for 'the Vygotsky book'. It had been accepted, but got off to a bad start when I immediately fractured my shoulder. He suggested we should have FaceTime calls every week and they continued for over a year. Gradually I began to make chapter plans and send them to him. He immersed himself in the study of Vygotsky and our weekly discussions were intense and probing; Gordon's free mind and his ability to invoke alternative perspectives were liberating. His death from Covid on 10 April 2020 came out of the blue and left an unfillable gap, for me and many others.

It was partly Gordon's undeviating focus on 'the Vygotsky book' and his belief in my ability to write it that made it happen; he was both friend and teacher to me. But I had learned my Vygotsky first from other teachers, during my studies at the University of London Institute of Education. I am grateful for the teaching of James Britton, Tony Burgess and Margaret Meek Spencer, for their enthusiasm, their scholarship, and their championing of Vygotsky's work about language and learning in education. I benefited hugely from their unfailing encouragement, and from our long professional conversations, lasting years.

Vygotsky began to be a central point of reference in all my writing and teaching, especially as an English adviser and a director of a professional centre for primary teachers. English teaching, and thinking about the curriculum generally, lacked a clear theoretical perspective that recognised the centrality of language to all learning and to education as a whole. Vygotsky's carefully argued theories of language development, concept development, the internalisation of language as inner speech and thought, and his revelatory

DOI: 10.4324/9780429203046-13

discussions of the development of writing, had direct practical implications for teaching and learning. I never tired of reading him; there were always more layers to discover.

After my PhD, I continued to read his work as it appeared in English translation, and began to work closely on *Tool and symbol*. In about 2009 I made contact online with Nikolai Veresov, and he sent me a copy of his invaluable book *Undiscovered Vygotsky*. He also sent, at my request, a copy of the original paper on the zone of proximal/proximate development, which I wanted to get translated. It had been published as ch. 6 of *Mind in society*, and I felt that the *Mind in society* editors had probably made significant changes to the text. When it was translated by Stanley Mitchell in 2010 this was shown to be the case. I went on to help Nikolai with a new translation into English of Vygotsky's famous paper on play.

I was eventually able to begin writing this book in March 2020, just before the first Covid lockdown. I asked friends to read individual chapters and gained a great deal from their emailed responses. Several people read one or more chapters and some read all of them. It was wonderfully supportive to have this kind of community to discuss the book with as it grew. I owe grateful thanks to the following people: Isobel Armstrong, Edith Bradley, Laura Contini, Henrietta Dombey, Hannah Rose Douglas, Debbie Flatt, Donatella Giovannini, Jean Gooder, Sarah Horrocks, Danuta Lipinska, Virginia Makins, Deirdre Osborne, Jan Parnell, Jeni Smith, Steve Williams and John Yandell.

Three people have read all the chapters of this book as they were completed, and I express my deepest thanks to them for their thoughtful feedback and positive suggestions. They are Tony Burgess, Sue Ellis and John Richmond.

I invited six people to make a direct contribution to Chapter 12 of the book, in the section 'What teachers say'. I am very grateful to them for sharing their reflections about the influence of Vygotskyan ideas on their thinking and practice. They are: Julian Grenier, Theo Bryer, Jeni Smith, Becky Lawrence, John Yandell and Donatella Giovannini.

Always with me, and encouraging me to 'do my work', has been the spirit of James Berry, my partner and teacher, who died in 2017.

The other community that I was in touch with as I continued to write was the large virtual community of Vygotskyans, the writers and academics whose work I was reading as I developed my own argument. Chief among the scholars whose work I found especially illuminating is Nikolai Veresov, still my mentor and friend. But there are also scholars that I know mostly through their writing. I owe a particular debt of thanks to Luciano Mecacci, whose bibliography of Vygotsky's works and deeply knowledgeable writings were invaluable. I also acknowledge the help of certain authors whose work enabled me to navigate my way through difficult territory, or who illuminated particular topics. These include: Tatiana Akhutina, David Bakhurst, Andy Blunden, Andy Byford, Manolis Dafermos, Jan Derry, Fernando González Rey, Ludmilla Hyman, David Joravsky, Benjamin Lee, Andrey Maidansky, Ronald Miller, Bernard Schneuwly, Jaan Valsiner, René Van der Veer, Gita Vygodskaya and Ekaterina Zavershneva.

Engaging with Vygotsky's ideas with the help of these writers created a real zone of proximate development for me; I was always working at the limits of what I could do and attempting things that I could not yet do.

The work of compiling lists of references in this book, and of logging the number of citations and seeking permissions, has been carried out with impeccable care by Darya Protopopova, Cathy Johns and Mattie Thaddeus Johns. I am hugely grateful to them.

My admiration and thanks to Fiona Firth for her understanding and professional approach to compiling the index.

Above all I thank John Richmond for his intense interest in the project, his meticulous work on the manuscript, his tactful suggestions, and his constant kindness and concern. John has prepared the book for publication, and it has greatly benefited from his detailed scrutiny. We arrived at a final manuscript at the beginning of the third lockdown in January 2021.

My editor, Alison Foyle, has been unfailingly sympathetic and supportive. I thank her for her encouragement and her enthusiasm for this book.

Index

Index entries in italics are books by Vygotsky, unless indicated otherwise. Locators in italics indicate that there is a figure on that page.

Ribot, T-A. 131
Rosen, H. 217
Rudneva, E.I. 205
Russia, political events in *see* political context
Russian psychology (Joravsky) 109–110

Said, E. 211
Saint Petersburg *see* Leningrad; Petrograd
Sakharov, L. 73, 80, 81, 94, 113, 174–175
sanatorium, treatment in 52, 197, 200
scaffolding, and the ZPD 157
schizophrenia 106
Schneuwly, B. (colleague of Leopoldoff-Martin) 147, 158–159, 222
schools: auxiliary schools and inclusion 42; role of 8; secondary school-teaching 217
scientific concepts 175–177, 178
scientific method, in psychology *see* methodology
Selected psychological works 212
self-control 101, 102–103, 105, 129, 177
Shemyakin, F.N. 164
Shif, Z. 48, 108, 153, 175, 203, 204
sign language 41–42
sign operations 76, 80–81
signs 102
Simon, B. 211–213
Simon, J. 211–213
Simon, T. 148
Slavina, L. 35, 73
Sobkin, V. 16
social experience 59
Socratic method 2, 11
special education 35, 37–38, 40, 42, 110, 147, 151, 152; for blind and deaf children 40–42; Vygotsky's approach to 37–39
speech 97, 101; and action 83–84; chimpanzees' lack of 91; development of 166–167; egocentric speech 71–72, 79, 95, 169–171, 189; genetic roots of 172; group talk 218; and imagination 131–132; inner speech 189–191, 192–194; and problem-solving 75–76
Speech and the development of mental processes in the child (Luria and Yudovitch) 212, 213–214
Spinoza, B., influence on Vygotsky 2, 15, 16, 67–68, 103, 129

Stalin, J.: Communist Party leadership and impact on pedology 109–110; Communist party leadership and impact on Vygotsky 163–164, 209–210, 221; dissemination of Vygotsky's work after his death 18, 203, 205–206; five-year plan and growing dictatorship 88; leadership of Communist party and control of scientific/intellectual activity 147, 188; Mandelstam arrested for poem about 196–197
Stanislavski, K.S. 16, 192, 196
Stern, D. 39, 109, 112, 114, 172
Stetsenko, A. 73
stubbornness 120
Studies on the history of behaviour (Vygotsky and Luria) 85, 89–95, 98, 108, 134, 222
Sutton, A. 47
symbolism 128–129

teachers: role of 11; views on Vygotsky 218–220
teaching 223; arts as central to 135; dialogic 218; discussion of term 143; early career 3–5; impact on development 150–151, 153–154; and the zone of proximal/proximate development 159 *see also* pedagogy
teaching about emotions, The (unfinished) 165, 184
theatre, importance of 12, 15–16, 29, 134; children's participation in 139
themes, in Vygotsky's work 222–223
theoretical analysis 65–66
thesis, doctoral 3, 14, 17, 24
Thinking and speech 5, 7–8, 15, 20, 80, 83, 84, 184, 204–205, xiv; argument in final chapter 187–199; and concept formation 113; discussion of methodology 165–167; distortion of 221; Italian translation (Meccaci) 210; and pedology 109; publication history 164–165, 203, 206–207, 212; structure of 167–168, 199–200; and the zone of proximal/proximate development 153–154 *see also Collected works*
Thought and language 158, 207, 213, 222, xiv
thoughts and thinking 11, 223; in adolescence 106; in chimpanzees 91; as complex human behaviour 7–8; and

Lightning Source UK Ltd.
Milton Keynes UK
UKHW011252110322
399900UK00002BA/14